Virtual Collaboration Spaces

Future Trends

Morgan Okafor

ISBN: 9781779666277
Imprint: Press for Play Books
Copyright © 2024 Morgan Okafor.
All Rights Reserved.

Contents

The Evolution of Virtual Collaboration	**1**
The Birth of Virtual Reality	1
Bibliography	**15**
Bibliography	**19**
The Rise of Virtual Collaboration	21
Bibliography	**47**
The Impact of Virtual Collaboration	50
Bibliography	**75**
The Future of Virtual Collaboration	**79**
Enhanced Virtual Meeting Experiences	79
Bibliography	**89**
Bibliography	**95**
Virtual Collaboration for Specific Industries	98
The Integration of Virtual and Augmented Reality	122
Ethical Considerations and Social Impact	129
Bibliography	**143**
The Challenges and Opportunities of Virtual Collaboration	**145**
Technical Challenges	145
Human Factors	161
Deploying and Managing Virtual Collaboration Spaces	178

Conclusion:	**197**
Conclusion:	197
The Future is Collaborative	**201**
Embracing the Virtual Collaboration Revolution	201
Bibliography	**205**
The Social and Cultural Impact	216
Future Challenges and Possibilities	226
Bibliography	**233**
Embracing the Future of Virtual Collaboration	241
Index	**257**

The Evolution of Virtual Collaboration

The Birth of Virtual Reality

The Origins of Virtual Reality

The concept of Virtual Reality (VR) can be traced back to the mid-20th century, although the roots of immersive experiences extend even further into the realms of art and literature. The origins of VR are marked by a confluence of technological advancements, theoretical explorations, and creative imaginings that have shaped its development into the sophisticated medium we recognize today.

Historical Context

The idea of creating simulated environments can be linked to early experiments in immersive experiences. One of the first notable examples was the invention of the *Sensorama* in the 1960s by Morton Heilig, a cinematographer who envisioned a multi-sensory experience for cinema. The Sensorama was a machine that combined 3D film, sound, vibrations, and even scents to create an immersive experience for its users. This device marked a significant step toward the development of VR, as it sought to engage multiple senses, a fundamental aspect of contemporary VR technology.

Theoretical Foundations

The theoretical underpinnings of VR can be found in several domains, including psychology, computer science, and philosophy. One of the key theoretical frameworks is the concept of *presence*, which refers to the feeling of being in a virtual environment. Researchers such as Mel Slater have explored the psychological effects of presence, demonstrating that users can experience a sense of reality within virtual spaces, often leading to emotional and behavioral responses similar to those experienced in the real world.

$$Presence = f(\text{Immersion, Interaction, Realism}) \qquad (1)$$

This equation suggests that the sense of presence is a function of three critical factors: immersion (the degree to which a user is enveloped in a virtual environment), interaction (the extent to which users can manipulate and engage with the virtual world), and realism (the fidelity of the virtual environment in replicating real-world elements).

Early Developments in VR Technology

The 1970s and 1980s saw significant advancements in computer graphics and display technologies, paving the way for more sophisticated VR systems. In 1968, Ivan Sutherland created the first head-mounted display (HMD) system, often referred to as the *Sword of Damocles*. This device was rudimentary by today's standards, but it represented a groundbreaking achievement in creating a visual display that could immerse users in a virtual environment.

The Role of Gaming and Simulation

As technology continued to evolve, the gaming industry became a significant driver for VR development. The 1990s witnessed the emergence of VR arcade games, such as *Virtuality*, which allowed players to engage in virtual worlds through arcade machines equipped with HMDs and motion tracking. These early gaming experiences were crucial in popularizing VR and demonstrating its potential as a medium for entertainment.

In parallel, the military and aerospace sectors began utilizing VR for simulation training. The use of flight simulators and combat training environments showcased VR's ability to provide safe, controlled, and repeatable training scenarios for personnel, emphasizing its practical applications beyond entertainment.

Challenges in Early VR Development

Despite the promising developments, early VR technology faced numerous challenges. The limitations of computing power, graphics rendering capabilities, and the bulkiness of HMDs hindered widespread adoption. Additionally, issues such as motion sickness and user discomfort due to prolonged use of VR systems raised concerns about the feasibility of VR as a mainstream technology.

Conclusion

The origins of virtual reality are rooted in a rich tapestry of historical, theoretical, and technological developments. From Morton Heilig's Sensorama to Ivan Sutherland's head-mounted displays, the journey of VR has been marked by both innovation and challenges. As we continue to explore the evolution of virtual collaboration spaces, understanding these origins provides valuable context for the advancements that have shaped contemporary VR experiences. The interplay between immersive technology and user interaction forms the foundation upon which the future of virtual collaboration will be built.

Early VR Applications

The advent of Virtual Reality (VR) marked a significant turning point in the way technology interacts with human perception. Early VR applications laid the groundwork for the immersive experiences we see today. The exploration of VR began in the 1960s, and while the technology was rudimentary, it set the stage for innovations that would follow.

Theoretical Foundations

The theoretical underpinnings of VR can be traced back to concepts of immersion and presence. Immersion refers to the degree to which a user feels enveloped by a virtual environment, while presence is the psychological sensation of being in that environment. These concepts are crucial for understanding how early VR applications were designed and experienced.

Early VR systems relied on basic sensory inputs, primarily visual and auditory, to create a sense of presence. The notion of *telepresence*, or the feeling of being physically present in a non-physical world, was central to these early applications.

Pioneering Applications

One of the earliest and most notable VR applications was the *Sensorama*, developed by Morton Heilig in 1962. The Sensorama was a multi-sensory machine that provided users with a simulated experience of riding a motorcycle through Brooklyn. It combined 3D visuals, sound, vibrations, and even smells to create an immersive experience. Although it was not a fully interactive VR system, it demonstrated the potential of combining various sensory modalities to enhance user experience.

Another significant early application was *The Aspen Movie Map*, developed at MIT in the late 1970s. This project allowed users to navigate a computer-generated model of Aspen, Colorado, by using a joystick. Users could explore the town, view landmarks, and even enter buildings. The Aspen Movie Map showcased the potential of VR for tourism and urban planning, providing a virtual tour experience that was innovative for its time.

Challenges Faced

Despite the excitement surrounding early VR applications, several challenges hindered widespread adoption.

- **Technical Limitations:** Early VR systems were often bulky and required specialized hardware. The graphics were rudimentary, leading to a lack of realism that diminished the immersive experience. Users frequently experienced discomfort due to motion sickness, a phenomenon known as *cybersickness*, caused by a disconnect between visual stimuli and physical motion.

- **High Costs:** The financial barrier to entry for both developers and users was significant. High costs associated with VR hardware and software limited access to a select few institutions and enthusiasts.

- **Limited Content:** The availability of engaging content was minimal. Most early VR applications were experimental and lacked the depth and interactivity that users craved.

Examples of Early VR Applications

1. **Virtual Reality Modeling Language (VRML)**: Developed in the 1990s, VRML was a file format for describing 3D interactive environments on the web. While not a VR system in itself, it allowed for the creation of virtual spaces that could be navigated by users, paving the way for future web-based VR experiences.

2. **NASA's Virtual Reality Applications**: In the 1990s, NASA began using VR for simulations in training astronauts and for visualizing complex data. For example, the *Virtual Reality Training Environment* (VRTE) was used to prepare astronauts for various missions, enabling them to practice operations in a simulated environment that closely mirrored real-life scenarios.

3. **The Virtuality Group's Arcade Machines**: In the early 1990s, The Virtuality Group created arcade machines that featured VR headsets. Games like *Dactyl Nightmare* allowed players to engage in multiplayer experiences within a virtual world, marking one of the first instances of VR gaming in public venues.

Conclusion

Early VR applications were characterized by innovation and experimentation, laying the groundwork for the more advanced systems we have today. While the technology faced numerous challenges, the foundational work done in this era was crucial for the evolution of VR. As we continue to explore the potential of virtual environments, it is essential to recognize the pioneering efforts that shaped the current landscape of virtual collaboration and interaction. The lessons learned from these early applications inform the design and implementation of modern VR systems, ensuring that they address the challenges faced by their predecessors while maximizing the potential for immersive experiences.

$$\text{Presence} = f(\text{Immersion}, \text{Interaction}) \qquad (2)$$

This equation illustrates the relationship between presence, immersion, and interaction in VR applications. As technology evolves, enhancing these factors will be critical for the success of future VR applications.

VR in the Gaming Industry

Virtual Reality (VR) has revolutionized the gaming industry, offering immersive experiences that were previously unimaginable. By creating a simulated environment that users can interact with, VR games transport players into fantastical worlds, allowing them to engage with the game in a more profound manner. This section explores the evolution, challenges, and future potential of VR in gaming.

The Evolution of VR Gaming

The journey of VR in gaming began in the early 1990s with systems like the Sega VR and Nintendo's Virtual Boy. However, these early attempts were limited by technology, resulting in low-quality graphics and motion sickness among players. It wasn't until the mid-2010s that significant advancements in VR technology occurred, primarily driven by the development of powerful GPUs, motion tracking systems, and affordable headsets.

The launch of devices such as the Oculus Rift, HTC Vive, and PlayStation VR marked a turning point in the VR gaming landscape. These headsets provided high-resolution displays, precise motion tracking, and a wide field of view, significantly enhancing the gaming experience. According to a report by *Statista*, the global VR gaming market is projected to reach $45.09 billion by 2025, illustrating the growing interest and investment in this sector.

Key Theoretical Frameworks

Several theoretical frameworks can help us understand the impact of VR in gaming:

- **Immersion Theory:** This theory posits that immersion is a critical factor in enhancing user experience. VR achieves this by engaging multiple senses, allowing players to feel as though they are part of the game world.

- **Presence Theory:** Presence refers to the psychological state where users feel as though they are physically present in a virtual environment. This is crucial for VR gaming, as a higher sense of presence can lead to greater emotional engagement and enjoyment.

- **Flow Theory:** Proposed by Mihaly Csikszentmihalyi, this theory describes a state of complete absorption in an activity. VR games are designed to facilitate flow by providing challenges that match the player's skill level, thus keeping them engaged.

Challenges in VR Gaming

Despite its potential, VR gaming faces several challenges:

- **Motion Sickness:** Many players experience motion sickness due to a disconnect between visual stimuli and physical movement. Developers are continuously working on solutions, such as reducing latency and incorporating comfort settings.

- **High Costs:** The cost of high-end VR systems can be prohibitive for many consumers. While prices have decreased, the initial investment for quality hardware remains a barrier.

- **Content Availability:** The success of VR gaming depends on the availability of engaging content. Developers must create games that fully utilize VR's capabilities to attract and retain players.

- **Physical Space Limitations:** Many VR experiences require a significant amount of physical space for players to move around. This can limit the accessibility of VR games in smaller living environments.

Examples of VR Games

Several notable VR games have made significant impacts on the industry:

- **Beat Saber:** This rhythm-based game combines music and lightsaber mechanics, providing a fun and physically engaging experience. Its popularity has made it a flagship title for VR gaming.

- **Half-Life: Alyx:** A critically acclaimed game that showcases the potential of VR storytelling and immersion. It utilizes advanced physics and interaction mechanics to create a compelling narrative experience.

- **The Walking Dead: Saints & Sinners:** This game offers players a survival horror experience where they must navigate a post-apocalyptic world. It effectively uses VR to enhance the sense of danger and urgency.

The Future of VR in Gaming

Looking ahead, the future of VR in gaming appears promising. Innovations such as haptic feedback, eye-tracking technology, and social VR experiences are on the horizon. Haptic feedback systems, which provide tactile sensations to users, can enhance immersion by simulating physical interactions within the game. Eye-tracking technology can facilitate more natural interactions, allowing players to control elements in the game merely by looking at them.

Moreover, social VR platforms are emerging, enabling players to interact in virtual spaces, fostering community and collaboration. Games like *Rec Room* and *VRChat* are examples of how social interactions can be integrated into VR gaming, paving the way for new gameplay experiences.

In conclusion, VR in the gaming industry has evolved dramatically over the past few decades. While challenges remain, the potential for immersive and engaging experiences continues to drive innovation. As technology advances, the future of VR gaming promises to be even more exciting, offering players new ways to explore virtual worlds and connect with others.

$$P = \frac{I}{A} \tag{3}$$

Where:

- P = Pressure experienced by the player in a VR environment
- I = Intensity of the VR experience
- A = Area of engagement in the VR space

This equation illustrates how an increase in the intensity of the VR experience can lead to greater pressure on the player, which can be interpreted as a heightened sense of immersion and emotional engagement.

VR in Education and Training

Virtual Reality (VR) has emerged as a transformative tool in the field of education and training, offering immersive experiences that enhance learning outcomes. This subsection explores the theoretical underpinnings, practical applications, challenges, and future prospects of VR in educational contexts.

Theoretical Framework

The use of VR in education is grounded in several learning theories, including constructivism, experiential learning, and cognitive load theory.

Constructivism posits that learners construct knowledge through experiences. VR environments allow students to engage with content actively, promoting deeper understanding. For instance, a biology student can explore the human body in a virtual environment, interacting with 3D models of organs and systems, which fosters a more profound comprehension of anatomical structures.

Experiential Learning emphasizes learning through experience. According to Kolb's experiential learning cycle, the process involves concrete experience, reflective observation, abstract conceptualization, and active experimentation. VR provides a platform for students to simulate real-world scenarios, such as medical training simulations where students can practice surgical procedures without the risks associated with real-life operations.

Cognitive Load Theory suggests that instructional design should consider the limitations of working memory. VR can help manage cognitive load by providing immersive experiences that reduce extraneous cognitive demands, allowing learners to focus on essential information. For example, a VR simulation can visually demonstrate complex concepts like climate change, making it easier for students to grasp the interconnectedness of various factors.

Practical Applications

VR has been successfully implemented in various educational settings, ranging from K-12 to higher education and professional training.

K-12 Education VR applications in K-12 education include interactive history lessons where students can "visit" ancient civilizations or explore ecosystems in science classes. Programs like Google Expeditions allow teachers to take students on virtual field trips, enhancing engagement and retention.

Higher Education In higher education, VR is utilized for immersive learning experiences in disciplines such as medicine, engineering, and architecture. For instance, medical students at institutions like Stanford University use VR simulations to practice patient interactions and surgical techniques, which prepares them for real-life clinical settings.

Corporate Training In the corporate sector, companies like Walmart and Boeing have adopted VR for employee training. Walmart employs VR to train employees on customer service and safety protocols, while Boeing uses VR for assembly line training, allowing workers to practice complex tasks in a safe environment.

Challenges and Limitations

Despite its potential, the integration of VR in education faces several challenges:

Cost and Accessibility The financial barrier associated with acquiring VR technology can limit its adoption, particularly in underfunded schools. High-quality VR headsets and software can be expensive, and not all institutions can afford them.

Technical Issues Technical challenges, such as hardware compatibility and software bugs, can hinder the effectiveness of VR in educational settings. Educators may require training to effectively implement VR tools, which can add to the complexity of integration.

Content Development The creation of high-quality, curriculum-aligned VR content is resource-intensive and often requires collaboration between educators and developers. There is a need for more accessible platforms that allow educators to create or customize VR experiences without extensive technical expertise.

Examples of Successful Implementation

Several institutions have demonstrated the successful implementation of VR in education:

Case Study: The University of Illinois   The University of Illinois has developed a VR program for architecture students, allowing them to walk through and interact with their designs in a virtual environment. This immersive experience enhances spatial awareness and design skills.

Case Study: Virtual Reality Medical Training   The Medical University of South Carolina utilizes VR for training medical students in patient interactions. This program has shown improved student confidence and competence in clinical skills, as students can practice in a risk-free environment.

Future Directions

As VR technology continues to evolve, its applications in education are expected to expand. Future advancements may include:

Increased Accessibility   As VR technology becomes more affordable and widespread, it is anticipated that more educational institutions will adopt VR as a standard teaching tool.

Enhanced Interactivity   Future VR applications may incorporate AI-driven elements that adapt to individual learning styles, providing personalized educational experiences.

Integration with Other Technologies   The convergence of VR with augmented reality (AR) and artificial intelligence (AI) may create hybrid learning environments that offer even richer educational experiences.

In conclusion, VR holds significant promise for enhancing education and training by providing immersive, interactive experiences that foster engagement and understanding. While challenges remain, the potential benefits of VR in educational contexts make it a compelling area for continued research and development.

VR in Healthcare

Virtual Reality (VR) has emerged as a transformative technology in the healthcare sector, offering innovative solutions for training, therapy, and patient care. This subsection explores the various applications of VR in healthcare, the theoretical foundations supporting its use, the challenges faced, and notable examples that illustrate its effectiveness.

Theoretical Foundations

The application of VR in healthcare is grounded in several theoretical frameworks, including:

- **Experiential Learning Theory:** This theory posits that learning occurs through experience. VR provides immersive experiences that enhance learning and retention, making it particularly effective for medical training.

- **Cognitive Behavioral Therapy (CBT):** VR can simulate environments that expose patients to their fears or anxieties in a controlled manner, facilitating therapeutic interventions based on CBT principles.

- **Social Learning Theory:** This theory emphasizes learning through observation. VR can create scenarios where healthcare professionals can observe and practice skills in a virtual environment before applying them in real life.

Applications of VR in Healthcare

2.1 Medical Training and Education   VR has revolutionized medical training by providing a safe and controlled environment for students and professionals to practice procedures. For instance, surgical simulations allow trainees to perform operations on virtual patients, honing their skills without the risks associated with real-life procedures.

$$\text{Skill Proficiency} = \frac{\text{Successful Simulations}}{\text{Total Simulations}} \times 100\% \qquad (4)$$

This equation quantifies the skill proficiency of trainees, emphasizing the importance of repeated practice in VR environments.

2.2 Patient Treatment and Rehabilitation   VR is increasingly used in therapeutic settings, particularly for rehabilitation. Patients recovering from strokes or injuries can engage in virtual exercises tailored to their specific needs. This not only motivates patients but also provides real-time feedback to healthcare providers.

2.3 Pain Management   Research indicates that VR can effectively manage pain during medical procedures. By immersing patients in calming virtual environments, their perception of pain can be significantly reduced. A study demonstrated that patients using VR during wound dressing changes reported a 50% reduction in pain levels compared to those who did not use VR.

Challenges in Implementing VR in Healthcare

Despite its potential, the integration of VR in healthcare faces several challenges:

- **Cost:** The initial investment in VR technology can be substantial, which may deter healthcare facilities from adopting it.

- **Accessibility:** Not all patients have equal access to VR technology, creating disparities in treatment options.

- **Training:** Healthcare professionals require training to effectively use VR tools, which can be time-consuming and costly.

- **Regulatory Issues:** The healthcare sector is heavily regulated, and the approval of VR applications can be a lengthy process.

Examples of VR in Healthcare

Several organizations and studies highlight the successful implementation of VR in healthcare:

4.1 The Virtual Reality Medical Center   The Virtual Reality Medical Center (VRMC) utilizes VR for various therapeutic applications, including exposure therapy for phobias and PTSD. Their approach allows patients to confront their fears in a controlled setting, leading to significant improvements in their conditions.

4.2 Surgical Simulators Companies like Osso VR and ImmersiveTouch have developed surgical simulators that allow surgeons to practice complex procedures in a risk-free environment. These simulators provide realistic haptic feedback, enhancing the training experience.

4.3 Pain Relief Studies Research conducted at the University of Washington demonstrated that patients undergoing burn wound care experienced less pain when using VR. The study highlighted the potential of VR as a non-pharmacological pain management tool.

Conclusion

The integration of VR in healthcare represents a significant advancement in medical training, patient treatment, and pain management. While challenges remain, the potential benefits of VR in enhancing healthcare delivery are substantial. As technology evolves and becomes more accessible, it is likely that VR will play an increasingly prominent role in the future of healthcare.

Bibliography

[1] Virtual Reality Medical Center. (n.d.). Retrieved from `https://www.vrmedicalcenter.com`

[2] Osso VR. (n.d.). Retrieved from `https://www.ossovr.com`

[3] University of Washington. (2020). Study on the effects of VR on pain management. Retrieved from `https://www.washington.edu`

The Potential of VR for Collaboration

Virtual Reality (VR) has emerged as a transformative technology with profound implications for collaboration across various sectors. This section explores the potential of VR for enhancing collaborative efforts, the theoretical frameworks that support these advancements, and the challenges that need to be addressed.

Theoretical Frameworks

The potential of VR for collaboration can be understood through several theoretical frameworks, including Social Presence Theory, Media Richness Theory, and the Theory of Distributed Cognition.

Social Presence Theory Social Presence Theory posits that the degree of salience of the other person in a communication interaction influences the quality of the interaction. In VR, the immersive environment can create a heightened sense of social presence, which enhances interpersonal interactions. When users feel more present with their collaborators, they are likely to engage more effectively and communicate more openly.

Media Richness Theory Media Richness Theory suggests that different communication media vary in their capacity to convey information and facilitate understanding. VR, as a rich medium, allows for multiple forms of communication—visual, auditory, and kinesthetic—thereby reducing ambiguity and improving clarity in collaborative tasks.

Theory of Distributed Cognition The Theory of Distributed Cognition emphasizes that cognitive processes are not confined to individuals but are distributed across people, tools, and environments. VR environments can facilitate this distribution by providing shared spaces where teams can interact with digital artifacts and each other, thereby enhancing collective problem-solving capabilities.

Applications of VR in Collaboration

Virtual Meeting Spaces One of the most significant applications of VR in collaboration is the creation of virtual meeting spaces. Platforms like Spatial and AltspaceVR allow teams to meet in immersive environments, where they can interact as avatars in a 3D space. This not only replicates the physical meeting experience but often enhances it by providing tools for real-time data visualization and interaction.

Remote Collaboration With the rise of remote work, VR presents a unique opportunity to bridge the gap between physical distance and collaborative engagement. For instance, companies like Facebook (now Meta) are developing Horizon Workrooms, which enable remote teams to collaborate in a shared virtual space, complete with whiteboards and 3D models.

Cross-Cultural Collaboration VR also has the potential to enhance cross-cultural collaboration. By providing a platform where individuals from diverse backgrounds can interact in a shared space, VR can facilitate cultural exchange and understanding. For example, initiatives like VR for Good use VR to connect communities across borders, fostering empathy and collaboration on global issues.

Challenges in Implementing VR Collaboration

Despite its potential, several challenges hinder the widespread adoption of VR for collaboration.

Technical Limitations Technical challenges such as bandwidth requirements, device compatibility, and latency issues can impede the effectiveness of VR collaboration. For example, high-quality VR experiences demand significant bandwidth, which may not be available in all regions, limiting access for some users.

User Acceptance User acceptance is another critical challenge. Many individuals may be hesitant to adopt VR technology due to unfamiliarity or discomfort with immersive experiences. Research indicates that perceived ease of use and perceived usefulness are significant factors influencing user acceptance of new technologies (Davis, 1989).

Cost and Accessibility The cost of VR hardware and software can be prohibitive for some organizations, particularly small businesses and startups. Ensuring that VR collaboration tools are accessible and affordable is essential for widespread adoption.

Future Directions

The future of VR collaboration looks promising, with ongoing advancements in technology and increasing interest from businesses. Potential future directions include:

Integration with AI Integrating AI with VR collaboration tools can enhance user experiences by providing personalized interactions and facilitating real-time language translation, which can be particularly beneficial for cross-cultural teams.

Enhanced User Interfaces Developing more intuitive user interfaces for VR collaboration tools can improve user acceptance and engagement. For instance, gesture-based controls and voice commands may make interactions more natural and accessible.

Focus on Inclusivity Ensuring that VR collaboration tools are designed with inclusivity in mind will be crucial. This includes considering the needs of users with disabilities and ensuring that VR environments are accessible to all.

Conclusion

In conclusion, the potential of VR for collaboration is vast, offering innovative solutions to enhance teamwork and communication in various fields. By addressing the challenges associated with its implementation and focusing on user-centered design, organizations can leverage VR to create more effective and engaging collaborative experiences. As technology continues to evolve, the possibilities for VR collaboration will only expand, paving the way for a more connected and collaborative future.

Bibliography

[1] Davis, F. D. (1989). Perceived usefulness, perceived ease of use, and user acceptance of information technology. *MIS Quarterly*, 13(3), 319-340.

Challenges and Limitations of Early VR

The early development of Virtual Reality (VR) technology was marked by significant enthusiasm and promise; however, it also faced a myriad of challenges and limitations that hindered its widespread adoption and effectiveness. This subsection explores the key challenges associated with early VR, including technological, psychological, and social limitations, and provides examples to illustrate these issues.

Technological Limitations

One of the primary challenges of early VR was the technology itself. The hardware and software available during the initial phases of VR development were often inadequate to provide a truly immersive experience. Key technological limitations included:

- **Low Resolution and Refresh Rates:** Early VR headsets, such as the Virtuality Group's arcade machines in the early 1990s, suffered from low resolution displays, typically around 320x240 pixels. This resulted in a pixelated visual experience that detracted from immersion. Furthermore, low refresh rates led to motion sickness, as the visual output could not keep up with the user's head movements.

- **Limited Field of View (FOV):** The FOV in early VR systems was often restricted, typically around 30-60 degrees. This narrow perspective limited the user's ability to perceive depth and spatial orientation, which are crucial for a convincing VR experience. A wider FOV, ideally above 100 degrees, is necessary for a more immersive experience.

- **Inadequate Tracking Systems:** Early VR systems relied on basic tracking technologies, such as magnetic or optical sensors, which were often inaccurate and susceptible to interference. For example, the Data Glove, a pioneering VR input device, struggled with precise hand tracking, leading to frustrating user experiences.

Psychological Limitations

The psychological effects of early VR technology also posed significant challenges. Users often experienced discomfort and disorientation due to the disparity between their physical and virtual environments. Some notable psychological limitations include:

- **Motion Sickness:** A common issue in early VR was motion sickness, also known as cybersickness. This phenomenon occurs when there is a mismatch between visual motion cues and the vestibular system's sense of motion. Studies have shown that up to 40% of users experienced symptoms such as nausea and dizziness when using early VR systems [?].

- **Presence and Immersion:** The sense of presence, or the feeling of being "there" in a virtual environment, was often lacking. Early VR experiences failed to create a convincing sense of immersion due to the aforementioned technological limitations. Users often felt disconnected from the virtual world, which diminished the overall experience.

- **User Acceptance:** The novelty of VR technology led to initial excitement; however, many users were quick to abandon early VR experiences due to discomfort and the lack of engaging content. A survey conducted in the 1990s indicated that while 80% of participants were initially enthusiastic about VR, only 20% continued using it after their first experience [?].

Social Limitations

Beyond technological and psychological challenges, early VR also faced social limitations that affected its acceptance and use. These included:

- **High Costs:** The cost of early VR systems was prohibitively high for most consumers and businesses. For instance, the Virtuality arcade machines cost upwards of $50,000, making them accessible only to niche markets. This limited the technology's exposure and growth in the consumer market.

- **Content Availability:** The lack of compelling content was a significant barrier to the adoption of early VR. Most VR experiences were limited to basic simulations and games, which failed to capture the interest of a broader audience. As a result, the potential applications of VR in fields such as education, training, and therapy were largely unexplored.

- **Cultural Perception:** Early VR was often associated with gaming and entertainment, leading to a perception that it was a novelty rather than a serious tool for collaboration or training. This cultural bias hindered investment and research into more practical applications of VR technology.

Conclusion

In conclusion, the early stages of VR development were marked by significant challenges and limitations that hindered its growth and acceptance. Technological shortcomings, psychological discomfort, and social barriers collectively contributed to the initial struggles of VR. Understanding these challenges is essential for appreciating the advancements made in subsequent years and the potential of VR technology in modern virtual collaboration spaces.

The Rise of Virtual Collaboration

Virtual Meeting Spaces

Virtual meeting spaces have emerged as a cornerstone of modern collaboration, enabling individuals and teams to connect in immersive environments regardless of their physical locations. These spaces leverage advancements in technology to create engaging, interactive platforms where participants can communicate, share ideas, and work together effectively. This subsection explores the theoretical foundations, practical applications, challenges, and examples of virtual meeting spaces.

Theoretical Foundations of Virtual Meeting Spaces

The concept of virtual meeting spaces is grounded in several theoretical frameworks, including social presence theory, media richness theory, and constructivist learning theory.

Social Presence Theory posits that the degree of social presence in a communication medium influences interpersonal interactions. In virtual meeting spaces, features such as video conferencing, avatars, and real-time feedback enhance social presence, making participants feel more connected and engaged.

Media Richness Theory suggests that different communication media have varying capabilities to convey information. Virtual meeting spaces, equipped with audio, video, and interactive tools, provide a rich medium that supports complex communication tasks. The richness of these environments can lead to better understanding and collaboration among team members.

Constructivist Learning Theory emphasizes the importance of active engagement and collaboration in the learning process. Virtual meeting spaces facilitate constructivist approaches by allowing participants to co-create knowledge through discussions, brainstorming sessions, and collaborative problem-solving activities.

Key Features of Virtual Meeting Spaces

Effective virtual meeting spaces incorporate several key features that enhance collaboration:

- **Video Conferencing:** High-quality video and audio capabilities enable face-to-face interactions, fostering a sense of presence and connection among participants.

- **Screen Sharing:** Participants can share their screens to present documents, slides, or applications, facilitating real-time collaboration and discussion.

- **Interactive Whiteboards:** Virtual whiteboards allow users to brainstorm, sketch ideas, and visualize concepts collaboratively, enhancing creativity and engagement.

- **Breakout Rooms:** These allow participants to split into smaller groups for focused discussions, making it easier to tackle specific topics or tasks.

- **Recordings and Transcripts:** The ability to record meetings and generate transcripts ensures that discussions are documented and can be revisited later, aiding in knowledge retention and accountability.

Challenges of Virtual Meeting Spaces

Despite their advantages, virtual meeting spaces face several challenges:

Technical Issues such as connectivity problems, software glitches, and hardware incompatibilities can disrupt meetings. According to a survey by [4], 40% of remote workers reported experiencing technical difficulties during virtual meetings, which can lead to frustration and decreased productivity.

Engagement and Participation can be challenging in virtual environments. Participants may become distracted by their surroundings or multitask during meetings, leading to reduced focus and participation. A study by [?] found that 60% of employees admitted to being less engaged in virtual meetings compared to in-person gatherings.

Time Zone Differences pose logistical challenges for global teams. Coordinating meetings across multiple time zones can be difficult, resulting in some participants having to join meetings at inconvenient times. This can lead to fatigue and decreased productivity, as noted by [?].

Examples of Virtual Meeting Spaces

Several platforms exemplify the capabilities of virtual meeting spaces:

Zoom has become synonymous with virtual meetings, offering features such as breakout rooms, virtual backgrounds, and integrations with various productivity tools. Its user-friendly interface and widespread adoption make it a popular choice for businesses and educational institutions.

Microsoft Teams integrates seamlessly with the Microsoft 365 suite, providing a collaborative environment where users can chat, share files, and conduct meetings. Its focus on team collaboration and productivity has made it a go-to solution for many organizations.

Spatial takes virtual meetings to the next level by creating immersive 3D environments where participants can interact as avatars. This platform emphasizes social presence and engagement, making virtual meetings feel more like in-person interactions.

Conclusion

Virtual meeting spaces represent a significant advancement in how teams collaborate and communicate. By leveraging technology to create engaging and interactive environments, organizations can overcome geographical barriers and enhance productivity. However, addressing the challenges associated with virtual meetings is crucial for maximizing their effectiveness. As technology continues to evolve, the potential for virtual meeting spaces to transform collaboration will only grow, paving the way for innovative approaches to teamwork in the digital age.

Virtual Teamwork

In the contemporary landscape of work, virtual teamwork has emerged as a crucial component of organizational success. Defined as the collaboration among team members who are geographically dispersed and communicate primarily through digital platforms, virtual teamwork leverages technology to facilitate coordination, communication, and cooperation. This section explores the theoretical underpinnings of virtual teamwork, the associated challenges, and practical examples that illuminate its significance.

Theoretical Framework of Virtual Teamwork

Theories of teamwork provide a foundation for understanding virtual collaboration. One prominent theory is the **Input-Process-Output (IPO) model**, which posits that team performance is influenced by various inputs (e.g., team composition, resources), processes (e.g., communication, decision-making), and outputs (e.g., performance, satisfaction). In a virtual context, the model adapts as follows:

$$\text{Team Performance} = f(\text{Inputs}, \text{Processes}, \text{Outputs}) \qquad (5)$$

Where: - Inputs include team diversity, technology availability, and organizational support. - Processes encompass communication patterns, conflict resolution, and collaboration strategies. - Outputs reflect the quality of deliverables and team cohesion.

Moreover, the **Social Presence Theory** suggests that the degree to which team members feel socially connected impacts their collaboration. In virtual teams, the lack of physical presence can lead to feelings of isolation, making it essential to foster social presence through effective communication tools and practices.

Challenges of Virtual Teamwork

Despite its advantages, virtual teamwork presents several challenges:

- **Communication Barriers:** The absence of non-verbal cues can lead to misunderstandings. For example, a message intended to be constructive may be perceived as critical due to the lack of tone and body language.

- **Technological Dependence:** Reliance on technology can create issues when tools fail or when team members lack the necessary skills to use them effectively. This dependence can lead to frustration and decreased productivity.

- **Cultural Differences:** Virtual teams often comprise members from diverse cultural backgrounds, which can influence communication styles and work ethics. Misinterpretations arising from cultural differences can hinder collaboration.

- **Trust Building:** Establishing trust in a virtual environment is more challenging than in face-to-face settings. Trust is essential for effective teamwork, and its absence can lead to reduced collaboration and increased conflict.

- **Time Zone Challenges:** Coordinating meetings and deadlines across different time zones can result in delays and misalignment, impacting team performance.

Strategies for Effective Virtual Teamwork

To address these challenges, organizations can implement several strategies:

- **Regular Communication:** Establishing a routine for check-ins and updates can enhance communication and build rapport among team members. Tools like Slack or Microsoft Teams can facilitate ongoing dialogue.

- **Use of Collaborative Tools:** Utilizing project management software such as Trello or Asana can help teams stay organized and aligned on tasks and deadlines.

- **Cultural Sensitivity Training:** Providing training on cultural awareness can help team members navigate differences and foster a more inclusive environment.

- **Building Trust through Transparency:** Encouraging open discussions about challenges and successes can help build trust. Regular feedback sessions can also promote transparency and accountability.

- **Flexible Scheduling:** Being mindful of time zone differences and allowing for flexible meeting times can accommodate all team members and enhance participation.

Examples of Successful Virtual Teams

Several organizations have successfully navigated the complexities of virtual teamwork:

- **GitHub:** As a platform for software development, GitHub relies on virtual teams to manage projects. The company emphasizes asynchronous communication and uses collaborative tools to facilitate coding and project management across global teams.

- **Zapier:** This fully remote company has cultivated a culture of transparency and communication. They utilize a combination of video calls, written documentation, and collaborative tools to maintain alignment and foster teamwork among their remote employees.

- **Automattic:** The company behind WordPress operates with a distributed workforce. Automatic employs a flexible approach to virtual teamwork, emphasizing written communication and regular team meetups to build relationships and maintain engagement.

Conclusion

Virtual teamwork represents a paradigm shift in how organizations operate. While it poses unique challenges, the strategic implementation of communication tools, cultural awareness, and trust-building practices can lead to successful collaboration. As organizations continue to embrace remote work, understanding and optimizing virtual teamwork will be essential for achieving organizational goals and fostering innovation. The future of work is undoubtedly collaborative, and virtual teamwork is at the forefront of this evolution.

Remote Collaboration

Remote collaboration has emerged as a pivotal aspect of modern work environments, driven by advancements in technology and the increasing necessity for flexibility in the workplace. This section delves into the theoretical foundations, challenges, and practical examples of remote collaboration, illustrating its significance in today's interconnected world.

Theoretical Foundations of Remote Collaboration

Remote collaboration refers to the process of working together from different geographical locations, utilizing technology to facilitate communication and cooperation. The theoretical framework for remote collaboration can be understood through several key concepts:

- **Social Presence Theory:** This theory posits that the degree of awareness individuals have of each other in a virtual environment affects their communication and collaboration. Higher social presence enhances trust and engagement among team members.

- **Media Richness Theory:** This framework suggests that different communication media vary in their ability to convey information. Richer media (e.g., video conferencing) are more effective for complex tasks, while leaner media (e.g., emails) suffice for simpler communications.

- **Collaboration Technology Acceptance Model (CTAM):** This model extends the Technology Acceptance Model (TAM) by focusing on the factors influencing the acceptance and use of collaboration technologies. Key determinants include perceived ease of use, perceived usefulness, and social influence.

Challenges of Remote Collaboration

Despite its advantages, remote collaboration presents several challenges that organizations must address to ensure effective teamwork:

1. **Communication Barriers:** Differences in time zones, cultural backgrounds, and communication styles can lead to misunderstandings and misinterpretations. For instance, a team member in one country may interpret a direct communication style as rudeness, while another may see it as efficiency.

2. **Technology Dependence:** Remote collaboration relies heavily on technology, which can be a double-edged sword. Technical issues, such as connectivity problems or software malfunctions, can disrupt workflow. For example, a sudden internet outage can halt a critical project discussion, causing delays.

3. **Isolation and Engagement:** Remote workers may experience feelings of isolation, leading to decreased motivation and engagement. A study by Gallup (2020) found that remote employees often report lower levels of engagement compared to their in-office counterparts.

4. **Trust and Relationship Building:** Building trust in remote teams can be challenging due to the lack of face-to-face interactions. Trust is crucial for effective collaboration, as it fosters open communication and risk-taking behaviors. One approach to mitigate this issue is through regular team-building activities, even in virtual settings.

Examples of Effective Remote Collaboration

Several organizations have successfully implemented remote collaboration strategies, showcasing best practices that others can emulate:

- **GitLab:** As a fully remote company, GitLab utilizes a comprehensive set of collaboration tools, including Git for version control, Slack for real-time communication, and Zoom for video meetings. Their extensive documentation and asynchronous communication culture empower team members to work independently while remaining connected.

- **Buffer:** Buffer has embraced a transparent remote work culture, sharing their internal processes and strategies publicly. They utilize tools like Trello for project management and Donut for virtual coffee meetups, fostering social connections among team members.

- **Zapier:** Zapier emphasizes the importance of documentation and clear communication in their remote collaboration efforts. By maintaining a centralized knowledge base and encouraging regular check-ins, they ensure that team members remain aligned on goals and expectations.

Conclusion

Remote collaboration is a transformative approach to teamwork, offering flexibility and the ability to harness diverse talent from around the globe. However, organizations must navigate the inherent challenges to maximize its effectiveness. By understanding the theoretical underpinnings, addressing communication barriers, and learning from successful examples, teams can thrive in remote collaboration environments. As technology continues to evolve, the future of remote collaboration holds immense potential for enhancing productivity and fostering innovation across various industries.

$$\text{Collaboration Effectiveness} = f(\text{Communication Quality, Trust, Technology Use}) \tag{6}$$

In conclusion, remote collaboration is not merely a trend but a fundamental shift in how we work together. Organizations that embrace this change and invest in the necessary tools and strategies will likely find themselves at the forefront of the future workplace.

Cross-Cultural Collaboration

The globalization of the workforce has made cross-cultural collaboration an essential aspect of virtual teamwork. As organizations increasingly operate in diverse environments, understanding and managing cultural differences becomes crucial for effective collaboration. This section explores the theories, challenges, and best practices associated with cross-cultural collaboration in virtual environments.

Theoretical Frameworks

Several theoretical frameworks provide insight into cross-cultural collaboration:

- **Hofstede's Cultural Dimensions Theory**: Geert Hofstede's framework identifies six dimensions of culture that influence behavior in professional settings. These dimensions include:
    1. *Power Distance Index (PDI)*: The degree of inequality that exists — and is accepted — between people with and without power.
    2. *Individualism vs. Collectivism (IDV)*: The strength of ties people have to others within their community.
    3. *Masculinity vs. Femininity (MAS)*: The distribution of emotional roles between the genders.
    4. *Uncertainty Avoidance Index (UAI)*: A society's tolerance for uncertainty and ambiguity.

5. *Long-Term Orientation vs. Short-Term Normative Orientation (LTO)*: The focus on future rewards versus respect for tradition.

6. *Indulgence vs. Restraint (IVR)*: The extent to which a society allows free gratification of basic and natural human desires.

- **Trompenaars' Model of National Culture Differences:** This model emphasizes the importance of understanding cultural differences in business interactions. Trompenaars identifies seven dimensions, including universalism vs. particularism and individualism vs. communitarianism, which can affect collaboration outcomes.

Challenges in Cross-Cultural Collaboration

Despite the potential benefits, cross-cultural collaboration presents several challenges:

- **Communication Barriers:** Language differences can lead to misunderstandings and misinterpretations. Even when a common language is used, idiomatic expressions and cultural references may not translate effectively.

- **Differing Work Ethics and Norms:** Cultural variations in attitudes toward deadlines, hierarchy, and teamwork can create friction. For example, in cultures with high power distance, team members may hesitate to challenge authority, while in more egalitarian cultures, open debate is encouraged.

- **Conflict Resolution Styles:** Different cultures have distinct approaches to conflict resolution. Some cultures may favor direct confrontation, while others may prefer indirect methods, leading to unresolved tensions.

- **Time Orientation:** Cultures may have different perceptions of time, affecting project timelines and meeting schedules. For instance, cultures with a monochronic time orientation (e.g., the United States) prioritize punctuality, while polychronic cultures (e.g., many Latin American countries) may view time more fluidly.

Best Practices for Effective Cross-Cultural Collaboration

To overcome challenges and enhance cross-cultural collaboration, organizations can adopt several best practices:

- **Cultural Awareness Training**: Providing training on cultural differences can equip team members with the knowledge to navigate diversity effectively. This training should include an overview of cultural dimensions, communication styles, and conflict resolution strategies.

- **Fostering Open Communication**: Creating an environment where team members feel comfortable expressing their thoughts and concerns can help bridge cultural gaps. Encouraging the use of clear, simple language and avoiding jargon can further facilitate understanding.

- **Building Trust and Relationships**: Trust is foundational in cross-cultural collaboration. Team-building activities, both virtual and in-person, can help establish rapport among team members from different cultural backgrounds.

- **Leveraging Technology for Collaboration**: Utilizing advanced collaboration tools that support diverse communication styles can enhance cross-cultural teamwork. For example, platforms that provide video conferencing, real-time translation, and collaborative document editing can help mitigate communication barriers.

- **Adapting Leadership Styles**: Leaders should adapt their styles to accommodate the cultural preferences of their team members. This may involve being more directive in high power distance cultures while adopting a more participative approach in low power distance cultures.

Examples of Successful Cross-Cultural Collaboration

Several organizations have successfully navigated cross-cultural collaboration:

- **Siemens AG**: Siemens has implemented a global collaboration platform that integrates cultural awareness training into its onboarding process. This initiative has resulted in improved teamwork across its diverse workforce.

- **Unilever**: Unilever promotes cross-cultural collaboration through its "Connected 4 Growth" program, which emphasizes collaborative leadership and local empowerment. This program has enabled teams to adapt their strategies based on local cultural contexts.

- **IBM**: IBM has a long-standing commitment to diversity and inclusion. The company utilizes virtual collaboration tools to connect global teams and encourages cross-cultural exchanges to foster understanding and innovation.

Conclusion

Cross-cultural collaboration in virtual environments is both a challenge and an opportunity. By understanding cultural differences, adopting best practices, and leveraging technology, organizations can enhance their collaborative efforts, leading to innovative solutions and improved outcomes. As the workforce continues to globalize, mastering the art of cross-cultural collaboration will be essential for success in the digital age.

Real-Time Collaboration Tools

In the ever-evolving landscape of virtual collaboration, real-time collaboration tools have emerged as essential components that facilitate seamless interaction among remote teams. These tools enable individuals to work together in a shared digital space, overcoming geographical barriers and fostering a sense of presence and engagement. This section delves into the theoretical foundations, challenges, and practical examples of real-time collaboration tools.

Theoretical Foundations

Real-time collaboration tools are grounded in several theoretical frameworks, including social presence theory, media richness theory, and the theory of distributed cognition.

Social Presence Theory posits that the degree of salience of the other person in the interaction affects the quality of the communication. Tools that provide high social presence, such as video conferencing platforms, enhance the feeling of being together, which can lead to better collaboration outcomes.

Media Richness Theory suggests that communication media can be classified based on their ability to convey information effectively. Richer media, which allow for multiple cues (e.g., video, audio, text), are more effective for complex tasks. Real-time collaboration tools that incorporate video and audio capabilities are considered richer than those relying solely on text.

Distributed Cognition emphasizes that cognitive processes are not solely contained within individuals but are distributed across people and tools. In this context, real-time collaboration tools serve as cognitive artifacts that support collective problem-solving and decision-making.

Challenges of Real-Time Collaboration Tools

Despite their advantages, real-time collaboration tools face several challenges:

Technical Limitations include issues such as bandwidth constraints, latency, and device compatibility. High-quality video and audio streams require significant bandwidth, which can be a barrier for users in low-connectivity regions. Latency can disrupt the flow of conversation, making it difficult for participants to engage naturally.

User Experience is another critical challenge. If the interface of a real-time collaboration tool is not intuitive, users may struggle to navigate its features, leading to frustration and decreased productivity. Ensuring that tools are user-friendly and accessible is vital for widespread adoption.

Security Concerns are paramount, especially when sensitive information is exchanged in real-time. Organizations must implement robust security measures, such as encryption and access controls, to protect data and maintain user trust.

Examples of Real-Time Collaboration Tools

Several tools exemplify the capabilities and functionalities of real-time collaboration:

1. **Zoom** is a widely used video conferencing platform that allows users to host virtual meetings, webinars, and collaborative sessions. Its features include screen sharing, breakout rooms, and chat functionalities, facilitating interactive discussions among participants.

2. **Microsoft Teams** integrates chat, video conferencing, and file sharing into a single platform, promoting collaboration within organizations. The ability to create channels for specific projects or teams enhances organization and communication.

3. **Google Workspace** provides a suite of tools, including Google Docs, Sheets, and Slides, that allow multiple users to edit documents in real-time. This feature supports collaborative writing and brainstorming, enabling teams to work simultaneously on shared content.

4. **Miro** is an online collaborative whiteboard platform that supports brainstorming and visual collaboration. Users can create diagrams, flowcharts, and mind maps in real-time, making it an excellent tool for creative teams.

Impact on Collaboration Dynamics

The integration of real-time collaboration tools has transformed how teams operate. The ability to communicate instantly and work together on shared documents enhances productivity and fosters a culture of collaboration.

Moreover, these tools allow for greater flexibility in work arrangements, enabling teams to operate asynchronously while still maintaining real-time communication when needed. This flexibility can lead to improved work-life balance and increased job satisfaction.

Conclusion

Real-time collaboration tools are indispensable in today's digital workspace, bridging gaps and facilitating effective teamwork. While challenges such as technical limitations and security concerns persist, the benefits of enhanced communication, increased productivity, and improved collaboration dynamics underscore the importance of these tools in the future of virtual collaboration.

As organizations continue to adapt to remote work and global teams, investing in robust real-time collaboration tools will be essential for fostering innovation, creativity, and efficiency in collaborative efforts.

VR and AI Integration

The integration of Virtual Reality (VR) and Artificial Intelligence (AI) represents a transformative shift in how we approach virtual collaboration. By merging these technologies, we can create immersive environments that not only enhance user experience but also provide intelligent systems that adapt to the needs of users in real-time. This subsection explores the theoretical foundations, challenges, and practical applications of VR and AI integration.

Theoretical Foundations

At its core, the integration of VR and AI is grounded in several theoretical frameworks, including human-computer interaction (HCI), cognitive science, and machine learning. HCI principles guide the design of user interfaces within VR environments, ensuring that interactions are intuitive and user-friendly. Cognitive science informs our understanding of how users perceive and navigate virtual spaces, while machine learning algorithms enable systems to learn from user behavior and improve over time.

One of the primary theoretical models relevant to this integration is the **Cognitive Load Theory** (CLT), which posits that learning is optimized when the cognitive load is managed effectively. In VR environments, AI can help reduce extraneous cognitive load by personalizing content delivery based on user preferences and performance, thus enhancing the overall learning experience.

Challenges of Integration

Despite the potential benefits, several challenges hinder the seamless integration of VR and AI:

- **Technical Limitations:** The computational power required for real-time AI processing in immersive VR environments can strain hardware capabilities. Latency issues may arise, leading to delays in AI responses, which can disrupt the immersive experience.

- **Data Privacy Concerns:** The use of AI in VR often necessitates the collection of user data to personalize experiences. This raises significant privacy concerns, especially in collaborative settings where sensitive information may be exchanged.

- **User Acceptance:** Users may exhibit resistance to AI-driven systems due to fears of surveillance or loss of control. Ensuring user trust and acceptance is crucial for the successful deployment of integrated systems.

- **Interoperability:** Integrating AI with existing VR platforms requires compatibility between various software and hardware components, which can be a complex and resource-intensive process.

Practical Applications

The integration of VR and AI has already begun to reshape various sectors through innovative applications:

1. **AI-Powered Virtual Assistants** In VR collaboration spaces, AI-powered virtual assistants can facilitate meetings by managing schedules, providing real-time data analysis, and offering contextual information based on participants'

discussions. For example, in a virtual design meeting, an AI assistant could analyze design proposals and suggest improvements based on user-defined criteria, thus enhancing the collaborative process.

2. Personalized Learning Experiences In educational VR environments, AI can tailor learning experiences to individual users by analyzing their interactions and performance metrics. For instance, an AI-driven educational platform could adapt the difficulty level of tasks in real-time, ensuring that students remain engaged without feeling overwhelmed. This adaptive learning approach is supported by the following equation:

$$\text{Adaptive Difficulty} = f(\text{User Performance, Engagement Level}) \quad (7)$$

Where f represents a function that adjusts the difficulty based on real-time data.

3. Enhanced Collaboration Tools AI can analyze user interactions within VR collaboration spaces to identify patterns and suggest optimal collaboration strategies. For example, if a team frequently struggles with communication during virtual meetings, the AI could recommend specific tools or techniques to improve interaction, such as breakout rooms or guided discussions.

4. Emotional Intelligence and Sentiment Analysis AI algorithms can be employed to assess the emotional states of participants during virtual meetings by analyzing voice tone, facial expressions, and body language through VR sensors. This information can be used to adjust the meeting dynamics, ensuring a more productive and emotionally aware collaboration environment. The underlying principle is represented by the following sentiment analysis model:

$$\text{Sentiment Score} = w_1 \cdot \text{Tone} + w_2 \cdot \text{Expression} + w_3 \cdot \text{Posture} \quad (8)$$

Where w_1, w_2, and w_3 are weights assigned based on the importance of each factor.

Conclusion

The integration of VR and AI offers immense potential for enhancing virtual collaboration. By addressing the challenges associated with this integration, organizations can leverage these technologies to create more immersive, personalized, and effective collaborative environments. As we continue to explore the synergies between VR and AI, it is essential to prioritize user experience, data privacy, and ethical considerations to ensure that these advancements benefit all stakeholders involved in virtual collaboration.

Virtual Collaboration Security

In the rapidly evolving landscape of virtual collaboration, security has emerged as a critical concern that can significantly influence the effectiveness and trustworthiness of virtual collaboration spaces. As organizations increasingly rely on these digital environments to conduct meetings, share sensitive information, and collaborate on projects, ensuring the integrity, confidentiality, and availability of data becomes paramount.

Theoretical Framework of Virtual Collaboration Security

Virtual collaboration security can be understood through the lens of three core principles: confidentiality, integrity, and availability, commonly referred to as the CIA triad.

- **Confidentiality:** This principle ensures that sensitive information is accessed only by authorized individuals. In virtual collaboration, this is achieved through encryption protocols and access controls.

- **Integrity:** Integrity guarantees that the information shared within virtual collaboration spaces remains accurate and unaltered. Implementing hashing algorithms and digital signatures can help maintain data integrity.

- **Availability:** This principle ensures that authorized users have access to information and resources when needed. Ensuring robust infrastructure and redundancy measures can enhance availability.

Common Security Threats in Virtual Collaboration

Despite advancements in security technology, virtual collaboration platforms face numerous threats that can jeopardize the safety of users and data. Some of the most common threats include:

- **Phishing Attacks:** Cybercriminals often use deceptive emails or messages to trick users into revealing sensitive information. For example, a user might receive a seemingly legitimate request for login credentials, leading to unauthorized access to collaboration tools.

- **Malware Infections:** Malware can infiltrate devices through malicious downloads or links shared during virtual meetings. Once installed, malware can steal sensitive information or disrupt collaboration efforts.

- **Man-in-the-Middle Attacks:** In this scenario, an attacker intercepts communication between two parties in a virtual collaboration space, potentially altering messages or stealing data without either party's knowledge.

- **Data Breaches:** Unauthorized access to collaboration platforms can lead to data breaches, where sensitive information is exposed to the public or competitors. High-profile breaches, such as those experienced by major corporations, highlight the importance of robust security measures.

Security Measures for Virtual Collaboration

To mitigate the risks associated with virtual collaboration, organizations must implement a comprehensive security strategy that encompasses various measures:

- **Encryption:** Utilizing encryption protocols, such as TLS (Transport Layer Security), ensures that data transmitted between users is secure and protected from interception.

- **Multi-Factor Authentication (MFA):** MFA adds an additional layer of security by requiring users to provide multiple forms of verification before gaining access to collaboration tools. This significantly reduces the likelihood of unauthorized access.

- **Regular Security Audits:** Conducting periodic security audits helps organizations identify vulnerabilities in their virtual collaboration platforms and address them proactively.

- **User Training and Awareness:** Educating users about security best practices, such as recognizing phishing attempts and using strong passwords, is crucial in fostering a security-conscious culture within organizations.

- **Access Controls:** Implementing role-based access controls ensures that users have access only to the information necessary for their roles, minimizing the risk of data exposure.

Case Studies and Real-World Examples

Several organizations have faced significant challenges related to virtual collaboration security, illustrating the importance of robust measures:

- **Zoom Security Issues:** In 2020, Zoom experienced a surge in usage due to the pandemic, but it also faced criticism for security vulnerabilities, including "Zoombombing," where unauthorized users disrupted meetings. In response, Zoom implemented end-to-end encryption and enhanced security features, demonstrating the need for continuous improvement in security practices.

- **Slack Data Breach:** In 2020, Slack revealed a data breach that exposed user information. The company responded by enhancing its security protocols and encouraging users to enable MFA, highlighting the necessity of proactive security measures in virtual collaboration tools.

- **Microsoft Teams and Security:** Microsoft Teams has integrated various security features, including data encryption and compliance certifications, to ensure secure collaboration. This commitment to security has made it a popular choice for organizations prioritizing data protection.

Future Directions in Virtual Collaboration Security

As virtual collaboration continues to evolve, so too will the security landscape. Emerging technologies, such as artificial intelligence (AI) and blockchain, offer promising avenues for enhancing security in virtual collaboration spaces:

- **AI-Driven Security Solutions:** AI can be leveraged to detect and respond to security threats in real-time, analyzing user behavior and identifying anomalies that may indicate a breach.

- **Blockchain for Data Integrity:** The decentralized nature of blockchain technology can be utilized to ensure data integrity in virtual collaboration. By creating immutable records of transactions, organizations can enhance trust in the information shared within collaboration spaces.

In conclusion, virtual collaboration security is a multifaceted challenge that requires a proactive and comprehensive approach. By understanding the theoretical framework, recognizing common threats, implementing robust security measures, and learning from real-world examples, organizations can create secure virtual collaboration environments that foster productivity and innovation while safeguarding sensitive information.

$$\text{Security Risk} = \text{Threat} \times \text{Vulnerability} \times \text{Impact} \tag{9}$$

This equation emphasizes the importance of addressing all three components to effectively manage security risks in virtual collaboration.

Collaborative Problem Solving in VR

In recent years, Virtual Reality (VR) has emerged as a powerful tool for collaborative problem solving, enabling teams to engage in complex tasks in immersive environments that facilitate creativity and innovation. This section explores the theoretical underpinnings of collaborative problem solving in VR, the challenges faced, and practical examples of its application.

Theoretical Framework

Collaborative problem solving (CPS) is a process where individuals work together to solve a problem, leveraging diverse perspectives and skills. The theoretical foundations of CPS can be traced to several key models:

- **Social Constructivism:** This theory posits that knowledge is constructed through social interactions. In VR, users can share ideas and insights in real-time, leading to a richer understanding of the problem at hand.
- **Cognitive Load Theory:** This theory emphasizes the importance of managing cognitive load to enhance learning and problem-solving capabilities. VR environments can reduce extraneous cognitive load by providing intuitive interfaces and visual aids, allowing users to focus on the problem.
- **Distributed Cognition:** This model suggests that cognitive processes are distributed across individuals and their environments. VR can enhance distributed cognition by allowing users to manipulate virtual objects and visualize complex data collaboratively.

Challenges in Collaborative Problem Solving in VR

Despite its potential, several challenges hinder the effectiveness of collaborative problem solving in VR:

- **Technical Limitations:** Issues such as latency, bandwidth constraints, and hardware compatibility can disrupt the collaborative experience, leading to frustration among users.

- **User Experience:** The design of VR interfaces must prioritize usability to ensure that all participants can engage effectively. Poorly designed interfaces can lead to cognitive overload and hinder collaboration.

- **Social Dynamics:** The virtual environment may alter social interactions, impacting communication styles and trust among team members. Users may feel less accountable in a virtual space, which can affect the group's overall performance.

- **Cultural Differences:** Teams composed of individuals from diverse cultural backgrounds may face challenges in communication and collaboration, as cultural norms and expectations can influence problem-solving approaches.

Examples of Collaborative Problem Solving in VR

Several organizations have successfully implemented VR for collaborative problem solving, demonstrating its effectiveness across various domains:

- **Architecture and Design:** Firms like *Foster + Partners* utilize VR to facilitate design discussions among architects and clients. By immersing clients in virtual walkthroughs of proposed structures, stakeholders can collaboratively identify design flaws and make real-time adjustments, enhancing the overall design process.

- **Healthcare:** The *University of Maryland* has developed a VR platform for medical training, allowing surgical teams to practice complex procedures collaboratively. The immersive environment enables team members to communicate effectively, share insights, and refine their skills in a risk-free setting.

- **Education:** The *University of Illinois* has implemented VR in its engineering curriculum, where students work together to solve engineering challenges. The VR environment fosters teamwork and creativity, allowing students to visualize complex systems and collaborate on solutions.

Mathematical Modeling of Collaborative Problem Solving

To better understand the dynamics of collaborative problem solving in VR, we can model the process mathematically. Let P represent the problem space, C the collaborative capabilities of the team, and E the effectiveness of the VR environment. The effectiveness of collaborative problem solving, E_{CPS}, can be expressed as:

$$E_{CPS} = f(P, C, E)$$

Where:

- f is a function that describes the interaction between the problem space, team capabilities, and the VR environment.

- P can be further defined by its complexity P_c and the clarity of information P_i:
$$P = P_c + P_i$$

- C can be characterized by the diversity of skills C_s and the level of trust C_t:
$$C = C_s \cdot C_t$$

Substituting these definitions into the effectiveness equation, we have:

$$E_{CPS} = f(P_c + P_i, C_s \cdot C_t, E)$$

This model allows researchers and practitioners to assess the impact of various factors on the effectiveness of collaborative problem solving in VR.

Conclusion

Collaborative problem solving in VR presents a unique opportunity to enhance teamwork and innovation across various fields. By understanding the theoretical frameworks, addressing the challenges, and learning from successful examples, organizations can harness the power of VR to foster collaborative environments that drive effective problem solving. As technology continues to evolve, the integration of advanced VR tools will likely further enhance the collaborative capabilities of teams, making it an essential component of modern problem-solving strategies.

Building Trust in Virtual Teams

Building trust in virtual teams is a critical factor that significantly influences collaboration, productivity, and overall team success. In a virtual environment, where face-to-face interactions are limited, establishing and maintaining trust can be particularly challenging. This section explores the theoretical foundations of trust in virtual teams, identifies common problems encountered, and provides examples of effective strategies for fostering trust among team members.

Theoretical Foundations of Trust

Trust is a multifaceted construct that has been extensively studied in organizational behavior and psychology. Mayer, Davis, and Schoorman (1995) propose a model of trust that includes three key components: ability, benevolence, and integrity.

$$\text{Trust} = f(\text{Ability, Benevolence, Integrity}) \qquad (10)$$

where:

- **Ability** refers to the skills and competencies of the team members.

- **Benevolence** indicates the extent to which team members care about one another's interests.

- **Integrity** reflects the adherence to a set of principles that team members find acceptable.

In virtual teams, the absence of physical presence can hinder the perception of these components, making it essential for team leaders to actively cultivate trust through intentional actions and communication strategies.

Common Problems in Building Trust

1. **Limited Non-Verbal Cues**: In face-to-face interactions, non-verbal cues such as body language and eye contact play a significant role in establishing trust. Virtual teams often rely on text-based communication or video conferencing, which can limit these cues and lead to misunderstandings.

2. **Geographical and Cultural Differences**: Virtual teams are often composed of members from diverse geographical locations and cultural backgrounds. These differences can lead to varying communication styles and expectations, which may complicate trust-building efforts.

3. **Isolation and Loneliness**: Team members working in isolation may feel disconnected from their peers, leading to feelings of mistrust and disengagement. The lack of informal interactions that typically occur in physical offices can exacerbate this issue.

4. **Inconsistent Communication**: Inconsistent or unclear communication can erode trust. When team members do not receive timely updates or feedback, it can lead to uncertainty and skepticism regarding each other's intentions and capabilities.

Strategies for Building Trust in Virtual Teams

To address the challenges of building trust in virtual teams, leaders can implement several effective strategies:

1. **Encourage Open Communication**: Establishing a culture of open communication is vital. Team leaders should encourage team members to express their thoughts, concerns, and ideas freely. Regular check-ins and feedback sessions can facilitate this process.

2. **Foster Personal Connections**: Taking time to build personal relationships among team members can enhance trust. Virtual team-building activities, such as icebreakers or informal coffee chats, can help team members get to know each other beyond their professional roles.

3. **Set Clear Expectations**: Clearly defining roles, responsibilities, and performance expectations can reduce ambiguity and build trust. When team members understand what is expected of them and their peers, it fosters accountability and reliability.

4. **Utilize Collaborative Tools**: Leveraging technology to create collaborative environments can enhance transparency and trust. Tools like shared project management platforms, communication apps, and collaborative documents allow team members to stay informed and engaged.

5. **Recognize and Celebrate Achievements**: Acknowledging individual and team accomplishments can reinforce trust and motivation. Celebrating milestones, both big and small, fosters a sense of belonging and appreciation within the team.

Examples of Successful Trust-Building Initiatives

Several organizations have successfully implemented strategies to build trust in their virtual teams:

- **GitLab**: As a fully remote company, GitLab emphasizes transparency and communication. They utilize an open handbook that outlines company policies and practices, ensuring that all team members have access to the same information, which fosters trust and alignment.

- **Buffer**: Buffer prioritizes team culture and connection through regular virtual retreats and team-building activities. They encourage team members to share personal stories and experiences, helping to create bonds that enhance trust.

- **Automattic**: The parent company of WordPress, Automattic, employs a unique approach to remote work by promoting asynchronous communication. They utilize tools like P2 (a WordPress theme for team collaboration) to keep everyone informed and engaged, building trust through consistent updates and shared knowledge.

Conclusion

Building trust in virtual teams is a dynamic and ongoing process that requires intentional effort from all team members. By understanding the theoretical foundations of trust, recognizing common challenges, and implementing effective strategies, organizations can create a collaborative environment that fosters trust, enhances team performance, and ultimately leads to greater success in virtual collaboration.

Bibliography

[1] Mayer, R. C., Davis, J. H., & Schoorman, F. D. (1995). An integrative model of organizational trust. *Academy of Management Review*, 20(3), 709-734.

Virtual Collaboration for Project Management

The landscape of project management has undergone a significant transformation with the advent of virtual collaboration tools. As organizations increasingly adopt remote work practices, the need for effective virtual collaboration in project management has become paramount. This section explores the theoretical foundations, challenges, and practical examples of virtual collaboration for project management.

Theoretical Foundations of Virtual Collaboration in Project Management

Virtual collaboration in project management is grounded in several key theories:

- **Social Presence Theory:** This theory posits that the degree of salience of the other person in a communication interaction influences the quality of communication. In virtual environments, tools that enhance social presence—such as video conferencing and collaborative platforms—can improve team cohesion and communication effectiveness.

- **Media Richness Theory:** This theory suggests that different communication media have varying capacities to convey information effectively. Rich media (e.g., video, virtual reality) are better suited for complex tasks, while lean media (e.g., emails, text messages) may suffice for straightforward communications. Project managers must choose appropriate tools based on the richness of the content being communicated.

- **Distributed Cognition Theory:** This theory emphasizes that knowledge is not only held by individuals but is distributed across tools, artifacts, and other individuals. Virtual collaboration tools enable teams to share knowledge and resources, enhancing collective problem-solving capabilities.

Challenges of Virtual Collaboration in Project Management

While virtual collaboration offers numerous advantages, it also presents several challenges:

- **Communication Barriers:** Virtual teams often face challenges related to miscommunication and misunderstandings due to the lack of non-verbal cues. To mitigate this, project managers should encourage the use of video calls and ensure that communication is clear and concise.

- **Time Zone Differences:** Global teams may struggle with scheduling meetings that accommodate all members. Utilizing asynchronous communication tools, such as project management software, can help alleviate this issue by allowing team members to contribute at their convenience.

- **Technology Dependence:** Virtual collaboration relies heavily on technology, which can lead to issues if tools malfunction or if team members lack technical proficiency. Project managers must provide adequate training and support to ensure all team members are comfortable with the tools being used.

- **Building Trust:** Trust is a critical component of effective collaboration. Virtual teams may find it challenging to build trust without face-to-face interactions. Regular check-ins, team-building activities, and transparent communication can help foster trust among team members.

Practical Examples of Virtual Collaboration in Project Management

Several organizations have successfully implemented virtual collaboration tools to enhance their project management processes. Here are a few notable examples:

- **Asana:** This project management software allows teams to track tasks, set deadlines, and communicate effectively within a single platform. Asana's visual project timelines and boards facilitate transparency and accountability, making it easier for teams to collaborate virtually.

- **Trello:** Trello uses a card-based system to help teams organize tasks and projects. Its intuitive interface allows team members to assign tasks, set due dates, and comment on progress, promoting collaboration and visibility across the project lifecycle.

- **Slack:** Slack is a communication platform that enables teams to collaborate in real-time through channels, direct messaging, and file sharing. Its integration with various project management tools allows teams to streamline communication and keep track of project updates seamlessly.

- **Microsoft Teams:** Microsoft Teams combines chat, video conferencing, and file collaboration in one platform. Its integration with Microsoft Office applications allows for real-time document editing, making it an effective tool for virtual project management.

Conclusion

Virtual collaboration has become an essential aspect of modern project management. By understanding the theoretical foundations, addressing challenges, and leveraging effective tools, project managers can enhance team collaboration and drive project success. As organizations continue to embrace remote work, the importance of virtual collaboration in project management will only increase.

$$P = \frac{C}{T} \tag{11}$$

Where:

- P = Project productivity

- C = Completed tasks

- T = Total time spent

By improving virtual collaboration, organizations can increase productivity (P), ensuring that more tasks are completed in less time, ultimately leading to successful project outcomes.

The Impact of Virtual Collaboration

Increased Productivity and Efficiency

The advent of virtual collaboration spaces has revolutionized the way teams operate, leading to significant increases in productivity and efficiency. This transformation is underpinned by several key factors, including the elimination of geographical barriers, enhanced communication tools, and the integration of advanced technologies.

Theoretical Framework

To understand the impact of virtual collaboration on productivity, we can refer to the *Input-Process-Output* (IPO) model of organizational behavior. According to this model, inputs (resources, information, and human capital) are transformed through processes (collaboration, communication, and decision-making) to produce outputs (products, services, and performance metrics). In the context of virtual collaboration, the inputs are often enhanced by technology, leading to more efficient processes and improved outputs.

$$\text{Productivity} = \frac{\text{Output}}{\text{Input}} \qquad (12)$$

As virtual collaboration tools streamline workflows, the output per unit of input increases, thereby enhancing productivity.

Elimination of Geographical Barriers

One of the most significant advantages of virtual collaboration is the ability to connect teams regardless of their physical location. This capability allows organizations to tap into a global talent pool, leading to a more diverse and skilled workforce. For instance, a software development company can hire developers from different countries, bringing together various perspectives and expertise.

This geographical flexibility not only facilitates the hiring of top talent but also allows for round-the-clock productivity. Teams can work in shifts across different time zones, ensuring that projects progress continuously. A prime example of this is the "follow-the-sun" model, where work is handed off between teams in different time zones, leading to faster project completion.

Enhanced Communication Tools

Modern virtual collaboration platforms, such as Slack, Microsoft Teams, and Zoom, provide a suite of communication tools that enhance interaction among team members. These tools include instant messaging, video conferencing, and collaborative document editing, which allow for real-time communication and feedback.

Research has shown that organizations utilizing these tools experience a 20-25% increase in productivity. For example, a study conducted by McKinsey Global Institute found that using social technologies can raise productivity by 20-25% in knowledge work.

Integration of Advanced Technologies

The integration of advanced technologies, such as artificial intelligence (AI) and machine learning, into virtual collaboration tools further boosts productivity. AI can automate repetitive tasks, analyze data, and provide insights that help teams make informed decisions faster.

For instance, AI-driven analytics can identify bottlenecks in workflows, allowing teams to address issues proactively. A case study involving a marketing firm showed that implementing AI tools reduced campaign planning time by 30%, enabling the team to focus on creative aspects rather than administrative tasks.

Challenges and Considerations

Despite the advantages, organizations must also be aware of potential challenges associated with virtual collaboration. Issues such as communication overload, technology dependency, and the risk of isolation can negatively impact productivity.

$$\text{Communication Overload} = \frac{\text{Total Messages}}{\text{Effective Messages}} \tag{13}$$

A high ratio of total messages to effective messages can lead to confusion and decreased productivity. To mitigate this, organizations should establish clear communication protocols and encourage the use of asynchronous communication methods when appropriate.

Conclusion

In summary, the shift towards virtual collaboration spaces has led to increased productivity and efficiency through the elimination of geographical barriers, enhanced communication tools, and the integration of advanced technologies. While challenges exist, organizations that strategically implement virtual collaboration can harness its full potential, leading to improved performance and competitive advantage in the marketplace.

As we move forward, it is essential for organizations to continuously evaluate and adapt their virtual collaboration strategies to ensure sustained productivity and efficiency in an ever-evolving digital landscape.

Cost Savings and Environmental Benefits

The advent of virtual collaboration spaces has fundamentally transformed the way organizations conduct their operations, leading to significant cost savings and environmental benefits. This section delves into the economic implications of virtual collaboration while highlighting its positive impact on the environment.

Economic Cost Savings

Virtual collaboration eliminates many traditional costs associated with in-person meetings and teamwork. These costs can be categorized as follows:

- **Travel Expenses:** One of the most significant costs incurred by organizations is travel. According to a study by the Global Business Travel Association, U.S. companies spent over $300 billion on business travel in 2019. With virtual collaboration tools, organizations can drastically reduce or even eliminate travel expenses. For example, by utilizing video conferencing platforms like Zoom or Microsoft Teams, teams can meet in real-time without the need for flights, hotels, or meals.

- **Office Space:** As remote work becomes more prevalent, organizations are re-evaluating their physical office requirements. A study by CBRE revealed that companies could save an average of $11,000 per employee annually by reducing office space. Virtual collaboration allows teams to work effectively from anywhere, reducing the need for large office spaces and associated costs such as utilities, maintenance, and rent.

- **Time Savings:** Virtual collaboration can enhance productivity by minimizing the time spent on commuting and in meetings. A report by the

Institute for Corporate Productivity found that remote workers are 35-40% more productive than their in-office counterparts. This productivity translates into cost savings as employees can focus on their core tasks rather than spending hours in transit or waiting for meetings to start.

Environmental Benefits

The environmental impact of virtual collaboration is equally noteworthy. By reducing the need for travel and large office spaces, organizations can significantly decrease their carbon footprints. The following points illustrate these benefits:

- **Reduced Carbon Emissions:** Transportation is a major contributor to greenhouse gas emissions. The Environmental Protection Agency (EPA) estimates that transportation accounts for 29% of total greenhouse gas emissions in the United States. By minimizing travel through virtual collaboration, organizations can help reduce these emissions. For instance, a study by the Carbon Trust found that remote working could save 3.6 million tonnes of CO_2 annually in the UK alone.

- **Decreased Resource Consumption:** Traditional office environments consume significant resources, including paper, electricity, and water. Virtual collaboration encourages digital documentation and communication, reducing the reliance on physical resources. For example, the use of collaborative platforms like Google Workspace or Microsoft 365 allows teams to share documents electronically, minimizing paper waste. A report by the World Wildlife Fund (WWF) indicates that moving to a paperless office could reduce paper usage by up to 90%.

- **Sustainable Practices:** Organizations that adopt virtual collaboration often implement sustainable practices, such as flexible work hours and remote work policies. These practices contribute to a healthier work-life balance and reduce the overall environmental impact. For instance, a company that allows employees to work from home can significantly decrease energy consumption in its office buildings, leading to lower utility bills and a smaller ecological footprint.

Theoretical Framework

The economic and environmental benefits of virtual collaboration can be analyzed through the lens of the *Triple Bottom Line* (TBL) framework, which emphasizes the importance of social, environmental, and economic performance. The TBL approach encourages organizations to consider the broader implications of their business practices, leading to a more sustainable and responsible operational model.

The following equation can be used to illustrate the cost savings associated with virtual collaboration:

$$\text{Total Cost Savings} = \text{Travel Savings} + \text{Office Space Savings} + \text{Time Savings} \quad (14)$$

Where: - Travel Savings is the total amount saved by reducing travel expenses. - Office Space Savings is the total reduction in costs associated with maintaining physical office space. - Time Savings can be quantified in monetary terms by calculating the value of time saved by employees.

Examples of Successful Implementation

Several organizations have successfully leveraged virtual collaboration to achieve cost savings and environmental benefits:

- **Salesforce:** The cloud-based software company Salesforce has adopted a flexible work model that emphasizes remote collaboration. As a result, the company has reduced its office space by 30%, leading to significant cost savings and a reduction in its carbon footprint.

- **Twitter:** Twitter announced in 2020 that employees could work from home indefinitely. This decision not only reduced operational costs associated with maintaining large office spaces but also contributed to a decrease in the company's overall carbon emissions as employees no longer needed to commute.

- **Dell Technologies:** Dell has implemented a flexible work policy that allows employees to work remotely. The company reported saving $12 million in travel costs in 2020 alone, demonstrating the financial benefits of virtual collaboration.

Conclusion

In conclusion, the cost savings and environmental benefits associated with virtual collaboration are substantial. By reducing travel expenses, minimizing the need for physical office spaces, and promoting sustainable practices, organizations can not only enhance their economic performance but also contribute to a healthier planet. As virtual collaboration continues to evolve, its role in shaping a more sustainable future will become increasingly significant.

Enhancing Communication and Connectivity

In the realm of virtual collaboration, enhancing communication and connectivity is paramount. Effective communication is the backbone of any successful collaborative effort, and in virtual environments, this becomes even more crucial due to the absence of physical cues and the potential for technological barriers. This section explores the theories, challenges, and practical examples that illustrate how communication and connectivity can be improved in virtual collaboration spaces.

Theoretical Framework

Theories of communication, such as Shannon-Weaver's Model of Communication, emphasize the importance of the sender, message, medium, receiver, and feedback in the communication process. In virtual collaboration, the medium often includes various digital tools, such as video conferencing platforms, chat applications, and collaborative software. The effectiveness of these tools hinges on their ability to facilitate clear and efficient communication.

$$C = \frac{S}{N} \qquad (15)$$

where C represents the channel capacity, S is the signal power, and N is the noise power. In the context of virtual collaboration, enhancing communication means maximizing the signal (clear communication) while minimizing noise (misunderstandings and technical issues).

Challenges in Virtual Communication

Despite the advancements in technology, several challenges persist in enhancing communication and connectivity within virtual collaboration spaces:

- **Technological Barriers:** Issues such as bandwidth limitations, latency, and device compatibility can hinder effective communication. For instance, a team member in a remote location may experience lag during a video call, leading to missed cues and fragmented conversations.

- **Cultural Differences:** In a globalized workforce, team members may come from diverse cultural backgrounds, which can affect communication styles and interpretations. For example, direct communication may be valued in some cultures, while others may prefer a more indirect approach.
- **Lack of Non-Verbal Cues:** Non-verbal communication, such as body language and facial expressions, plays a significant role in conveying messages. In virtual settings, these cues are often diminished, which can lead to misunderstandings.
- **Collaboration Fatigue:** The constant use of virtual communication tools can lead to fatigue, known as "Zoom fatigue," where individuals feel drained after prolonged video meetings. This fatigue can decrease engagement and hinder effective communication.

Strategies for Enhancing Communication

To address these challenges, organizations can implement several strategies to enhance communication and connectivity in virtual collaboration:

- **Utilizing Advanced Communication Tools:** Leveraging platforms that integrate multiple communication channels—such as video, audio, and chat—can enhance connectivity. Tools like Microsoft Teams, Slack, and Zoom offer features that facilitate seamless communication and collaboration.
- **Establishing Clear Communication Protocols:** Organizations should define communication norms and expectations, such as response times, preferred communication channels, and guidelines for virtual meetings. This clarity helps reduce misunderstandings and ensures that all team members are on the same page.
- **Fostering an Inclusive Environment:** Encouraging team members to share their cultural perspectives and communication preferences can help bridge gaps and enhance understanding. This may involve training sessions focused on cultural competence and effective virtual communication.
- **Incorporating Interactive Elements:** Engaging team members through interactive activities during virtual meetings—such as polls, breakout rooms, and collaborative brainstorming sessions—can enhance participation and connectivity. For example, using tools like Miro or MURAL allows teams to visualize ideas collaboratively.

- **Providing Technical Support:** Offering resources and support for team members experiencing technical difficulties can minimize disruptions. This may include training sessions on using collaboration tools effectively or providing IT support during meetings.

Real-World Examples

Several organizations have successfully enhanced communication and connectivity in their virtual collaboration efforts:

- **Remote Work at GitLab:** GitLab, a fully remote company, emphasizes asynchronous communication, allowing team members to contribute at their convenience. They utilize a combination of documentation, issue tracking, and video calls to ensure clear communication and connectivity across time zones.

- **Virtual Reality Meetings at Spatial:** Spatial, a virtual reality platform, allows teams to meet in immersive 3D environments. This technology enhances communication by providing a sense of presence and enabling non-verbal cues through avatars, thus bridging some gaps inherent in traditional video conferencing.

- **Cross-Cultural Teams at Buffer:** Buffer, a social media management platform, promotes transparency and inclusivity by encouraging team members from diverse backgrounds to share their communication styles and preferences. This practice fosters understanding and enhances overall team connectivity.

Conclusion

Enhancing communication and connectivity in virtual collaboration spaces is essential for fostering effective teamwork and achieving organizational goals. By understanding the theoretical underpinnings of communication, addressing the challenges faced in virtual environments, and implementing strategic solutions, organizations can create a more connected and collaborative workforce. As technology continues to evolve, the potential for enhanced communication in virtual collaboration will only grow, paving the way for innovative and productive teamwork.

Breaking Down Physical Barriers

The advent of virtual collaboration technologies has fundamentally transformed the way individuals and teams interact, thereby breaking down physical barriers that once limited communication and cooperation. In this section, we explore the theoretical underpinnings of virtual collaboration, the problems associated with physical barriers, and real-world examples that illustrate the impact of these technologies.

Theoretical Framework

Virtual collaboration is grounded in several theories, including Social Presence Theory, Media Richness Theory, and the Distributed Cognition Framework.

Social Presence Theory posits that the degree of awareness of another person in a communication interaction affects the quality of the interaction. In virtual environments, tools that enhance social presence—such as avatars, video conferencing, and immersive virtual reality—can create a sense of closeness and immediacy that helps to mitigate the feelings of isolation often associated with remote work.

Media Richness Theory suggests that different communication media have varying capabilities to convey information. Richer media (e.g., video conferencing) can provide more cues and reduce ambiguity compared to leaner media (e.g., email). This is particularly important in virtual collaboration, where the richness of the medium can enhance understanding and reduce the likelihood of miscommunication.

Distributed Cognition Framework emphasizes that cognition is not solely an individual process but is distributed across people, tools, and environments. In virtual collaboration, the tools used—such as collaborative software and virtual environments—act as extensions of cognitive processes, allowing teams to solve problems collectively and efficiently.

Problems Associated with Physical Barriers

Despite the advantages of virtual collaboration, several challenges persist:

1. Limited Access to Technology   In many regions, access to high-speed internet and advanced computing devices remains limited. This digital divide can exacerbate existing inequalities, preventing certain groups from fully participating in virtual collaboration.

2. Time Zone Differences   Global teams often face difficulties coordinating meetings across different time zones. This can lead to delays in communication and collaboration, as team members may struggle to find mutually convenient times to connect.

3. Cultural Differences   Physical barriers are often accompanied by cultural differences that can influence communication styles, decision-making processes, and conflict resolution strategies. Misunderstandings arising from these differences can hinder effective collaboration.

4. Lack of Non-Verbal Cues   While virtual collaboration tools can provide visual and auditory cues, they often lack the richness of face-to-face interactions, where body language and non-verbal signals play a crucial role in communication. This can lead to misinterpretations and reduced trust among team members.

Examples of Breaking Down Physical Barriers

Virtual collaboration technologies have successfully addressed many of the challenges posed by physical barriers.

Example 1: Remote Work During the COVID-19 Pandemic   The COVID-19 pandemic forced organizations worldwide to adopt remote work practices almost overnight. Tools such as Zoom, Microsoft Teams, and Slack became essential for maintaining communication and collaboration among distributed teams. Companies that previously relied on in-person meetings quickly adapted to virtual formats, demonstrating that physical barriers could be effectively overcome.

Example 2: International Project Teams   Consider the case of an international project team working on renewable energy solutions. Team members from different countries, such as Brazil, Germany, and South Africa, utilized virtual collaboration platforms to share ideas, conduct brainstorming sessions, and develop project proposals. By leveraging tools like Miro for collaborative brainstorming and Trello for project management, the team was able to break down geographical barriers and work cohesively towards a common goal.

Example 3: Virtual Reality in Education Educational institutions have also embraced virtual collaboration to enhance learning experiences. Virtual reality (VR) platforms allow students from diverse backgrounds to collaborate on projects in immersive environments. For instance, architecture students from different universities can work together in a virtual space to design buildings, overcoming the limitations of physical distance and fostering a collaborative learning atmosphere.

Conclusion

Breaking down physical barriers through virtual collaboration is not merely about technology; it involves understanding and addressing the underlying challenges that come with remote interactions. As organizations and individuals continue to adapt to a virtual-first world, the ability to effectively collaborate across distances will remain critical to achieving collective goals. By leveraging theoretical frameworks, addressing challenges, and learning from successful examples, we can harness the full potential of virtual collaboration to create inclusive and productive environments that transcend physical limitations.

Fostering Creativity and Innovation

In the rapidly evolving landscape of virtual collaboration, the ability to foster creativity and innovation has become paramount. Virtual environments offer unique opportunities that can enhance creative processes and facilitate innovative solutions to complex problems. This section explores the theoretical frameworks, challenges, and practical examples of how virtual collaboration can be leveraged to stimulate creativity and innovation.

Theoretical Frameworks

The relationship between collaboration and creativity has been extensively studied in various fields, including psychology, organizational behavior, and design thinking. One prominent theory is the **Social Interaction Theory**, which posits that creativity is often a product of collaborative interactions among individuals with diverse perspectives and expertise. According to this theory, the exchange of ideas in a virtual setting can lead to novel solutions that may not have emerged in isolation.

Another relevant framework is the **Systems Theory of Innovation**, which emphasizes the interconnectedness of various elements in the innovation ecosystem. This theory suggests that fostering an environment conducive to creativity requires not only collaboration but also the integration of technology, culture, and organizational practices. Virtual collaboration spaces can serve as platforms that support this interconnectedness, facilitating idea generation and the iterative process of innovation.

Challenges to Creativity in Virtual Environments

Despite the potential advantages of virtual collaboration for fostering creativity, several challenges must be addressed:

- **Communication Barriers:** Virtual environments may hinder non-verbal communication cues, such as body language and tone of voice, which are crucial for effective collaboration. This can lead to misunderstandings and reduce the richness of creative exchanges.

- **Isolation:** Remote collaboration can sometimes lead to feelings of isolation among team members, diminishing motivation and engagement. This emotional disconnect can stifle creativity and innovation.

- **Technological Limitations:** The effectiveness of virtual collaboration tools can vary significantly. Inadequate technology can impede the flow of ideas and the collaborative process, making it challenging to foster an innovative atmosphere.

Strategies for Fostering Creativity and Innovation

To overcome these challenges, organizations can implement several strategies to enhance creativity and innovation in virtual collaboration:

- **Creating Inclusive Virtual Spaces:** Designing virtual collaboration spaces that encourage participation from all team members is crucial. This can involve using tools that allow for anonymous idea sharing or brainstorming sessions, where everyone's input is valued equally.

- **Utilizing Advanced Collaboration Tools:** Leveraging technology that enhances communication and collaboration can significantly impact creative outcomes. Tools such as virtual whiteboards, real-time brainstorming applications, and immersive environments can facilitate more dynamic interactions.

- **Encouraging Diverse Teams:** Bringing together individuals from various backgrounds and disciplines can lead to a richer exchange of ideas. Research shows that diversity fosters creativity, as different perspectives can challenge conventional thinking and inspire innovative solutions.

- **Implementing Structured Creativity Techniques:** Techniques such as Design Thinking, Agile methodologies, and the Six Thinking Hats can provide frameworks for structured creativity in virtual settings. These methods encourage divergent thinking and help teams navigate complex problems collaboratively.

Examples of Successful Virtual Collaboration for Innovation

Several organizations have successfully harnessed the power of virtual collaboration to foster creativity and innovation:

- **Google's Virtual Innovation Labs:** Google has created virtual innovation labs where cross-functional teams collaborate on new product ideas. By utilizing immersive virtual environments, team members can interact in real-time, share ideas, and prototype solutions, leading to successful product launches.

- **IBM's Design Thinking Workshops:** IBM employs Design Thinking workshops in virtual formats, allowing diverse teams to collaborate on user-centered design projects. These workshops have led to innovative software solutions that address customer needs effectively.

- **NASA's Collaborative Innovation Platform:** NASA has developed a collaborative platform that connects scientists and engineers from around the world. This platform facilitates the sharing of ideas and resources, leading to groundbreaking innovations in space exploration technologies.

Conclusion

Fostering creativity and innovation in virtual collaboration spaces is not merely a byproduct of technology; it requires intentional strategies, diverse teams, and an understanding of the dynamics of virtual interactions. By addressing the challenges and leveraging the opportunities presented by virtual collaboration, organizations can create environments that not only enhance creativity but also drive meaningful innovation. As we move forward in an increasingly digital world, the ability to cultivate creativity within virtual settings will be a critical determinant of success in various industries.

Improving Work-Life Balance

The concept of work-life balance has gained significant attention in recent years, particularly as the boundaries between professional and personal lives have blurred due to advancements in technology and the rise of remote work. Virtual collaboration spaces have emerged as a crucial component in addressing this challenge, offering tools and strategies that can enhance individuals' ability to manage their work and personal commitments effectively.

Theoretical Framework

Work-life balance can be defined as the equilibrium between the time and energy dedicated to work-related activities and those allocated to personal life, including family, leisure, and self-care. According to Greenhaus and Allen (2011), achieving a satisfactory work-life balance is essential for overall well-being and job satisfaction. Theories such as the Role Theory suggest that individuals occupy multiple roles in life, and the ability to manage these roles effectively can lead to improved performance in both personal and professional domains.

Challenges to Work-Life Balance

Despite the potential benefits of virtual collaboration, several challenges can hinder the achievement of work-life balance:

- **Increased Workload:** The flexibility of remote work can lead to an expectation of constant availability, resulting in longer working hours and burnout. According to a study by the International Labour Organization (ILO), remote workers often report working more hours than their office-based counterparts.

- **Distractions at Home:** Working from home can introduce various distractions, such as household chores, family responsibilities, and the temptation to engage in leisure activities, which can disrupt focus and productivity.

- **Lack of Clear Boundaries:** The absence of a physical separation between work and home can make it difficult for individuals to disconnect from work, leading to stress and decreased overall satisfaction. Research by the American Psychological Association (APA) indicates that 60% of remote workers feel they are unable to unplug from work.

Strategies for Improvement

To improve work-life balance through virtual collaboration, organizations and individuals can adopt several strategies:

- **Establishing Clear Boundaries:** Organizations should promote the importance of setting boundaries between work and personal life. This can include defining specific working hours and encouraging employees to disconnect after hours. For instance, companies like Basecamp have implemented policies that discourage after-hours communication, fostering a culture of respect for personal time.

- **Flexible Work Arrangements:** Providing employees with the flexibility to choose their working hours can lead to increased job satisfaction and productivity. A study by FlexJobs found that 73% of respondents reported improved work-life balance when given flexible work options.

- **Utilizing Technology Wisely:** While technology can facilitate collaboration, it is essential to use it judiciously. Tools like Slack and Zoom should be used to enhance communication without overwhelming employees. Implementing "no meeting" days can also help reduce the burden of constant connectivity.

- **Encouraging Regular Breaks:** Research shows that taking regular breaks can improve focus and productivity. Organizations can promote the use of techniques such as the Pomodoro Technique, which encourages short breaks after focused work sessions, to help employees recharge.

Examples of Successful Implementation

Several organizations have successfully integrated virtual collaboration tools to enhance work-life balance:

- **Zapier:** This fully remote company emphasizes a results-oriented work environment, allowing employees to set their own schedules. They also encourage regular time off to prevent burnout, leading to high employee satisfaction and retention rates.

- **GitLab:** As a pioneer in remote work, GitLab has established a comprehensive remote work handbook that outlines best practices for maintaining work-life balance. Their emphasis on asynchronous communication allows team members to work at their own pace, accommodating personal commitments.

- **Buffer:** Buffer promotes a culture of transparency and flexibility, encouraging employees to take time off as needed. Their commitment to mental health resources and regular check-ins has resulted in a supportive work environment that prioritizes well-being.

Conclusion

Improving work-life balance in the context of virtual collaboration is not only beneficial for individual well-being but also essential for organizational success. By implementing strategies that promote flexibility, clear boundaries, and effective use of technology, organizations can create an environment that supports employees in managing their professional and personal lives. As the future of work continues to evolve, prioritizing work-life balance will be crucial for attracting and retaining top talent, fostering innovation, and enhancing overall productivity.

$$\text{Work-Life Balance} = \frac{\text{Work Satisfaction} + \text{Personal Satisfaction}}{\text{Time Allocated to Work} + \text{Time Allocated to Personal Life}} \tag{16}$$

This equation illustrates the delicate interplay between work and personal satisfaction, emphasizing the need for a balanced approach to time allocation in the pursuit of a fulfilling life.

References

- Greenhaus, J. H., & Allen, T. D. (2011). Work-family balance: A review and extension of the literature. *The Handbook of Industrial, Work & Organizational Psychology*, 3, 165-188.

- International Labour Organization (ILO). (2020). *Working from Home: From Pandemic to Future of Work*.

- American Psychological Association (APA). (2021). *The Impact of Remote Work on Employee Well-Being*.

- FlexJobs. (2021). *2021 State of Remote Work*.

Virtual Collaboration in the Post-Pandemic Era

The COVID-19 pandemic has fundamentally transformed the landscape of work, accelerating the adoption of virtual collaboration tools and reshaping the way teams interact. As organizations navigate the post-pandemic era, understanding the implications of this shift is crucial for fostering effective collaboration. This section explores the evolution of virtual collaboration during and after the pandemic, highlighting relevant theories, challenges, and examples.

The Acceleration of Virtual Collaboration

Before the pandemic, many organizations were already utilizing virtual collaboration tools, but the necessity of remote work during lockdowns catalyzed widespread adoption. According to a report by [1], the use of digital tools for remote collaboration increased by 300% in some sectors. This rapid transition has led to a paradigm shift in workplace dynamics, compelling organizations to rethink their collaboration strategies.

Theoretical Frameworks

To understand the impact of virtual collaboration in the post-pandemic era, we can draw on several theoretical frameworks:

- **Social Presence Theory:** This theory posits that the effectiveness of communication is influenced by the degree of social presence perceived by participants. In a virtual environment, factors such as video quality, audio clarity, and the use of avatars can enhance or diminish social presence, affecting collaboration outcomes.

- **Media Richness Theory:** This framework categorizes communication channels based on their capacity to convey information. Richer media (e.g., video conferencing) are more effective for complex tasks that require immediate feedback, while leaner media (e.g., emails) are suitable for straightforward communication. The pandemic highlighted the importance of selecting appropriate media for various collaboration tasks.

- **Distributed Team Theory:** This theory focuses on the dynamics of teams that operate across geographical boundaries. The pandemic forced many organizations to adopt distributed team models, leading to new challenges in coordination, trust-building, and cultural integration.

Challenges of Virtual Collaboration Post-Pandemic

While the shift to virtual collaboration has opened new avenues for teamwork, it has also introduced several challenges:

- **Collaboration Fatigue:** Prolonged reliance on virtual meetings has led to a phenomenon known as "Zoom fatigue," characterized by decreased engagement and productivity. [?] found that the cognitive load of maintaining eye contact and interpreting non-verbal cues in virtual settings can be exhausting, leading to burnout.
- **Communication Barriers:** The absence of physical presence can hinder effective communication. Misinterpretations are more likely in virtual settings, where non-verbal cues are less discernible. Organizations must invest in training employees to communicate effectively in virtual environments.
- **Equity and Inclusion:** The digital divide remains a significant challenge. Not all employees have equal access to technology and high-speed internet, leading to disparities in participation and collaboration. Organizations must ensure equitable access to virtual collaboration tools to foster inclusivity.

Examples of Successful Virtual Collaboration

Several organizations have successfully navigated the challenges of virtual collaboration in the post-pandemic era:

- **GitLab:** As a fully remote company, GitLab has effectively leveraged virtual collaboration tools to maintain productivity and engagement. Their comprehensive handbook on remote work serves as a valuable resource for organizations seeking to implement best practices in virtual collaboration.
- **Zoom Video Communications:** The company behind the popular video conferencing tool has continuously adapted its platform to meet the evolving needs of users. Features such as breakout rooms and virtual backgrounds have enhanced the collaborative experience, enabling more interactive meetings.
- **Slack Technologies:** By integrating various applications within its platform, Slack has created a centralized hub for team communication and collaboration. The use of channels allows for organized discussions, while integrations with project management tools streamline workflows.

Future Directions for Virtual Collaboration

Looking ahead, organizations must consider the following strategies to enhance virtual collaboration:

- **Hybrid Work Models:** As companies transition to hybrid work environments, they must develop strategies to integrate in-person and virtual collaboration seamlessly. This includes investing in technology that supports hybrid meetings and fostering a culture that values both remote and on-site contributions.

- **Continuous Training and Development:** Organizations should prioritize ongoing training in virtual collaboration skills, including effective communication, conflict resolution, and cultural competency. This will empower employees to navigate the complexities of remote teamwork.

- **Emphasizing Well-Being:** To combat collaboration fatigue and promote employee well-being, organizations should encourage regular breaks, implement flexible work hours, and create opportunities for informal interactions among team members.

In conclusion, the post-pandemic era presents both challenges and opportunities for virtual collaboration. By leveraging theoretical frameworks, addressing challenges, and adopting best practices, organizations can foster effective collaboration in an increasingly digital world. The lessons learned during this transformative period will shape the future of work, emphasizing the importance of adaptability, inclusivity, and innovation in virtual collaboration.

Virtual Collaboration for Diversity and Inclusion

Virtual collaboration has emerged as a powerful tool for promoting diversity and inclusion within organizations and teams. In an increasingly globalized world, the ability to connect individuals from various backgrounds, cultures, and experiences is crucial for fostering innovative ideas and solutions. This section explores the theoretical foundations, challenges, and practical examples of how virtual collaboration can enhance diversity and inclusion in the workplace.

Theoretical Foundations

The concept of diversity encompasses a wide range of characteristics, including race, gender, age, sexual orientation, disability, and cultural background. Inclusion, on the other hand, refers to the practices and policies that ensure individuals from diverse backgrounds feel valued and integrated within a team or organization. According to [?], diversity can lead to improved performance when combined with effective inclusion strategies. This is particularly relevant in virtual collaboration, where the dynamics of interaction can significantly influence team effectiveness.

One theoretical framework that supports the integration of diversity and inclusion in virtual collaboration is Social Identity Theory. This theory posits that individuals categorize themselves and others into social groups, which influences their behavior and interactions. In virtual environments, understanding social identities is essential for creating inclusive spaces where all voices are heard. Furthermore, the *Contact Hypothesis* suggests that increased interaction among diverse groups can reduce prejudice and promote understanding, making virtual collaboration an ideal platform for fostering relationships across cultural boundaries [?].

Challenges in Virtual Collaboration

While virtual collaboration presents opportunities for enhancing diversity and inclusion, several challenges must be addressed:

- **Communication Barriers:** Different cultural backgrounds can lead to misunderstandings in communication styles. For example, direct communication may be preferred in some cultures, while others may favor indirect approaches. These differences can hinder effective collaboration if not managed properly.

- **Technology Access and Literacy:** Not all team members may have equal access to technology or the necessary skills to use virtual collaboration tools effectively. This digital divide can exacerbate existing inequalities and limit participation from underrepresented groups.

- **Implicit Bias:** Virtual environments can sometimes amplify biases, as individuals may rely on stereotypes when interacting with avatars or profiles rather than engaging with the person behind them. This can lead to exclusionary practices and hinder the formation of genuine connections.

- **Isolation and Engagement:** Virtual collaboration can inadvertently lead to feelings of isolation among team members, particularly those from minority backgrounds. Ensuring that all voices are heard and valued is essential for maintaining engagement and motivation.

Examples of Successful Virtual Collaboration for Diversity and Inclusion

Several organizations have successfully leveraged virtual collaboration to enhance diversity and inclusion:

- **Global Teams at IBM:** IBM has implemented virtual collaboration tools that allow teams from diverse geographical and cultural backgrounds to work together seamlessly. By promoting inclusive practices, such as regular check-ins and feedback sessions, IBM has fostered an environment where all employees feel empowered to contribute their unique perspectives.

- **Remote Work Initiatives at Buffer:** Buffer, a social media management platform, has embraced remote work as a means to diversify its workforce. By hiring talent from around the world, Buffer has created a culturally rich team that benefits from varied viewpoints. The company utilizes virtual collaboration tools to ensure that every team member, regardless of location, has an equal opportunity to participate in discussions and decision-making processes.

- **Diversity and Inclusion Training:** Organizations like Google have developed virtual training programs focused on diversity and inclusion. These programs utilize interactive virtual environments to engage employees in discussions about unconscious bias and cultural competency, fostering a more inclusive workplace culture.

Best Practices for Promoting Diversity and Inclusion in Virtual Collaboration

To maximize the benefits of virtual collaboration for diversity and inclusion, organizations should consider the following best practices:

- **Establish Clear Communication Norms:** Develop guidelines for communication that respect diverse styles and preferences. Encourage team members to share their communication preferences and adapt accordingly.

- **Invest in Technology Access:** Provide resources and training to ensure all team members have access to the necessary technology and skills for effective virtual collaboration. This includes offering workshops on using collaboration tools and providing financial assistance for equipment.

- **Create Inclusive Virtual Spaces:** Design virtual meeting environments that promote engagement and participation from all team members. This may include using breakout rooms for smaller group discussions or employing facilitation techniques that encourage quieter voices to contribute.

- **Foster a Culture of Feedback:** Regularly solicit feedback from team members regarding their experiences in virtual collaboration. Use this feedback to inform practices and policies that enhance inclusivity.

- **Celebrate Diversity:** Recognize and celebrate the diverse backgrounds and contributions of team members. This can include sharing cultural insights during meetings or highlighting diverse achievements within the team.

Conclusion

Virtual collaboration holds significant potential for enhancing diversity and inclusion within organizations. By understanding the theoretical underpinnings, addressing challenges, and implementing best practices, organizations can create virtual environments that value and leverage diversity. As the workforce continues to evolve, embracing diversity through virtual collaboration will be essential for fostering innovation and driving success in the digital age.

Virtual Collaboration for Globalization

Globalization refers to the process by which businesses or other organizations develop international influence or start operating on an international scale. In the context of virtual collaboration, globalization is significantly enhanced through the use of digital technologies that enable seamless communication and cooperation across geographical boundaries. This section explores the role of virtual collaboration in facilitating globalization, the challenges it presents, and the practical implications for organizations and individuals.

The Role of Virtual Collaboration in Globalization

Virtual collaboration tools allow teams from different parts of the world to work together as if they were in the same room. Technologies such as video conferencing, collaborative project management software, and cloud-based document sharing have transformed the way organizations operate internationally. According to a report by McKinsey Global Institute, organizations that leverage digital collaboration tools can increase productivity by up to 25% ([1]).

The rise of remote work has further accelerated globalization. Companies can now hire talent from anywhere in the world, leading to a more diverse workforce. For instance, companies like GitHub and Automattic operate entirely remotely, allowing them to tap into global talent pools, which enhances creativity and innovation.

Challenges of Virtual Collaboration in a Global Context

Despite the benefits, virtual collaboration for globalization comes with its own set of challenges:

- **Time Zone Differences:** Coordinating meetings across multiple time zones can lead to scheduling conflicts and can impact team cohesion. For example, a team based in New York and another in Tokyo may find it challenging to find overlapping working hours.

- **Cultural Differences:** Different cultural backgrounds can influence communication styles, work ethics, and decision-making processes. For example, a direct communication style common in the United States may clash with a more indirect style prevalent in Japan, leading to misunderstandings.

- **Technological Barriers:** Not all regions have the same access to high-speed internet and advanced technology. This digital divide can hinder participation from certain areas, exacerbating inequalities in global collaboration.

- **Security and Privacy Issues:** Collaborating across borders raises concerns about data security and privacy. Different countries have varying regulations regarding data protection, which can complicate compliance for multinational organizations.

Theoretical Perspectives on Virtual Collaboration and Globalization

From a theoretical perspective, the concept of *Networked Globalization* ([2]) posits that the internet has created a new form of globalization characterized by interconnectedness and interdependence. This framework emphasizes the importance of digital networks in facilitating real-time communication and collaboration, enabling organizations to operate on a global scale.

Moreover, the *Social Capital Theory* ([3]) suggests that social networks have value. In a global context, virtual collaboration enhances social capital by connecting individuals from diverse backgrounds, fostering relationships that can lead to collaborative opportunities. The ability to build trust and rapport in virtual environments is crucial for effective global teamwork.

Examples of Successful Virtual Collaboration in Globalization

Several organizations have successfully leveraged virtual collaboration to enhance their global operations:

- **Slack Technologies:** The company's collaboration platform allows teams from around the world to communicate in real time, share files, and integrate with other tools. This has enabled businesses to operate more efficiently across borders.

- **Airbnb:** By utilizing virtual collaboration tools for its global teams, Airbnb has been able to maintain a cohesive culture despite its widespread geographical presence. Regular virtual meetings and collaborative platforms allow for consistent communication and alignment on goals.

- **UNESCO:** The United Nations Educational, Scientific and Cultural Organization utilizes virtual collaboration tools to connect experts and stakeholders from different countries to work on global education initiatives. This has resulted in the sharing of best practices and resources across borders.

Conclusion

Virtual collaboration plays a pivotal role in the process of globalization, enabling organizations to operate on a global scale and fostering diverse, inclusive work environments. However, it is essential to address the challenges that come with it, such as time zone differences, cultural disparities, and technological barriers. By leveraging theoretical frameworks like Networked Globalization and Social Capital Theory, organizations can better understand the dynamics of virtual collaboration in a global context. The successful examples of companies like Slack and Airbnb demonstrate the potential of virtual collaboration to enhance productivity, innovation, and connectivity in an increasingly globalized world.

Bibliography

[1] McKinsey Global Institute. (2017). *Digital Globalization: The New Era of Global Flows.*

[2] Castells, M. (1996). *The Rise of the Network Society.* Blackwell Publishers.

[3] Putnam, R. D. (2000). *Bowling Alone: The Collapse and Revival of American Community.* Simon & Schuster.

Virtual Collaboration for Social Impact

Virtual collaboration has emerged as a powerful tool for addressing social issues and driving positive change across various sectors. By leveraging technology to connect individuals and organizations, virtual collaboration enables the pooling of resources, knowledge, and skills to tackle pressing global challenges. This section explores the theoretical underpinnings, practical applications, and challenges associated with using virtual collaboration for social impact.

Theoretical Framework

The concept of social impact refers to the significant, positive changes that address social challenges, improve quality of life, and enhance community well-being. Theories such as the *Social Change Theory* and *Collective Impact Framework* provide a foundation for understanding how virtual collaboration can facilitate social change. The Social Change Theory posits that meaningful change occurs when individuals and groups work together towards common goals. The Collective Impact Framework emphasizes the importance of a shared agenda, aligned efforts, and continuous communication among stakeholders to achieve substantial social outcomes.

$$\text{Social Impact} = \text{Collective Effort} \times \text{Shared Vision} \qquad (17)$$

This equation highlights that the magnitude of social impact is proportional to the collective efforts of participants and the clarity of their shared vision.

Practical Applications

Virtual collaboration platforms have been utilized in various initiatives aimed at social impact. Here are some notable examples:

- **Global Health Initiatives:** Organizations like the *World Health Organization (WHO)* and *Doctors Without Borders* use virtual collaboration tools to coordinate responses to health crises, such as the COVID-19 pandemic. By connecting healthcare professionals across borders, they can share knowledge, resources, and best practices to improve health outcomes globally.

- **Education and Skill Development:** Platforms such as *Coursera* and *edX* enable educators to collaborate on developing courses that reach underserved populations. For instance, during the pandemic, many institutions partnered to offer free online courses, empowering individuals with skills that enhance employability and economic stability.

- **Environmental Advocacy:** Organizations like *Greenpeace* utilize virtual collaboration to mobilize activists and coordinate campaigns. By leveraging social media and collaborative tools, they can raise awareness about environmental issues and drive community engagement.

- **Disaster Response:** The *Crisis Text Line* employs virtual collaboration to provide immediate support during emergencies. Volunteers across the globe can offer real-time assistance, ensuring that individuals in crisis receive help promptly.

Challenges in Virtual Collaboration for Social Impact

Despite the potential benefits, there are several challenges that hinder the effectiveness of virtual collaboration for social impact:

- **Digital Divide:** Access to technology remains uneven, with marginalized communities often lacking the necessary tools and internet connectivity to participate in virtual collaboration. This disparity can exacerbate existing inequalities.

- **Trust and Relationship Building:** Establishing trust among collaborators can be challenging in virtual environments. Without face-to-face interaction, it may take longer to build relationships, which are essential for effective collaboration.

- **Coordination Complexity:** Managing diverse stakeholders with varying interests and goals can complicate collaboration efforts. Misalignment can lead to inefficiencies and diluted impact.

- **Sustainability of Engagement:** Keeping participants engaged over time is crucial for long-term success. Virtual fatigue can set in, leading to decreased participation and commitment.

Strategies for Enhancing Virtual Collaboration for Social Impact

To overcome these challenges, organizations can adopt several strategies:

- **Inclusive Access:** Implementing programs that provide technology and internet access to underserved communities can help bridge the digital divide. Partnerships with local organizations can facilitate outreach and support.

- **Building Trust:** Establishing clear communication protocols and fostering an inclusive environment can enhance trust among collaborators. Regular check-ins and team-building activities can strengthen relationships.

- **Effective Coordination:** Utilizing project management tools and frameworks can streamline coordination efforts. Defining roles, responsibilities, and shared goals can help align interests and maximize impact.

- **Engagement Strategies:** Incorporating interactive elements, such as gamification and feedback loops, can maintain participant engagement. Recognizing contributions and celebrating successes can also motivate continued involvement.

Conclusion

Virtual collaboration offers significant potential for driving social impact by connecting diverse stakeholders and facilitating collective action. While challenges exist, strategic approaches can enhance the effectiveness of these collaborative efforts. As technology continues to evolve, the possibilities for leveraging virtual collaboration to address social issues will expand, ultimately contributing to a more equitable and sustainable future.

$$\text{Social Impact Success} = \text{Effective Collaboration} + \text{Sustainable Engagement} \quad (18)$$

This equation encapsulates the idea that achieving social impact is contingent upon not only effective collaboration but also the sustainability of engagement among participants.

The Future of Virtual Collaboration

Enhanced Virtual Meeting Experiences

Haptic Feedback and Sensory Immersion

The evolution of virtual collaboration spaces has been significantly influenced by advancements in haptic feedback technology and sensory immersion. Haptic feedback refers to the use of tactile sensations to simulate the sense of touch in a virtual environment, allowing users to experience a more immersive and realistic interaction with digital objects. Sensory immersion, on the other hand, encompasses the integration of multiple sensory modalities—such as sight, sound, and touch—to create a cohesive and engaging virtual experience. Together, these technologies have the potential to revolutionize the way individuals collaborate in virtual environments.

Theoretical Framework

The theoretical underpinnings of haptic feedback and sensory immersion can be traced back to several key concepts in psychology and human-computer interaction (HCI). The concept of *embodiment* suggests that users perceive their presence within a virtual environment when they can interact with it in a meaningful way. According to the *Theory of Presence*, the more sensory modalities that are engaged, the greater the sense of presence and immersion experienced by the user [?].

Haptic feedback systems often utilize devices such as gloves, vests, or handheld controllers equipped with actuators that provide tactile sensations corresponding to virtual interactions. This feedback can include vibrations, forces, or motions that simulate the texture, weight, and resistance of virtual objects. The integration of haptic feedback into virtual collaboration tools can enhance user engagement by reinforcing the physicality of actions performed in the virtual space.

Challenges in Implementation

Despite the promising potential of haptic feedback and sensory immersion, several challenges impede their widespread adoption in virtual collaboration spaces.

- **Technical Limitations:** Current haptic devices often suffer from limitations in resolution, range of sensations, and responsiveness. High-fidelity haptic feedback requires sophisticated hardware and software integration, which can be costly and complex to implement.

- **User Experience Design:** Designing intuitive and effective haptic feedback experiences poses a challenge. Developers must consider the appropriateness of feedback for different tasks and contexts, ensuring that it enhances rather than detracts from the user experience.

- **Physical Discomfort:** Prolonged use of haptic devices can lead to discomfort or fatigue, limiting the duration of effective collaboration sessions. Ergonomics must be a priority in the design of haptic interfaces to ensure user comfort.

Examples of Haptic Feedback in Virtual Collaboration

Several innovative applications of haptic feedback and sensory immersion demonstrate their potential in virtual collaboration:

- **Virtual Prototyping in Engineering:** Companies like *HaptX* have developed haptic gloves that allow engineers to manipulate virtual prototypes as if they were real objects. This technology enables teams to collaborate on product design in a virtual space, providing tactile feedback that enhances the evaluation process.

- **Medical Training Simulations:** In healthcare, haptic feedback is being utilized in surgical simulations. Platforms such as *Osso VR* allow medical professionals to practice procedures with realistic tactile sensations, improving their skills and confidence before performing actual surgeries.

- **Remote Team Collaboration:** Tools like *Spatial* incorporate haptic feedback to facilitate remote teamwork. Users can interact with virtual objects and convey information through touch, enhancing communication and collaboration among distributed teams.

Conclusion

In conclusion, haptic feedback and sensory immersion play a crucial role in shaping the future of virtual collaboration spaces. By providing users with realistic tactile sensations and engaging multiple sensory modalities, these technologies enhance the sense of presence and immersion, fostering more effective collaboration. However, addressing the technical challenges and user experience design considerations is essential for realizing their full potential. As advancements continue, the integration of haptic feedback into virtual collaboration tools will likely become increasingly sophisticated, paving the way for a new era of immersive teamwork.

Avatar Customization

In the realm of virtual collaboration, avatar customization plays a pivotal role in enhancing user experience and fostering a sense of presence. Avatars serve as digital representations of users, allowing them to express their identity and individuality in virtual spaces. This section delves into the theoretical foundations, challenges, and practical examples of avatar customization in virtual collaboration environments.

Theoretical Foundations

The concept of avatars can be traced back to early online gaming and virtual worlds, where users created digital representations of themselves. Theories of social presence and identity in virtual environments underscore the significance of avatar customization. According to the *Social Presence Theory* (Short, Williams, & Christie, 1976), the degree of salience in communication can be influenced by the representation of individuals. A well-customized avatar can enhance social presence, leading to more meaningful interactions.

Additionally, the *Self-Determination Theory* (Deci & Ryan, 1985) posits that individuals have innate psychological needs for autonomy, competence, and relatedness. Avatar customization satisfies the need for autonomy by allowing users to express their unique identities. This personalization fosters a deeper connection to the virtual environment, enhancing overall engagement.

Challenges in Avatar Customization

Despite its benefits, avatar customization presents several challenges:

- **Complexity of Customization Options:** Users may face overwhelming choices when customizing their avatars, leading to decision fatigue. Research indicates that too many options can hinder user satisfaction (Iyengar & Lepper, 2000).

- **Cultural Sensitivity:** Customization options must consider cultural diversity. Certain representations may be offensive or inappropriate in specific cultural contexts, necessitating careful design and implementation.

- **Technical Limitations:** The quality of avatar customization can be constrained by hardware capabilities. Low-end devices may not support high-resolution graphics or complex animations, limiting the user experience.

- **Identity Misrepresentation:** Users may create avatars that do not accurately reflect their real-life identity, leading to potential misunderstandings and trust issues in collaborative settings.

Examples of Avatar Customization in Virtual Collaboration

Several platforms have effectively implemented avatar customization features to enhance user engagement and collaboration:

- **VRChat:** This social VR platform allows users to create highly personalized avatars, from humanoid figures to fantastical creatures. Users can upload custom models, promoting creativity and self-expression. VRChat's community-driven approach enables users to share their creations, fostering a vibrant ecosystem of avatar design.

- **Microsoft Teams:** The integration of avatars in Microsoft Teams provides users with the ability to customize their digital presence during meetings. Users can select from a range of professional attire and accessories, enhancing the sense of professionalism while still allowing for personal flair.

- **Mozilla Hubs:** This open-source virtual reality platform emphasizes accessibility and ease of use. Users can create avatars with minimal effort, focusing on inclusivity. Mozilla Hubs allows users to customize their avatars' appearance and attire, promoting a sense of belonging in virtual spaces.

Conclusion

Avatar customization is a vital component of virtual collaboration, influencing user engagement, social presence, and identity expression. By understanding the theoretical foundations, addressing challenges, and examining successful examples, organizations can leverage avatar customization to enhance virtual collaboration experiences. As technology continues to evolve, the potential for more sophisticated and inclusive avatar customization options will further enrich the virtual collaboration landscape.

$$\text{User Engagement} = f(\text{Customization Options, Cultural Sensitivity, Technical Capabilities}) \quad (19)$$

This equation illustrates the interdependent relationship between user engagement and the factors influencing avatar customization. By optimizing these factors, organizations can foster a more engaging and collaborative virtual environment.

Realistic Virtual Environments

The concept of realistic virtual environments (RVE) is pivotal in enhancing the user experience in virtual collaboration spaces. As technology progresses, the demand for immersive and interactive environments has grown, enabling users to engage in virtual settings that closely mimic real-world interactions. This section explores the theoretical foundations, challenges, and applications of realistic virtual environments in the context of virtual collaboration.

Theoretical Foundations

Realistic virtual environments are grounded in several theoretical frameworks, including presence theory, immersion theory, and social presence theory.

Presence Theory posits that users experience a sense of being in a virtual space, which is crucial for effective collaboration. The concept of presence can be measured using various metrics, such as the *Presence Questionnaire* (PQ) developed by Witmer and Singer (1998), which assesses the subjective experience of presence in virtual environments.

$$PQ = \sum_{i=1}^{n} (\text{Score}_i) \cdot \text{Weight}_i \quad (20)$$

where $Score_i$ represents the user's rating of different presence-related items, and $Weight_i$ indicates the importance of each item.

Immersion Theory emphasizes the role of sensory inputs in creating a compelling virtual experience. Immersion can be categorized into two types: *physical immersion* (the extent to which users are physically engaged with the environment) and *psychological immersion* (the degree to which users feel absorbed in the virtual experience).

Social Presence Theory focuses on the perception of social interactions within virtual environments. The ability to perceive social cues, such as body language and facial expressions, significantly impacts collaboration outcomes. Research by Biocca et al. (2003) indicates that higher social presence leads to improved communication and trust among team members.

Challenges in Creating Realistic Virtual Environments

Despite advancements in technology, several challenges hinder the creation of truly realistic virtual environments:

1. Technical Limitations: High-fidelity graphics and real-time rendering require significant computational power. Limitations in hardware can result in lag, reduced frame rates, and lower quality visuals, which detract from the immersive experience.

2. User Adaptability: Users may experience discomfort or disorientation when transitioning from physical to virtual environments. This phenomenon, known as *cybersickness*, can lead to decreased engagement and productivity.

3. Interaction Design: Designing intuitive and natural interaction methods is crucial for user satisfaction. Users often struggle with complex controls or interfaces that do not align with their expectations of real-world interactions.

4. Content Creation: Developing high-quality, realistic virtual environments requires substantial resources and expertise. The process of creating detailed 3D models, animations, and soundscapes can be time-consuming and costly.

Examples of Realistic Virtual Environments

Several platforms exemplify the successful implementation of realistic virtual environments in collaborative settings:

1. Spatial: Spatial is a virtual collaboration platform that allows users to create and interact in 3D environments. Users can customize their avatars and engage in real-time discussions, utilizing features such as spatial audio to enhance the realism of conversations. The platform has been adopted by companies for remote meetings and brainstorming sessions.

2. Mozilla Hubs: Mozilla Hubs is an open-source platform that enables users to create virtual spaces accessible via web browsers. Users can design their environments using 3D models and interact with others through voice and text chat. Hubs' flexibility allows for diverse applications, from educational workshops to social gatherings.

3. VirBELA: VirBELA is a virtual world designed for remote collaboration, offering realistic environments for conferences, meetings, and training sessions. The platform emphasizes social presence through avatar interactions, enabling users to navigate virtual offices and engage in collaborative tasks.

Future Directions

The future of realistic virtual environments in virtual collaboration is promising, driven by advancements in technology and user expectations. Key trends include:

1. AI-Driven Environments: Artificial intelligence can enhance realism by creating adaptive environments that respond to user behavior and preferences. AI can also generate realistic avatars and facilitate more natural interactions.

2. Integration of Haptic Feedback: Incorporating haptic feedback devices can provide users with tactile sensations, further enhancing the immersive experience. This technology allows users to feel virtual objects, making interactions more intuitive.

3. Cross-Platform Compatibility: As virtual environments become increasingly popular, ensuring compatibility across different devices and platforms will be essential. This includes optimizing experiences for VR headsets, desktop computers, and mobile devices.

4. User-Centric Design: Focusing on user experience and feedback will be critical in developing realistic virtual environments. Engaging users in the design process can lead to more intuitive and satisfying experiences.

In conclusion, realistic virtual environments play a crucial role in the effectiveness of virtual collaboration. By addressing current challenges and leveraging emerging technologies, organizations can create immersive spaces that foster creativity, communication, and teamwork. As the demand for virtual collaboration continues to grow, the pursuit of increasingly realistic and engaging environments will be essential for success.

Multi-Sensory Communication

In the realm of virtual collaboration, the concept of multi-sensory communication is emerging as a pivotal component that enhances user engagement and interaction. Multi-sensory communication refers to the integration of multiple sensory modalities—such as visual, auditory, tactile, and olfactory cues—into the communication process. This approach not only enriches the user experience but also facilitates a deeper understanding of information being shared in virtual environments.

Theoretical Framework

The theoretical underpinnings of multi-sensory communication can be traced back to the principles of sensory integration, which suggest that the brain processes information from various sensory modalities simultaneously to create a cohesive understanding of the environment. According to the *Dual Coding Theory* proposed by Allan Paivio, information is better retained and recalled when it is presented in both verbal and non-verbal forms. This theory implies that integrating multiple senses can significantly enhance cognitive processing and memory retention.

Mathematically, the effectiveness of multi-sensory communication can be represented as follows:

$$E = f(V, A, T, O) \qquad (21)$$

Where:

- E = Effectiveness of communication

- V = Visual stimuli

- A = Auditory stimuli

- T = Tactile stimuli

- O = Olfactory stimuli

This equation suggests that the effectiveness of communication increases as the variety of sensory stimuli utilized increases.

Challenges in Multi-Sensory Communication

Despite its potential benefits, multi-sensory communication in virtual environments faces several challenges:

- **Technical Limitations:** The current technological infrastructure may not support the seamless integration of multi-sensory cues. For instance, while visual and auditory components are relatively straightforward to implement, tactile and olfactory feedback require advanced hardware that is not widely available.

- **User Overload:** Introducing too many sensory inputs can lead to cognitive overload, where users may struggle to process the information being presented. This phenomenon is often referred to as *sensory saturation*, which can hinder effective communication rather than enhance it.

- **Individual Differences:** People have varying preferences and sensitivities to different sensory modalities. Some users may benefit more from visual cues, while others may prefer auditory or tactile feedback. This diversity necessitates a customizable approach to multi-sensory communication.

Examples of Multi-Sensory Communication in Virtual Collaboration

Several applications and platforms are pioneering the use of multi-sensory communication in virtual collaboration:

- **Virtual Reality (VR) Environments:** Platforms like *Spatial* and *Engage* enable users to interact in immersive 3D spaces where they can see avatars, hear spatial audio, and even use haptic feedback devices to simulate touch. For instance, a user might feel a vibration when interacting with virtual objects, enhancing the realism of the experience.

- **Augmented Reality (AR) Applications:** In AR settings, applications such as *Microsoft HoloLens* allow users to overlay digital information onto the physical world. Users can see visual cues while receiving auditory instructions, thereby creating a multi-sensory learning environment. A practical example is in medical training, where students can visualize anatomical structures while receiving real-time auditory feedback from instructors.

- **Collaborative Tools:** Tools like *Miro* and *Jamboard* incorporate visual and auditory elements to facilitate brainstorming sessions. Users can draw, add sticky notes, and verbally discuss ideas simultaneously, creating a rich multi-sensory experience that fosters creativity and collaboration.

Conclusion

In conclusion, multi-sensory communication holds significant promise for enhancing virtual collaboration experiences. By engaging multiple senses, we can improve information retention, foster deeper connections among participants, and create more immersive environments. However, it is crucial to address the technical challenges, potential cognitive overload, and individual differences to fully leverage the benefits of this approach. As technology continues to advance, the integration of multi-sensory communication will likely play a vital role in shaping the future of virtual collaboration spaces, making them more effective, engaging, and inclusive for users around the globe.

Bibliography

[1] Paivio, A. (1986). *Mental Representations: A Dual Coding Approach*. Oxford University Press.

[2] Mayer, R. E. (2001). *Multimedia Learning*. Cambridge University Press.

[3] Liu, M., & Chen, X. (2010). Multi-sensory communication in virtual environments: A review. *Virtual Reality*, 14(3), 193-206.

[4] Microsoft. (2021). *HoloLens 2: Mixed Reality for Business*. Retrieved from https://www.microsoft.com/en-us/hololens

Advanced Spatial Audio

The concept of spatial audio has gained significant traction in virtual collaboration spaces, enhancing the immersive experience and improving communication among users. Advanced spatial audio technology aims to replicate the natural hearing experience by simulating how sound waves interact with the environment and how they reach the listener's ears. This subsection delves into the theory behind spatial audio, its implementation in virtual environments, the challenges faced, and examples of its application in various contexts.

Theory of Spatial Audio

Spatial audio refers to the technique of placing sound in a three-dimensional space to create a more realistic auditory experience. The human auditory system is adept at localizing sound sources based on several cues, including:

- **Interaural Time Difference (ITD):** The difference in the time it takes for a sound to reach each ear. Sounds arriving at the ear closer to the source will reach that ear slightly earlier than the other.

- **Interaural Level Difference (ILD):** The difference in sound pressure level reaching each ear. Sounds coming from one side are louder in the ear closer to the source.

- **Head-Related Transfer Function (HRTF):** The way the shape of the head, ears, and torso affect the sound that reaches the ears, providing cues about the elevation and distance of sound sources.

Mathematically, the localization of sound can be described using the following equations:

$$ITD = \frac{d}{c} \qquad (22)$$

where d is the distance between the ears, and c is the speed of sound in air (approximately 343 m/s).

$$ILD = 20 \log_{10}\left(\frac{p_1}{p_2}\right) \qquad (23)$$

where p_1 and p_2 are the sound pressures at each ear.

The combination of these cues allows users to perceive sound directionality and distance, which is critical in collaborative environments where multiple participants may be interacting simultaneously.

Implementation in Virtual Collaboration Spaces

In virtual environments, advanced spatial audio can be implemented using various technologies and techniques, such as:

- **3D Audio Engines:** Software frameworks like Unity and Unreal Engine provide built-in support for spatial audio, allowing developers to easily position sound sources in a three-dimensional space.

- **Binaural Audio Processing:** This technique simulates how sound would reach the ears using HRTFs, creating an immersive experience for users wearing headphones.

- **Ambisonics:** A method of recording and reproducing sound that captures the sound field in a spherical format, allowing for dynamic sound placement and movement.

An example of spatial audio in action is the use of binaural audio in virtual meetings. By positioning speakers in a virtual space, participants can perceive where each speaker is located, making it easier to follow conversations and reducing the cognitive load associated with traditional flat audio.

Challenges of Advanced Spatial Audio

Despite its advantages, implementing advanced spatial audio in virtual collaboration spaces comes with several challenges:

- **Hardware Limitations:** Not all devices support high-quality spatial audio processing. Users may experience degraded audio quality if their hardware is not capable of rendering spatial audio accurately.

- **User Variability:** Individual differences in hearing ability and headphone characteristics can affect the perception of spatial audio, leading to inconsistent experiences across users.

- **Complexity of Sound Environments:** In highly dynamic environments with multiple sound sources, accurately simulating spatial audio can become computationally intensive and may lead to latency issues.

Examples of Spatial Audio Applications

Several organizations and platforms have successfully integrated advanced spatial audio into their virtual collaboration tools:

- **Spatial.io:** This virtual collaboration platform uses spatial audio to create immersive meeting environments where users can interact naturally, with sound reflecting their positions in the virtual space.

- **Mozilla Hubs:** An open-source virtual reality platform that incorporates spatial audio, allowing users to engage in discussions and collaborate on projects while experiencing a sense of presence and immersion.

- **Facebook Horizon Workrooms:** This virtual meeting space leverages spatial audio to enhance communication, making it easier for participants to identify who is speaking based on their virtual location.

Conclusion

Advanced spatial audio represents a significant advancement in the field of virtual collaboration. By mimicking natural auditory cues, it enhances user experiences, improves communication, and fosters a sense of presence in virtual environments. As technology continues to evolve, the integration of spatial audio into virtual collaboration spaces will likely become more sophisticated, paving the way for richer and more engaging collaborative experiences.

Virtual Reality for User Engagement

Virtual Reality (VR) has emerged as a transformative medium in enhancing user engagement across various sectors. By immersing users in interactive and lifelike environments, VR not only captures attention but also fosters deeper emotional connections with content. This section explores the theoretical foundations of user engagement in VR, identifies existing challenges, and provides examples of successful applications.

Theoretical Foundations of User Engagement

User engagement refers to the degree of attention, interest, and involvement that a user exhibits while interacting with a system or content. In the context of VR, engagement is often framed through several theoretical lenses:

- **Flow Theory:** Proposed by Csikszentmihalyi, flow theory posits that users experience heightened engagement when they are immersed in activities that balance challenge and skill. In VR, the immersive nature of the environment can induce a state of flow, where users lose track of time and become fully absorbed in the experience.

- **Presence Theory:** Presence refers to the sense of "being there" in a virtual environment. Research indicates that higher levels of presence correlate with increased user engagement, as users feel more connected to the virtual world and its elements.

- **Cognitive Load Theory:** This theory suggests that user engagement is influenced by the amount of cognitive effort required to process information. VR can either enhance or hinder engagement based on how well it manages cognitive load, with overly complex environments potentially leading to disengagement.

Challenges in Enhancing User Engagement

Despite the potential of VR to enhance user engagement, several challenges persist:

- **Technical Limitations:** Issues such as latency, hardware compatibility, and the need for high-quality graphics can detract from the immersive experience. For instance, a study by Jerald (2015) highlighted that even slight delays in motion tracking can disrupt the sense of presence, leading to disengagement.

- **User Adaptation:** Users may experience discomfort or motion sickness, which can hinder their ability to engage fully with VR content. A study by LaViola (2000) found that approximately 40% of users experience some form of discomfort in VR, which can significantly affect engagement levels.

- **Content Relevance:** The effectiveness of VR in enhancing engagement is contingent upon the relevance of the content to the user. If users perceive the VR experience as irrelevant or uninteresting, their engagement will diminish.

Successful Applications of VR for User Engagement

Numerous industries have successfully leveraged VR to enhance user engagement, with notable examples including:

- **Education:** Educational institutions are increasingly adopting VR to create immersive learning experiences. For instance, platforms like Labster provide virtual laboratories where students can conduct experiments in a risk-free environment. Research by Mikropoulos and Natsis (2011) showed that students using VR for science education exhibited higher engagement and retention rates compared to traditional methods.

- **Marketing:** Brands are utilizing VR to create engaging marketing campaigns. For example, the automotive industry has embraced VR showrooms, allowing potential customers to explore vehicles in a virtual space. Audi's VR experience enables users to customize and visualize their car choices, leading to increased customer engagement and satisfaction.

- **Healthcare:** VR is being used in therapeutic settings to enhance patient engagement in treatment. For instance, the use of VR in pain management has shown promising results. A study by Hoffman et al. (2000) demonstrated that patients who engaged with VR during painful procedures reported lower pain levels and higher satisfaction, attributing this to the immersive distraction provided by the VR environment.

Conclusion

In summary, Virtual Reality presents significant opportunities for enhancing user engagement through its immersive and interactive capabilities. By understanding the theoretical underpinnings of engagement, addressing existing challenges, and learning from successful applications, stakeholders can harness the full potential of VR to create compelling and engaging user experiences. As technology continues to evolve, the future of VR in user engagement holds immense promise, paving the way for innovative applications across various sectors.

Bibliography

[1] Jerald, J. (2015). *The VR Book: Human-Centered Design for Virtual Reality*. Association for Computing Machinery.

[2] LaViola, J. J. (2000). *A Discussion of Cybersickness in Virtual Environments*. Proceedings of the SPIE, 3959, 111-124.

[3] Mikropoulos, T. A., & Natsis, A. (2011). *Educational Virtual Environments: A Meta-Analysis of the Effectiveness of Educational VR Applications*. Computers & Education, 57(2), 1072-1080.

[4] Hoffman, H. G., Patterson, D. R., Carrougher, G. J., & Furness, T. A. (2000). *Use of Virtual Reality for Pain Control During Wound Care in Patients with Burns*. The Clinical Journal of Pain, 16(3), 244-250.

Virtual Collaboration in Extended Reality

Extended Reality (XR) encompasses a spectrum of immersive technologies, including Virtual Reality (VR), Augmented Reality (AR), and Mixed Reality (MR). These technologies significantly enhance virtual collaboration by providing immersive environments that facilitate interaction and engagement among participants, regardless of their physical locations. This section explores the applications, benefits, challenges, and future prospects of virtual collaboration in XR.

Definition and Scope of Extended Reality

Extended Reality is defined as an umbrella term that combines the physical and digital worlds. It allows users to interact with digital content in a way that feels real. The integration of XR into collaboration spaces transforms traditional workflows, enabling new forms of interaction and communication. According to

Milgram and Kishino's (1994) Reality-Virtuality Continuum, XR can be visualized as a continuum ranging from the real environment to fully immersive virtual environments, where AR is situated between the two.

Applications of XR in Virtual Collaboration

The applications of XR in virtual collaboration are diverse and span various industries:

- **Remote Team Meetings:** XR platforms facilitate immersive meetings where participants can interact with 3D models and visualizations, enhancing understanding and engagement. For example, platforms like Spatial and Engage allow teams to collaborate in a shared virtual space, manipulating objects as if they were physically present.

- **Training and Simulation:** XR is extensively used in training environments, particularly in fields such as healthcare, aviation, and military. For instance, medical professionals can practice surgical procedures in a risk-free virtual environment, improving their skills and confidence before performing on real patients.

- **Design and Prototyping:** In architecture and product design, XR allows teams to visualize and manipulate designs in real-time. Tools like Microsoft Mesh enable collaborative design sessions where stakeholders can view and modify 3D models, streamlining the design process.

- **Education:** XR can enhance educational experiences by providing interactive learning environments. For example, students can explore historical sites or complex scientific concepts through immersive simulations, fostering deeper understanding and retention of knowledge.

Benefits of Virtual Collaboration in XR

The incorporation of XR into virtual collaboration offers several advantages:

1. **Enhanced Engagement:** XR provides immersive experiences that capture attention and foster active participation. This leads to increased engagement during meetings and collaborative sessions.

2. **Improved Communication:** XR allows for richer communication through visual and spatial cues. Participants can share and manipulate 3D objects, leading to clearer understanding and reduced miscommunication.

3. **Increased Accessibility:** XR can bridge geographical gaps, allowing teams from different locations to collaborate seamlessly. This is particularly beneficial for organizations with a distributed workforce.

4. **Cost Efficiency:** By reducing the need for physical prototypes and travel, XR can lead to significant cost savings. Organizations can conduct virtual meetings and training sessions without incurring travel expenses.

Challenges of XR in Virtual Collaboration

Despite its potential, the implementation of XR in virtual collaboration faces several challenges:

- **Technical Limitations:** The need for high-performance hardware and reliable internet connectivity can hinder the widespread adoption of XR technologies. Latency and bandwidth issues can disrupt the user experience, leading to frustration.

- **User Acceptance:** The transition to XR collaboration requires users to adapt to new technologies and workflows. Resistance to change and lack of familiarity with XR can impede adoption.

- **Privacy and Security Concerns:** The use of XR raises concerns about data privacy and security. Organizations must ensure that sensitive information shared in virtual environments is adequately protected from unauthorized access.

- **Cognitive Overload:** The immersive nature of XR can lead to cognitive overload, where users may struggle to process excessive information or distractions in a virtual environment.

Future Prospects of XR in Virtual Collaboration

The future of virtual collaboration in XR is promising, with several trends emerging:

- **Integration with AI:** The integration of artificial intelligence (AI) with XR can enhance collaboration by providing intelligent virtual assistants that help manage tasks and facilitate communication.

- **Advancements in Hardware:** As hardware technology continues to evolve, we can expect more affordable and accessible XR devices that offer improved performance and user experience.

- **Development of Standards:** The establishment of industry standards for XR collaboration tools will facilitate interoperability, allowing different platforms to work together seamlessly.

- **Focus on Inclusivity:** Future XR solutions will likely prioritize inclusivity, ensuring that individuals with disabilities can participate fully in virtual collaboration environments.

Conclusion

Virtual collaboration in Extended Reality represents a significant advancement in how teams interact and work together. By leveraging the immersive capabilities of XR, organizations can enhance engagement, communication, and productivity. However, addressing the challenges associated with XR adoption is crucial for realizing its full potential. As technology continues to evolve, the future of virtual collaboration in XR holds exciting possibilities that can transform the way we work and collaborate across distances.

Virtual Collaboration for Specific Industries

Virtual Collaboration in Architecture and Design

In the rapidly evolving landscape of architecture and design, virtual collaboration has emerged as a transformative force, reshaping the way architects, designers, and clients interact throughout the design process. This section explores the theoretical underpinnings, challenges, and practical applications of virtual collaboration in architecture and design.

Theoretical Foundations

The integration of virtual collaboration in architecture and design is rooted in several theoretical frameworks, including:

- **Constructivist Theory:** This theory posits that knowledge is constructed through social interactions and experiences. In virtual collaboration, architects and designers engage with stakeholders in real-time, allowing for a shared understanding of design concepts and fostering collective creativity.

- **Distributed Cognition:** This framework emphasizes that cognitive processes are distributed across individuals and tools. Virtual collaboration platforms enable the sharing of information and resources, allowing teams to leverage collective intelligence and enhance problem-solving capabilities.

- **Collaborative Design Theory:** This theory focuses on the collaborative nature of design processes. Virtual environments facilitate participatory design, where clients and stakeholders can contribute to the design process, ensuring that their needs and preferences are incorporated.

Challenges in Virtual Collaboration

Despite its potential, virtual collaboration in architecture and design faces several challenges:

- **Technical Barriers:** Issues such as bandwidth limitations, software compatibility, and hardware constraints can hinder effective virtual collaboration. For example, high-resolution 3D models may require substantial bandwidth, leading to latency and performance issues during collaborative sessions.

- **Communication Gaps:** Virtual collaboration can sometimes result in misunderstandings due to the lack of non-verbal cues. Architects and clients may misinterpret design intentions, leading to conflicts and revisions. Effective communication strategies, such as regular check-ins and feedback loops, are essential to mitigate these issues.

- **Cultural Differences:** In global projects, team members may come from diverse cultural backgrounds, which can influence collaboration styles and expectations. Understanding and respecting these differences is crucial for fostering a cohesive virtual team environment.

Applications of Virtual Collaboration in Architecture and Design

Several applications highlight the effectiveness of virtual collaboration in architecture and design:

- **Building Information Modeling (BIM):** BIM is a digital representation of the physical and functional characteristics of a building. Virtual collaboration tools integrated with BIM allow architects, engineers, and contractors to work together seamlessly, sharing updates and modifications in real-time. This collaborative approach reduces errors and enhances project efficiency.

- **Virtual Reality (VR) Walkthroughs:** Architects can create immersive VR experiences that allow clients to explore design concepts before construction begins. For instance, using VR headsets, clients can navigate through a virtual model of their future home, providing feedback on spatial arrangements and design elements. This interactive approach significantly improves client engagement and satisfaction.

- **Cloud-Based Design Platforms:** Platforms like Autodesk Revit and SketchUp facilitate real-time collaboration among design teams. These tools enable multiple users to work on the same project simultaneously, allowing for instant updates and revisions. A notable example is the use of Autodesk's BIM 360, which provides a cloud-based environment for project teams to collaborate efficiently, regardless of location.

- **Augmented Reality (AR) Applications:** AR technology overlays digital information onto the physical world, enabling architects to visualize designs in real-time. For example, using AR applications, architects can project 3D models onto a construction site, allowing clients to see how the design integrates with the existing environment. This enhances understanding and facilitates informed decision-making.

- **Collaborative Design Workshops:** Virtual workshops utilizing tools like Miro or MURAL enable teams to brainstorm and develop design concepts collaboratively. These platforms allow participants to share ideas, sketches, and notes in an interactive digital space, promoting creativity and innovation.

Case Studies

Several case studies illustrate the successful application of virtual collaboration in architecture and design:

- **The Edge, Amsterdam:** This innovative office building, designed by PLP Architecture, utilized virtual collaboration tools extensively during its design phase. The team employed BIM and virtual reality to engage stakeholders, resulting in a highly efficient design process and a building that maximizes energy efficiency and user comfort.

- **Zaha Hadid Architects' Design Process:** Zaha Hadid Architects have embraced virtual collaboration tools to enhance their design workflow. By using VR and AR technologies, the firm has been able to create immersive presentations for clients, allowing them to experience designs in a realistic context. This approach has led to more informed decisions and a smoother design approval process.

- **The New National Stadium, Tokyo:** The design team for the Tokyo 2020 Olympics utilized virtual collaboration to manage the complexities of the project. By leveraging cloud-based platforms, the team coordinated efforts among architects, engineers, and contractors, ensuring that the project met its ambitious timeline and budget constraints.

Conclusion

Virtual collaboration in architecture and design represents a paradigm shift in how projects are conceived, developed, and executed. By leveraging advanced technologies and collaborative frameworks, architects and designers can enhance creativity, improve communication, and streamline workflows. Despite the challenges, the potential for virtual collaboration to revolutionize the industry is immense, paving the way for more innovative and inclusive design practices. As the field continues to evolve, embracing virtual collaboration will be essential for architects and designers seeking to thrive in an increasingly interconnected world.

Virtual Collaboration in Engineering

Virtual collaboration in engineering represents a transformative shift in how engineering teams operate, design, and innovate. As projects become increasingly complex and globalized, the need for effective collaboration tools and methodologies has never been greater. This section explores the theoretical foundations, challenges, and practical examples of virtual collaboration in the engineering sector.

Theoretical Foundations

The theoretical underpinnings of virtual collaboration in engineering can be framed within the context of systems theory and collaborative engineering. Systems theory posits that complex systems are best understood through the interactions of their components. In engineering, this means recognizing that a project comprises various interdependent elements—design, materials, processes, and human resources—that must work together seamlessly.

Collaborative engineering emphasizes the importance of teamwork and communication among diverse stakeholders, including engineers, architects, project managers, and clients. According to [?], effective collaboration can significantly enhance project outcomes, leading to increased innovation and reduced time-to-market.

Challenges of Virtual Collaboration in Engineering

Despite the advantages, virtual collaboration in engineering is not without its challenges. Key issues include:

- **Communication Barriers:** Differences in time zones, languages, and cultural contexts can hinder effective communication. As noted by [?], misunderstandings can lead to costly errors in design and implementation.

- **Technical Limitations:** The effectiveness of virtual collaboration tools depends on reliable internet connectivity and compatible software. A lack of bandwidth can result in latency issues, which disrupt real-time collaboration. According to [?], engineers often face difficulties with software integration, leading to inefficiencies.

- **Data Security:** Engineering projects often involve sensitive information. Ensuring data security in virtual environments is crucial. As highlighted by [?], breaches can have severe consequences, including intellectual property theft and reputational damage.

- **Cultural Differences:** Collaborating across cultures can lead to conflicts in work styles and expectations. Understanding these differences is essential for fostering a collaborative environment, as outlined by [?].

Examples of Virtual Collaboration in Engineering

1. **Building Information Modeling (BIM):** BIM is a prime example of virtual collaboration in engineering. It allows multiple stakeholders to work on a single, shared model, facilitating real-time updates and modifications. According to [?], BIM enhances communication and coordination among architects, engineers, and contractors, reducing errors and improving project timelines.

2. **Virtual Reality (VR) for Design Reviews:** Companies like *Ford Motor Company* have adopted VR technology to conduct design reviews. Engineers can immerse themselves in a virtual environment to evaluate designs, identify potential issues, and collaborate with team members from around the world. This approach not only accelerates the design process but also enhances creativity and innovation [?].

3. **Cloud-Based Collaboration Platforms:** Tools such as *Autodesk Fusion 360* enable engineers to collaborate on designs in real-time, regardless of their physical location. These platforms support version control, ensuring that all team members are working with the most up-to-date information. According to [?], this level of collaboration has been shown to increase productivity and reduce project lead times.

Future Directions

As the engineering field continues to evolve, the future of virtual collaboration looks promising. Emerging technologies such as artificial intelligence (AI) and machine learning (ML) are expected to further enhance collaboration by automating routine tasks and providing data-driven insights. For instance, predictive analytics can help teams anticipate project risks and make informed decisions, as discussed by [?].

Additionally, the integration of augmented reality (AR) in engineering processes is gaining traction. AR can overlay digital information onto the physical world, allowing engineers to visualize complex systems and collaborate more effectively. This technology has the potential to revolutionize training and on-site collaboration, as evidenced by its application in maintenance and repair tasks [?].

Conclusion

Virtual collaboration in engineering is reshaping how projects are conceived, developed, and executed. While challenges remain, the benefits of enhanced communication, increased efficiency, and improved innovation are driving the adoption of virtual collaboration tools and practices. As technology continues to advance, the engineering industry is poised to embrace a future where collaboration transcends geographical boundaries, fostering a more interconnected and innovative global community.

Virtual Collaboration in Manufacturing

The manufacturing industry has undergone significant transformations over the past few decades, largely driven by advancements in technology. Among these advancements, virtual collaboration has emerged as a pivotal force, enabling manufacturers to improve efficiency, reduce costs, and foster innovation. This section explores the applications, benefits, challenges, and future prospects of virtual collaboration in manufacturing.

The Role of Virtual Collaboration in Manufacturing

Virtual collaboration in manufacturing refers to the use of digital tools and platforms that facilitate teamwork and communication among individuals or teams, regardless of their physical locations. This can encompass a range of technologies, including virtual reality (VR), augmented reality (AR), and collaborative software applications. The integration of these tools allows for real-time interaction, data sharing, and decision-making, which are crucial in a fast-paced manufacturing environment.

Applications of Virtual Collaboration in Manufacturing

1. **Design and Prototyping:** Virtual collaboration tools enable design teams to work together on product development from different locations. For instance, using VR, engineers can visualize and manipulate 3D models of products, allowing for immediate feedback and iteration. This reduces the time and cost associated with physical prototypes.

2. **Remote Monitoring and Maintenance:** Virtual collaboration facilitates remote monitoring of manufacturing processes. Technicians can use AR to overlay digital information onto physical machinery, allowing them to diagnose issues without being on-site. This capability not only saves time but also minimizes downtime in production.

3. **Training and Skill Development:** Virtual collaboration tools provide immersive training experiences for new employees. For example, VR simulations can replicate complex manufacturing environments, enabling trainees to practice skills in a safe and controlled setting. This enhances learning outcomes and reduces the risk of accidents.

4. **Supply Chain Management:** Virtual collaboration enhances communication across the supply chain, allowing manufacturers to coordinate more effectively with suppliers and distributors. Real-time data sharing ensures that all stakeholders are informed about inventory levels, production schedules, and logistics, leading to improved efficiency.

Benefits of Virtual Collaboration in Manufacturing

The adoption of virtual collaboration in manufacturing offers several advantages:

- **Increased Efficiency:** By enabling teams to collaborate in real-time, virtual collaboration reduces the time spent on meetings and approvals. This streamlining of processes leads to faster product development cycles.

- **Cost Reduction:** Virtual collaboration minimizes the need for travel and physical resources, resulting in significant cost savings. Additionally, reduced downtime due to remote support can lead to increased productivity.

- **Enhanced Innovation:** Virtual collaboration fosters a culture of innovation by bringing together diverse teams with different perspectives. This diversity can lead to creative problem-solving and the development of novel solutions.

- **Improved Quality:** With real-time feedback and collaboration, manufacturing teams can identify and address quality issues more effectively. This proactive approach helps maintain high standards throughout the production process.

Challenges of Virtual Collaboration in Manufacturing

Despite its numerous benefits, virtual collaboration in manufacturing is not without challenges:

1. **Technical Barriers:** The effectiveness of virtual collaboration relies heavily on technology. Issues such as bandwidth limitations, software compatibility, and hardware malfunctions can hinder communication and collaboration.

2. **Cultural Resistance:** Some organizations may face resistance to adopting virtual collaboration tools, particularly from employees accustomed to traditional methods of working. Change management strategies are essential to facilitate the transition.

3. **Security Concerns:** The sharing of sensitive information across digital platforms raises concerns regarding data security. Manufacturers must implement robust cybersecurity measures to protect proprietary information.

4. **Training and Support:** Employees may require training to effectively use virtual collaboration tools. Ongoing support and resources are necessary to ensure that teams can maximize the benefits of these technologies.

Examples of Virtual Collaboration in Manufacturing

Several companies have successfully implemented virtual collaboration in their manufacturing processes:

- **Ford Motor Company:** Ford utilizes VR technology for design and engineering collaboration. By allowing teams to visualize and interact with 3D models, Ford has accelerated its product development timeline and improved design quality.

- **General Electric (GE):** GE employs AR for remote maintenance and support. Technicians can receive real-time guidance from experts located elsewhere, reducing the time required for repairs and minimizing production downtime.

- **Siemens:** Siemens has integrated virtual collaboration tools into its manufacturing processes, enabling cross-functional teams to collaborate on projects in real-time. This approach has led to increased efficiency and innovation within the organization.

Future Prospects of Virtual Collaboration in Manufacturing

Looking ahead, the future of virtual collaboration in manufacturing appears promising. As technology continues to evolve, we can expect several trends to shape the landscape:

1. **Advancements in AI and Machine Learning:** The integration of AI and machine learning into virtual collaboration tools will enhance decision-making capabilities, enabling manufacturers to analyze data and predict outcomes more effectively.

2. **Expansion of 5G Technology:** The rollout of 5G networks will improve connectivity and reduce latency, making virtual collaboration more seamless and effective. This will particularly benefit remote monitoring and maintenance applications.

3. **Increased Focus on Sustainability:** Virtual collaboration will play a crucial role in driving sustainable manufacturing practices. By reducing the need for travel and optimizing resource use, manufacturers can minimize their environmental impact.

4. **Greater Emphasis on Cybersecurity:** As reliance on virtual collaboration increases, so too will the need for robust cybersecurity measures. Manufacturers will need to prioritize data protection to safeguard their operations.

In conclusion, virtual collaboration is transforming the manufacturing industry by enhancing communication, improving efficiency, and fostering innovation. While challenges remain, the benefits far outweigh the drawbacks, making virtual collaboration an essential component of modern manufacturing practices. As technology continues to advance, the potential for virtual collaboration in manufacturing will only grow, paving the way for a more connected and efficient future.

Virtual Collaboration in Healthcare

The healthcare industry is undergoing a significant transformation, driven by advancements in technology and the increasing need for efficient and effective collaboration among healthcare professionals. Virtual collaboration in healthcare is not just a trend; it is a necessity that enhances patient care, streamlines operations, and fosters innovative solutions to complex medical challenges.

Theoretical Framework

Virtual collaboration in healthcare can be understood through the lens of several theoretical frameworks, including the Technology Acceptance Model (TAM) and the Socio-Technical Systems Theory. The TAM posits that perceived ease of use and perceived usefulness are critical factors influencing the acceptance of technology among healthcare professionals. In the context of virtual collaboration, tools that are user-friendly and demonstrably improve patient outcomes are more likely to be adopted.

Socio-Technical Systems Theory emphasizes the interdependent relationship between social and technical aspects of an organization. In healthcare, this means that successful virtual collaboration requires not only advanced technological tools but also a supportive organizational culture that encourages teamwork and communication among healthcare providers.

Applications of Virtual Collaboration in Healthcare

1. **Telemedicine**: One of the most prominent applications of virtual collaboration in healthcare is telemedicine. Telemedicine allows healthcare providers to consult with patients remotely, reducing the need for in-person visits. This is particularly beneficial for patients in rural or underserved areas. Studies have shown that telemedicine can lead to improved patient satisfaction and adherence to treatment plans.

2. **Collaborative Platforms**: Healthcare professionals are increasingly using collaborative platforms to share information and coordinate care. Tools such as Microsoft Teams, Slack, and specialized healthcare platforms like Doximity facilitate real-time communication and document sharing among multidisciplinary teams. This enhances decision-making and ensures that all team members are on the same page regarding patient care.

3. **Virtual Reality (VR) for Training**: Virtual reality is being utilized for training healthcare professionals. VR simulations can replicate complex surgical procedures or emergency scenarios, allowing trainees to practice in a risk-free

environment. For example, the use of VR in surgical training has shown to improve skills acquisition and retention among surgical residents.

4. **Remote Monitoring and Wearable Technology**: Wearable devices that monitor patients' vital signs can transmit data to healthcare providers in real-time. This allows for continuous monitoring and timely interventions when necessary. Virtual collaboration tools enable healthcare teams to analyze this data collaboratively, improving patient outcomes through proactive care.

Challenges in Virtual Collaboration in Healthcare

Despite its benefits, virtual collaboration in healthcare faces several challenges:

1. **Data Security and Privacy**: The healthcare industry is subject to strict regulations regarding patient data privacy, such as the Health Insurance Portability and Accountability Act (HIPAA) in the United States. Ensuring that virtual collaboration tools comply with these regulations is paramount to protect patient information.

2. **Technology Adoption**: Resistance to change is a common barrier in healthcare settings. Some healthcare professionals may be hesitant to adopt new technologies due to concerns about their effectiveness or the learning curve associated with using them.

3. **Interoperability**: Different healthcare systems and tools may not be compatible with each other, leading to fragmented care. Achieving interoperability among various platforms is essential for seamless virtual collaboration.

4. **Digital Divide**: There is a risk that virtual collaboration may exacerbate existing inequalities in healthcare access. Patients without reliable internet access or technological literacy may be left behind in a system increasingly reliant on digital solutions.

Examples of Successful Virtual Collaboration in Healthcare

1. **Mayo Clinic's Telehealth Services**: The Mayo Clinic has implemented a robust telehealth program that allows patients to consult with specialists remotely. This program has been instrumental in providing care during the COVID-19 pandemic, ensuring that patients receive timely medical attention without the risk of exposure to the virus.

2. **Cleveland Clinic's Virtual Second Opinions**: The Cleveland Clinic offers a service where patients can receive virtual second opinions from top specialists. This initiative not only empowers patients but also facilitates collaboration among healthcare providers across different institutions.

3. **Doctors Without Borders (MSF) and Virtual Collaboration**: MSF has utilized virtual collaboration tools to coordinate care in remote areas during humanitarian crises. By using mobile applications and cloud-based platforms, MSF teams can share patient data and treatment plans, ensuring continuity of care in challenging environments.

Conclusion

Virtual collaboration in healthcare represents a paradigm shift that has the potential to enhance patient care, improve operational efficiencies, and foster innovation. While challenges such as data security, technology adoption, and interoperability remain, the successful implementation of virtual collaboration tools can lead to significant improvements in healthcare delivery. As the industry continues to evolve, embracing these technologies will be crucial for healthcare professionals aiming to provide high-quality, patient-centered care in an increasingly digital world.

Virtual Collaboration in Education

Virtual collaboration in education has emerged as a transformative force, reshaping how educators and students interact, learn, and share knowledge. The integration of virtual collaboration tools and environments has opened new avenues for learning, breaking down geographical barriers and fostering an inclusive educational landscape. This section explores the theoretical foundations, challenges, and real-world applications of virtual collaboration in education.

Theoretical Foundations

The theoretical underpinnings of virtual collaboration in education can be linked to several key educational theories:

- **Constructivism:** This theory posits that learners construct their own understanding and knowledge of the world, through experiencing things and reflecting on those experiences. Virtual collaboration platforms facilitate constructivist learning by allowing students to engage in discussions, share resources, and collaborate on projects, thus creating knowledge collectively.

- **Social Learning Theory:** Proposed by Albert Bandura, this theory emphasizes learning through observation and interaction with others. Virtual collaboration tools enable students to observe peers, engage in discussions, and learn from diverse perspectives, enhancing their understanding of complex concepts.

- **Connectivism:** This theory, introduced by George Siemens, asserts that learning occurs across a network of connections. In the context of virtual collaboration, students can connect with experts, peers, and resources worldwide, fostering a rich learning environment that transcends traditional classroom boundaries.

Challenges in Virtual Collaboration in Education

While the benefits of virtual collaboration in education are significant, several challenges must be addressed:

- **Technological Barriers:** Access to reliable internet and appropriate devices is crucial for effective virtual collaboration. Disparities in technology access can hinder participation, particularly in underprivileged communities.

- **Digital Literacy:** Students and educators must possess the skills to navigate virtual collaboration tools effectively. A lack of digital literacy can impede engagement and collaboration.

- **Engagement and Motivation:** Maintaining student engagement in virtual environments can be challenging. Educators must implement strategies to foster motivation and active participation.

- **Assessment and Evaluation:** Evaluating student performance in virtual collaborative settings requires innovative assessment methods that account for the collaborative nature of learning.

Examples of Virtual Collaboration in Education

Numerous educational institutions and organizations have successfully implemented virtual collaboration initiatives:

- **Global Classrooms:** Programs like *ePals* connect classrooms from different countries, allowing students to collaborate on projects, exchange ideas, and learn about different cultures. For instance, a project between a classroom in the United States and one in Kenya focused on environmental issues, culminating in a joint presentation shared through a virtual platform.

- **Virtual Reality in Education:** Institutions are leveraging virtual reality (VR) to create immersive learning experiences. For example, the *Virtual Reality Education Pathfinders* program uses VR to simulate historical events, allowing students to explore and collaborate in a virtual environment that enhances their understanding of history.

- **Online Collaborative Platforms:** Tools like *Google Classroom* and *Microsoft Teams* facilitate virtual collaboration by providing spaces for discussions, resource sharing, and project management. A notable case is the use of these platforms during the COVID-19 pandemic, which enabled schools to transition to remote learning seamlessly.

- **International Research Collaborations:** Universities often engage in collaborative research projects that span multiple countries. For example, the *Global Education Conference* brings together educators and students worldwide to discuss best practices and share research findings, fostering a global dialogue on educational innovation.

Conclusion

Virtual collaboration in education represents a paradigm shift in teaching and learning. By embracing collaborative technologies and methodologies, educators can create more engaging, inclusive, and effective learning experiences. However, addressing the challenges associated with technology access, digital literacy, and student engagement is essential for maximizing the potential of virtual collaboration in education. As we move forward, it is crucial to continue exploring innovative approaches and strategies that enhance collaborative learning in diverse educational settings.

$$\text{Effective Learning} = \text{Engagement} + \text{Collaboration} + \text{Technology} \qquad (24)$$

In summary, the future of education lies in harnessing the power of virtual collaboration to foster a global learning community that transcends traditional boundaries and prepares students for the complexities of the modern world.

Virtual Collaboration in Entertainment

The entertainment industry has undergone a transformative shift with the advent of virtual collaboration technologies. This evolution has not only redefined how content is created and consumed but has also fostered new forms of artistic expression and audience engagement. This section explores the various facets of virtual collaboration in entertainment, highlighting relevant theories, challenges, and practical examples.

Theoretical Framework

Virtual collaboration in entertainment can be examined through the lens of several theoretical frameworks, including Social Constructivism and Media Richness Theory.

Social Constructivism posits that knowledge is constructed through social interactions and experiences. In the context of entertainment, this suggests that collaborative projects in virtual environments allow creators to co-construct narratives and experiences that reflect diverse perspectives.

Media Richness Theory argues that different media have varying capacities for conveying information. Virtual collaboration tools, such as immersive VR environments, offer rich media experiences that can enhance storytelling by providing sensory engagement beyond traditional formats. This theory supports the idea that the richness of virtual environments can lead to deeper emotional connections with audiences.

Applications of Virtual Collaboration in Entertainment

Virtual collaboration is applied across various sectors of the entertainment industry, including film, music, gaming, and live performances. Each sector utilizes unique technologies and approaches to enhance collaboration.

2.1 Film Production In film production, virtual collaboration tools enable remote teams to work together seamlessly. Platforms like *Frame.io* allow filmmakers to share video edits, receive feedback in real-time, and collaborate on post-production tasks. For instance, during the production of the film *The Mandalorian*, the use of virtual sets and real-time rendering technologies allowed the crew to collaborate effectively from different locations, reducing the need for extensive travel and physical sets.

2.2 Music Collaboration The music industry has also embraced virtual collaboration, allowing artists from around the world to create music together without being in the same physical space. Software such as *Soundtrap* and *BandLab* facilitates real-time music creation and editing. A notable example is the collaboration between artists like *Travis Scott* and *Fortnite*, where a virtual concert was held, merging gaming with live music performance, attracting millions of viewers and redefining live entertainment.

2.3 Gaming Development   In the gaming sector, virtual collaboration is essential for development teams spread across different geographical locations. Tools like *Unity* and *Unreal Engine* provide collaborative environments where developers can work on game design, coding, and testing in real-time. The game *Fortnite* serves as an excellent case study, where continuous updates and events are developed collaboratively, engaging players in a shared virtual space.

2.4 Live Performances   Live performances have also benefited from virtual collaboration technologies. Artists are now able to perform live in virtual spaces, reaching global audiences. Platforms like *VRChat* and *AltspaceVR* allow performers to interact with fans in immersive environments. The virtual concert by *Lil Nas X* in *Roblox* exemplifies this trend, where the artist performed for a virtual audience, creating an interactive experience that transcended physical limitations.

Challenges of Virtual Collaboration in Entertainment

While virtual collaboration presents numerous opportunities, it also poses several challenges that must be addressed to maximize its potential.

3.1 Technological Barriers   One of the primary challenges is the technological barriers that can hinder collaboration. High-quality virtual collaboration requires robust internet connectivity and access to advanced hardware. Disparities in technology access can lead to inequalities among collaborators, particularly in regions with limited resources.

3.2 Creative Differences   Creative differences among collaborators can be exacerbated in virtual environments. The lack of face-to-face interaction may lead to misunderstandings and conflicts, requiring effective communication strategies to navigate these challenges. Establishing clear roles and responsibilities, along with regular check-ins, can help mitigate these issues.

3.3 Intellectual Property Concerns   Intellectual property (IP) concerns are another significant challenge in virtual collaboration. As multiple creators contribute to a project, determining ownership and rights can become complex.

Establishing clear agreements and using blockchain technology for transparent IP management may provide solutions to these challenges.

Future Directions

The future of virtual collaboration in entertainment looks promising, with advancements in technology continuously enhancing the collaborative experience. Emerging technologies such as artificial intelligence and machine learning are expected to play a significant role in automating aspects of content creation, thereby allowing artists to focus on the creative process.

4.1 Enhanced User Experiences The integration of augmented reality (AR) and virtual reality (VR) will likely lead to more immersive and interactive experiences for audiences. Future collaborations may involve mixed-reality performances where audiences can participate in the creative process, blurring the lines between creators and consumers.

4.2 Global Collaboration Networks As virtual collaboration tools become more sophisticated, we may witness the rise of global collaboration networks, where artists from diverse backgrounds come together to create content that reflects a multitude of cultural perspectives. This shift has the potential to enrich the entertainment landscape and foster greater inclusivity.

Conclusion

Virtual collaboration in entertainment represents a dynamic intersection of technology and creativity. As the industry continues to evolve, embracing these collaborative tools will be essential for artists and creators seeking to innovate and connect with audiences in meaningful ways. By addressing the challenges and leveraging the opportunities presented by virtual collaboration, the entertainment industry can pave the way for a more inclusive and engaging future.

Virtual Collaboration in Retail

The retail industry is undergoing a significant transformation, driven by advancements in technology and changing consumer behaviors. Virtual collaboration in retail has emerged as a powerful tool for enhancing customer experiences, streamlining operations, and fostering innovation. This section explores the role of virtual collaboration in retail, its theoretical underpinnings, associated challenges, and practical examples.

Theoretical Framework

The integration of virtual collaboration in retail can be understood through several theoretical lenses, including:

- **Social Presence Theory:** This theory posits that the level of social presence in a communication medium affects the quality of interaction. In retail, virtual collaboration tools that enhance social presence, such as video conferencing and immersive environments, can lead to improved customer engagement and satisfaction.

- **Technology Acceptance Model (TAM):** TAM suggests that perceived ease of use and perceived usefulness influence user acceptance of technology. Retailers adopting virtual collaboration tools must ensure these tools are user-friendly and demonstrably beneficial to both employees and customers.

- **Collaborative Consumption:** This concept emphasizes shared access to goods and services. Virtual collaboration facilitates collaborative consumption by enabling retailers to connect with customers and partners more effectively, fostering a community around shared experiences and resources.

Challenges in Virtual Collaboration

Despite its potential, virtual collaboration in retail faces several challenges:

- **Technological Barriers:** Retailers may encounter issues related to bandwidth, device compatibility, and software integration. These barriers can hinder the seamless implementation of virtual collaboration tools.

- **Cultural Resistance:** Employees and management may resist adopting new technologies due to fear of change or lack of familiarity. Overcoming this resistance requires effective change management strategies and training programs.

- **Data Security Concerns:** Retailers must address data privacy and security risks associated with virtual collaboration. Protecting customer information and ensuring compliance with regulations like GDPR is paramount.

- **Maintaining Customer Engagement:** In a virtual environment, maintaining customer engagement can be challenging. Retailers must innovate continuously to create compelling virtual experiences that resonate with consumers.

Examples of Virtual Collaboration in Retail

Several retailers have successfully implemented virtual collaboration strategies to enhance their operations and customer experiences:

- **Virtual Showrooms:** Companies like *IKEA* have introduced virtual showrooms that allow customers to explore products in immersive 3D environments. This approach enhances the shopping experience by enabling customers to visualize how products will fit into their homes.

- **Remote Consultations:** *Sephora* has leveraged virtual collaboration by offering remote consultations through video calls. Customers can receive personalized beauty advice from experts, thereby enhancing customer satisfaction and driving sales.

- **Collaborative Supply Chain Management:** Retailers such as *Walmart* utilize virtual collaboration platforms to coordinate with suppliers and streamline inventory management. These platforms facilitate real-time communication and data sharing, improving efficiency and reducing costs.

- **Community Engagement:** Brands like *Nike* have created virtual communities where customers can connect, share experiences, and participate in events. This fosters brand loyalty and encourages collaborative consumption among customers.

Conclusion

Virtual collaboration in retail represents a paradigm shift in how retailers engage with customers and manage operations. By leveraging technology to create immersive experiences, enhance communication, and foster collaboration, retailers can navigate the complexities of a rapidly changing market. However, addressing the challenges associated with virtual collaboration is crucial for success. Retailers must invest in technology, training, and security to fully realize the benefits of virtual collaboration and create a competitive advantage in the retail landscape.

$$\text{Customer Satisfaction} = f(\text{Engagement, Usability, Value}) \quad (25)$$

Where:

- Engagement refers to the level of interaction and involvement customers have with the virtual collaboration tools.

- Usability indicates how easy and intuitive the tools are for customers to use.

- Value represents the perceived benefits customers derive from their interactions.

Virtual Collaboration in Research and Development

Virtual collaboration in research and development (R&D) has emerged as a transformative approach to innovation, enabling teams to work together across geographical boundaries and diverse disciplines. The integration of virtual collaboration tools has the potential to enhance productivity, foster creativity, and accelerate the pace of research. This section explores the theoretical foundations, challenges, and practical examples of virtual collaboration in R&D.

Theoretical Foundations

The theory of collaborative innovation posits that diverse teams, equipped with varied expertise and perspectives, can generate more innovative solutions than individuals working in isolation. This is particularly relevant in R&D, where complex problems often require interdisciplinary approaches. According to [?], open innovation frameworks encourage organizations to leverage external ideas and technologies in conjunction with internal R&D efforts, creating a more dynamic and collaborative environment.

Mathematically, the effectiveness of collaborative innovation can be represented as:

$$I = f(E, D, C) \qquad (26)$$

where I is the level of innovation achieved, E represents the diversity of expertise within the team, D is the degree of collaboration, and C is the communication effectiveness among team members. Higher values of E, D, and C lead to increased innovation outcomes.

Challenges in Virtual Collaboration for R&D

Despite the advantages, virtual collaboration in R&D is not without its challenges:

- **Technical Barriers:** High-quality virtual collaboration requires robust technological infrastructure. Issues such as bandwidth limitations, software compatibility, and latency can hinder effective collaboration. A study by [?]

found that 30% of researchers experienced significant disruptions due to technical issues during virtual meetings.

- **Cultural Differences:** R&D teams often comprise members from various cultural backgrounds, leading to differences in communication styles, work ethics, and problem-solving approaches. This can create misunderstandings and conflict, as highlighted by [?], who emphasized the importance of cultural awareness in international collaborations.

- **Trust Building:** Trust is a critical component of effective collaboration. In virtual environments, the lack of face-to-face interaction can impede trust development. According to [?], trust can be modeled as a function of perceived competence, integrity, and benevolence among team members.

Examples of Virtual Collaboration in R&D

Several organizations and research institutions have successfully implemented virtual collaboration strategies in their R&D efforts:

- **NASA's Collaborative Research:** NASA utilizes virtual collaboration tools to facilitate research across its various centers. For instance, the agency's use of virtual reality environments allows scientists and engineers to simulate and visualize complex data, enhancing their ability to collaborate on projects such as the Mars Rover missions [?].

- **Global Research Networks:** The Human Genome Project is a prime example of successful virtual collaboration in R&D. It involved researchers from around the world working together to map the human genome. The project utilized online databases and communication platforms to share findings and coordinate efforts, resulting in significant advancements in genomics [?].

- **Pharmaceutical Industry Collaborations:** Companies like Pfizer and BioNTech have leveraged virtual collaboration to expedite vaccine development. During the COVID-19 pandemic, these companies utilized cloud-based platforms to share data, collaborate on research, and streamline the development process, leading to the rapid creation of effective vaccines [?].

Conclusion

Virtual collaboration in R&D presents both opportunities and challenges. By understanding the theoretical foundations and addressing the barriers to effective collaboration, organizations can harness the power of diverse teams to drive innovation. The examples highlighted demonstrate that successful virtual collaboration is not only possible but can also lead to groundbreaking advancements in various fields. As technology continues to evolve, the potential for virtual collaboration in R&D will only expand, paving the way for a more interconnected and innovative future.

Virtual Collaboration in Marketing

The marketing landscape has undergone a seismic shift in recent years, driven by technological advancements and changing consumer behaviors. As businesses increasingly adopt virtual collaboration tools, the marketing sector is reaping the benefits of enhanced communication, creativity, and efficiency. This section explores the role of virtual collaboration in marketing, examining its theoretical foundations, practical applications, challenges, and real-world examples.

Theoretical Foundations

The integration of virtual collaboration in marketing can be understood through several theoretical frameworks:

- **Social Exchange Theory:** This theory posits that social behavior is the result of an exchange process aiming to maximize benefits and minimize costs. In marketing, virtual collaboration enhances relationships between brands and consumers, allowing for real-time feedback and engagement, which can lead to improved customer loyalty and satisfaction.

- **Diffusion of Innovations:** Rogers' theory explains how, why, and at what rate new ideas and technology spread. Virtual collaboration tools are rapidly adopted in marketing due to their ability to facilitate innovative campaigns and reach broader audiences efficiently.

- **Collaborative Consumption:** This concept emphasizes the sharing of resources and services, which is increasingly relevant in marketing strategies that leverage user-generated content and community engagement through virtual platforms.

Applications of Virtual Collaboration in Marketing

Virtual collaboration in marketing manifests in various forms, including:

- **Remote Brainstorming Sessions:** Teams can utilize virtual whiteboards and brainstorming tools such as Miro or MURAL to generate creative ideas for campaigns. These tools promote inclusivity and allow for diverse inputs regardless of geographical location.

- **Virtual Focus Groups:** Marketers can conduct focus groups using video conferencing tools like Zoom or Microsoft Teams. This approach enables real-time interaction with participants, facilitating deeper insights into consumer preferences and behaviors.

- **Collaborative Content Creation:** Tools such as Google Docs and Adobe Creative Cloud allow multiple team members to work on marketing materials simultaneously. This not only streamlines the content creation process but also enhances creative collaboration, leading to higher-quality outputs.

- **Social Media Campaigns:** Virtual collaboration tools enable marketing teams to coordinate social media strategies across different platforms. Teams can share content calendars, track engagement metrics, and adjust campaigns in real-time based on performance data.

- **Influencer Partnerships:** Virtual collaboration allows brands to engage with influencers more effectively. Tools like Asana or Trello can be used to manage campaigns, track deliverables, and ensure that brand messaging aligns with influencer content.

Challenges of Virtual Collaboration in Marketing

While virtual collaboration offers numerous advantages, it also presents challenges:

- **Communication Barriers:** Misunderstandings can arise from the lack of non-verbal cues in virtual settings. Marketers must be vigilant in ensuring clear communication and may need to rely more on written documentation to avoid ambiguity.

- **Technology Dependence:** The effectiveness of virtual collaboration hinges on the availability and reliability of technology. Technical issues such as poor internet connectivity can disrupt meetings and hinder productivity.

- **Cultural Differences:** In global marketing teams, cultural differences can influence collaboration styles and decision-making processes. Marketers must cultivate cultural awareness and adaptability to foster effective teamwork.

- **Collaboration Fatigue:** The increased reliance on virtual meetings can lead to fatigue among team members. Marketers need to balance virtual collaboration with asynchronous communication methods to maintain engagement and productivity.

Real-World Examples

Several companies have successfully leveraged virtual collaboration in their marketing strategies:

- **Coca-Cola:** During the pandemic, Coca-Cola utilized virtual brainstorming sessions with global teams to develop innovative marketing campaigns that resonated with consumers. By embracing virtual collaboration, they maintained a strong brand presence despite physical distancing.

- **Nike:** Nike's marketing team employs virtual collaboration tools to coordinate global campaigns. By utilizing platforms like Slack and Google Drive, they ensure that all team members are aligned and can contribute to creative processes, regardless of location.

- **Unilever:** Unilever has embraced virtual focus groups to gather consumer insights quickly. By conducting these sessions online, they can reach diverse demographics and adapt their marketing strategies in real-time based on participant feedback.

Conclusion

In conclusion, virtual collaboration has become an integral component of modern marketing strategies. By facilitating enhanced communication, creativity, and efficiency, it empowers marketing teams to navigate the complexities of a rapidly evolving landscape. However, challenges such as communication barriers and cultural differences must be addressed to fully harness the potential of virtual collaboration. As technology continues to advance, the future of marketing will increasingly rely on collaborative efforts that transcend geographical boundaries, fostering innovation and engagement in ways previously unimaginable.

$$\text{ROI} = \frac{\text{Net Profit}}{\text{Cost of Investment}} \times 100 \qquad (27)$$

The effectiveness of virtual collaboration in marketing can ultimately be measured by its impact on return on investment (ROI), emphasizing the importance of optimizing collaborative efforts to achieve desired business outcomes.

The Integration of Virtual and Augmented Reality

Virtual and Augmented Reality Hybrid Environments

The convergence of Virtual Reality (VR) and Augmented Reality (AR) has led to the emergence of hybrid environments that leverage the strengths of both technologies. Hybrid environments provide users with immersive experiences that blend virtual content with the real world, creating interactive and engaging spaces for collaboration, training, and entertainment. This section explores the theoretical foundations, potential applications, challenges, and examples of hybrid VR and AR environments.

Theoretical Foundations

Hybrid environments are grounded in several key theories from both virtual reality and augmented reality research. One foundational theory is the **Spatial Presence Theory**, which posits that users experience a sense of being in a virtual environment when they perceive themselves as interacting with it. This theory is crucial for understanding how hybrid environments can create a seamless integration of real and virtual elements.

Another important theoretical framework is the **Media Richness Theory**, which suggests that the effectiveness of communication depends on the richness of the medium used. Hybrid environments enhance media richness by allowing for multiple forms of communication, including visual, auditory, and haptic feedback, thereby improving collaboration and interaction among users.

Applications of Hybrid Environments

Hybrid environments have a wide range of applications across various sectors:

- **Education and Training:** Hybrid environments can facilitate hands-on training by overlaying virtual simulations onto real-world settings. For instance, medical students can practice surgical procedures using AR overlays on physical models, enhancing their learning experience.

- **Architecture and Design:** Architects can use hybrid environments to visualize designs in real-time. By overlaying 3D models onto physical spaces, stakeholders can experience and provide feedback on designs before construction begins.

- **Manufacturing:** In manufacturing, workers can benefit from AR instructions displayed in their field of view while they perform tasks in a physical environment. This can lead to improved accuracy and efficiency in assembly lines.

- **Remote Collaboration:** Hybrid environments can enable remote teams to collaborate more effectively. For example, team members can gather in a virtual space while interacting with real-world objects through AR, allowing for a more immersive brainstorming session.

Challenges in Hybrid Environments

Despite the advantages, several challenges hinder the widespread adoption of hybrid environments:

- **Technical Limitations:** The integration of VR and AR requires advanced hardware and software capabilities. Issues such as latency, bandwidth limitations, and device compatibility can impact the user experience. For example, the need for powerful graphics processing units (GPUs) can be a barrier for smaller organizations.

- **User Experience:** Designing intuitive interfaces for hybrid environments is crucial. Users may face difficulties in navigating these environments, especially if the integration of virtual and real elements is not seamless. Studies indicate that poor user experience can lead to frustration and decreased engagement.

- **Data Security and Privacy:** The use of hybrid environments raises concerns regarding data security and user privacy. As these environments often involve real-time data sharing and communication, ensuring secure connections and protecting sensitive information is paramount.

- **Cognitive Overload:** The simultaneous presentation of virtual and real information can lead to cognitive overload, where users struggle to process the overwhelming amount of stimuli. This can hinder decision-making and reduce the effectiveness of collaboration.

Examples of Hybrid Environments

Several notable examples illustrate the application of hybrid environments:

- **Microsoft HoloLens:** This AR headset allows users to interact with holograms in their physical environment. It has been used in various sectors, including healthcare, where surgeons can visualize patient data while performing procedures, enhancing precision and outcomes.

- **IKEA Place:** This mobile app utilizes AR to allow users to visualize furniture in their homes before making a purchase. By overlaying 3D models of furniture onto real-world spaces, customers can make informed decisions and reduce the likelihood of returns.

- **Google's Project Tango:** This initiative aimed to create devices capable of understanding their physical environment. By combining AR with spatial awareness, users could interact with both virtual and real objects, enhancing navigation and interaction in various applications, from gaming to education.

Conclusion

In conclusion, hybrid environments that integrate VR and AR technologies offer significant potential for enhancing collaboration, training, and user engagement across various industries. However, addressing the technical, experiential, and security challenges is essential for realizing the full benefits of these environments. As technology continues to advance, the future of hybrid environments looks promising, paving the way for innovative applications that redefine how we interact with both the virtual and physical worlds.

$$\text{User Engagement} = f(\text{Media Richness, Spatial Presence, User Experience}) \tag{28}$$

Augmented Reality Overlays in Virtual Collaboration

Augmented Reality (AR) overlays in virtual collaboration represent a groundbreaking integration of digital information with the physical world, enhancing the collaborative experience by providing contextual data and interactive elements. This subsection explores the theory behind AR overlays, the challenges associated with their implementation, and practical examples of their application in various collaborative environments.

Theoretical Framework

The theoretical foundation of AR overlays is rooted in the concept of *mixed reality*, which combines real and virtual worlds to produce new environments where physical and digital objects coexist and interact in real-time. This is facilitated by advanced technologies such as computer vision, simultaneous localization and mapping (SLAM), and depth tracking. The integration of these technologies allows for the precise placement of digital information in the user's physical environment, creating an immersive experience that enhances understanding and communication.

Challenges of AR Overlays in Virtual Collaboration

Despite the potential benefits of AR overlays, several challenges hinder their widespread adoption in virtual collaboration:

- **Technical Limitations:** High-performance hardware is required to render AR overlays seamlessly. Limitations in processing power, battery life, and display quality can detract from the user experience.

- **User Experience:** Designing intuitive and user-friendly interfaces for AR applications is critical. Users may struggle with navigation and interaction if the interface is not well-designed, leading to frustration and decreased productivity.

- **Data Security and Privacy:** The use of AR overlays often involves the collection of sensitive data from users' environments. Ensuring the privacy and security of this data is paramount, as breaches can lead to significant repercussions.

- **Interoperability:** Different AR platforms may not be compatible with one another, creating barriers for collaboration across various systems and devices. Establishing standards for AR content and interactions is essential for seamless integration.

Practical Examples of AR Overlays in Virtual Collaboration

Several industries have successfully implemented AR overlays to enhance virtual collaboration:

- **Architecture and Design:** In architectural design, AR overlays allow teams to visualize building plans in real-world environments. For instance, using AR applications like *IKEA Place*, designers can overlay 3D models of furniture in a physical space to assess design choices before implementation.

- **Healthcare:** Surgeons have begun using AR overlays during operations to visualize critical information, such as patient anatomy and surgical pathways. The *Microsoft HoloLens* has been utilized in operating rooms to project vital patient data onto the surgeon's field of view, improving precision and outcomes.

- **Manufacturing:** In manufacturing, AR overlays assist in training and maintenance. For example, *Porsche* has implemented AR glasses that provide technicians with real-time data and instructions while they work on vehicles, reducing errors and increasing efficiency.

- **Remote Collaboration:** Tools like *Spatial* enable remote teams to collaborate in a shared virtual space where AR overlays provide contextual information, such as annotations and 3D models, enhancing discussions and decision-making processes.

Conclusion

The integration of augmented reality overlays in virtual collaboration offers a promising avenue for enhancing communication, understanding, and productivity across various fields. While challenges remain, advancements in technology and design are paving the way for broader adoption. As AR continues to evolve, its potential to reshape collaborative practices and improve outcomes in diverse industries cannot be overstated. Future research should focus on addressing the technical and user experience challenges to fully harness the capabilities of AR in virtual collaboration.

Virtual Reality Training Enhanced with Augmented Reality

The integration of Augmented Reality (AR) into Virtual Reality (VR) training represents a significant advancement in the educational and professional development landscape. By combining the immersive environments of VR with the contextual enhancements of AR, training programs can offer more interactive, engaging, and effective learning experiences. This section explores the theoretical foundations, challenges, and practical examples of VR training enhanced with AR.

Theoretical Foundations

The theoretical underpinnings of VR and AR training can be traced to several key learning theories, including Constructivism, Experiential Learning, and Situated Learning.

Constructivism posits that learners construct knowledge through experiences and reflections. In a VR environment enriched with AR elements, learners can interact with virtual objects while receiving real-time contextual information, fostering deeper understanding and retention.

Experiential Learning, as articulated by Kolb (1984), emphasizes learning through experience, which is particularly relevant in VR training. The cycle of Concrete Experience, Reflective Observation, Abstract Conceptualization, and Active Experimentation is enhanced when AR provides immediate feedback and additional layers of information.

Situated Learning argues that knowledge is best acquired in context. By overlaying AR content in a VR training scenario, learners can visualize and interact with complex concepts in a realistic setting, bridging the gap between theory and practice.

Challenges in Integration

Despite the potential benefits, integrating AR into VR training presents several challenges:

Technical Limitations include issues related to hardware compatibility, latency, and the need for robust software solutions that can seamlessly merge AR and VR experiences. High-quality AR requires significant processing power, which may not always be available in existing VR systems.

User Experience is critical. If the AR elements distract from the VR experience or create cognitive overload, the training effectiveness may diminish. Designers must carefully balance the amount of information presented in AR to ensure it enhances rather than detracts from the learning experience.

Cost is another significant factor. Developing and implementing AR-enhanced VR training programs can be expensive, requiring investment in both technology and content creation. Organizations must weigh these costs against the potential benefits of improved training outcomes.

Practical Examples

Several industries have begun to adopt AR-enhanced VR training solutions, showcasing their effectiveness in various contexts:

Healthcare is one of the most prominent fields utilizing this technology. For instance, surgical training programs can use VR to simulate complex procedures while AR overlays provide real-time anatomical information, helping trainees visualize critical structures and understand spatial relationships during operations.

Manufacturing also benefits from this integration. Companies like Boeing have implemented AR in their VR training modules for assembly line workers. Trainees can practice assembling parts in a virtual environment while AR provides step-by-step guidance and highlights potential errors, significantly reducing training time and increasing accuracy.

Emergency Services training has seen advancements through AR-enhanced VR simulations. Firefighters, for example, can engage in realistic fire scenarios in VR while AR overlays provide crucial data on fire behavior, structural integrity, and safety protocols, enabling them to make informed decisions in high-pressure situations.

Conclusion

The convergence of VR and AR in training environments offers a transformative approach to learning, providing immersive, interactive, and contextually rich experiences. While challenges remain, the potential for enhanced engagement, retention, and practical application makes this integration a compelling avenue for future training programs. As technology continues to evolve, the synergy between

ETHICAL CONSIDERATIONS AND SOCIAL IMPACT

VR and AR is likely to redefine the standards of training across various industries, fostering a new era of learning that is both effective and efficient.

$$E = mc^2 \qquad (29)$$

In summary, VR training enhanced with AR not only aligns with established learning theories but also addresses real-world training needs across sectors, paving the way for innovative educational practices that can adapt to the demands of a rapidly changing workforce.

Ethical Considerations and Social Impact

Privacy and Data Security

In the rapidly evolving landscape of virtual collaboration, privacy and data security have emerged as critical concerns. As organizations increasingly rely on virtual environments for communication and collaboration, the protection of sensitive information becomes paramount. This section explores the theoretical foundations, prevalent issues, and practical examples related to privacy and data security in virtual collaboration spaces.

Theoretical Foundations

Privacy can be defined as the right of individuals to control their personal information and to decide how it is collected, used, and shared. Data security, on the other hand, refers to the measures taken to protect digital information from unauthorized access, corruption, or theft. The intersection of these two concepts is particularly relevant in virtual collaboration, where data is often shared across multiple platforms and among various stakeholders.

The concept of *confidentiality* is central to data security. It ensures that sensitive information is only accessible to authorized users. This is often achieved through encryption techniques, which transform readable data into an unreadable format, only reversible by those who possess the appropriate decryption keys. Mathematically, encryption can be represented as:

$$C = E(K, M)$$

where C is the ciphertext, E is the encryption function, K is the encryption key, and M is the plaintext message.

Additionally, the principle of *least privilege* dictates that users should have the minimum level of access necessary to perform their tasks. This approach mitigates the risk of unauthorized access and potential data breaches.

Challenges in Virtual Collaboration

Despite the theoretical frameworks available, several challenges persist in ensuring privacy and data security in virtual collaboration environments:

- **Data Breaches:** As organizations increasingly store sensitive information in cloud-based platforms, they become prime targets for cyberattacks. High-profile breaches, such as the 2017 Equifax incident, where personal data of approximately 147 million individuals was compromised, highlight the vulnerabilities inherent in data storage and management practices.

- **Inadequate Security Protocols:** Many organizations lack robust security measures. A survey conducted by the Ponemon Institute revealed that 60% of organizations do not have a formal incident response plan in place, increasing their susceptibility to data breaches.

- **User Behavior:** The human factor remains a significant vulnerability. Employees may inadvertently expose sensitive data through phishing attacks or by using weak passwords. Research indicates that 81% of data breaches are linked to compromised passwords, emphasizing the need for user education and awareness programs.

Examples of Privacy and Data Security Issues

1. **Zoom Data Privacy Concerns:** During the COVID-19 pandemic, Zoom became a popular platform for virtual meetings. However, it faced scrutiny over its data privacy practices, including allegations of sharing user data with Facebook without consent. This raised significant concerns about user privacy and prompted the company to enhance its security measures, including end-to-end encryption for meetings.

2. **Microsoft Teams and Data Compliance:** Microsoft Teams, widely used for remote collaboration, adheres to various compliance standards, such as the General Data Protection Regulation (GDPR) and Health Insurance Portability and Accountability Act (HIPAA). However, organizations must ensure that their usage of Teams aligns with these regulations, particularly regarding data retention and user consent.

3. **Slack and Data Retention Policies:** Slack's data retention policies have been a point of contention. Users may unintentionally share sensitive information in channels that are not adequately protected. The platform offers features to manage data retention, but organizations must actively implement these settings to safeguard sensitive information.

Best Practices for Enhancing Privacy and Data Security

To address the challenges associated with privacy and data security in virtual collaboration, organizations should consider implementing the following best practices:

- **Data Encryption:** Utilize end-to-end encryption for all communication and file sharing. This ensures that even if data is intercepted, it remains unreadable without the decryption keys.

- **Access Controls:** Implement role-based access controls to limit data access based on user roles. Regularly review and update permissions to reflect changes in personnel and responsibilities.

- **User Training:** Conduct regular training sessions to educate employees about security best practices, including recognizing phishing attempts and creating strong passwords.

- **Regular Audits:** Perform regular security audits to identify vulnerabilities and assess compliance with data protection regulations. This proactive approach can help mitigate risks before they escalate into significant issues.

Conclusion

As virtual collaboration continues to expand, the importance of privacy and data security cannot be overstated. Organizations must prioritize the protection of sensitive information by adopting robust security measures, fostering a culture of awareness, and remaining vigilant against emerging threats. By addressing these challenges head-on, organizations can create a secure environment that enhances collaboration while safeguarding the privacy of individuals and the integrity of their data.

Digital Inclusivity

Digital inclusivity refers to the practice of ensuring that all individuals, regardless of their socio-economic status, geographic location, age, gender, or ability, have equal access to digital technologies and the opportunities they provide. In the context of virtual collaboration, digital inclusivity is crucial for fostering a diverse and equitable environment where all participants can contribute effectively.

Theoretical Framework

The concept of digital inclusivity is grounded in several theoretical frameworks, including the Digital Divide theory and the Capability Approach. The Digital Divide theory posits that disparities in access to technology can lead to unequal opportunities and outcomes in society. This divide can be seen in various forms, such as:

- **Access Divide:** Differences in access to hardware, software, and high-speed internet.

- **Skill Divide:** Variations in digital literacy and the ability to use technology effectively.

- **Usage Divide:** Disparities in how individuals utilize technology for different purposes.

The Capability Approach, developed by economist Amartya Sen, emphasizes the importance of providing individuals with the capabilities to achieve their desired outcomes. In the context of digital inclusivity, this means equipping individuals with the necessary tools, skills, and support to participate fully in digital environments.

Challenges to Digital Inclusivity

Despite the recognized importance of digital inclusivity, several challenges persist:

- **Infrastructure Limitations:** In many regions, particularly rural and underserved urban areas, the lack of reliable internet access remains a significant barrier. According to the Federal Communications Commission (FCC), approximately 19 million Americans lack access to broadband internet, which hinders their ability to engage in virtual collaboration.

- **Economic Barriers:** The cost of devices and internet services can be prohibitive for low-income individuals and families. A report from the Pew Research Center found that 25% of adults with an annual household income of less than $30,000 do not own a smartphone, compared to only 3% of those with an income of $75,000 or more.

- **Digital Literacy:** A lack of digital skills can prevent individuals from effectively using virtual collaboration tools. The International Telecommunication Union (ITU) has highlighted that digital literacy is essential for participating in the digital economy, yet many people, particularly older adults, may lack the necessary training.

- **Cultural and Linguistic Barriers:** Language differences and cultural nuances can create challenges in virtual collaboration. Tools that do not support multiple languages or fail to consider cultural contexts may alienate participants from diverse backgrounds.

Examples of Digital Inclusivity Initiatives

To address these challenges, various initiatives have emerged to promote digital inclusivity:

- **Community Wi-Fi Programs:** Many cities have launched community Wi-Fi projects to provide free internet access in public spaces. For example, San Francisco's "Free Wi-Fi in Parks" initiative allows residents and visitors to connect to the internet in designated areas, bridging the access gap.

- **Digital Literacy Training:** Organizations such as the Goodwill Industries and the Digital Literacy Project offer training programs aimed at enhancing digital skills among underserved populations. These programs often focus on essential skills such as using email, navigating the internet, and utilizing collaboration tools.

- **Inclusive Design Principles:** Companies developing virtual collaboration tools are increasingly adopting inclusive design principles. For instance, Microsoft has implemented accessibility features in its Teams platform, such as live captions and screen reader compatibility, to accommodate users with disabilities.

- **Language Support:** Platforms like Zoom and Google Meet have introduced features that support real-time translation and transcription, making it easier for participants who speak different languages to communicate effectively during virtual meetings.

Measuring Digital Inclusivity

To assess the effectiveness of digital inclusivity efforts, organizations can utilize various metrics, including:

$$\text{Digital Inclusivity Index} = \frac{\text{Number of Users with Access}}{\text{Total Target Population}} \times 100 \qquad (30)$$

This index provides a quantitative measure of how many individuals within a target population have access to necessary digital resources. Additionally, qualitative feedback from participants can provide insights into their experiences and challenges in virtual collaboration.

Conclusion

Digital inclusivity is essential for ensuring that virtual collaboration spaces are equitable and accessible to all. By addressing the barriers of access, affordability, digital literacy, and cultural differences, organizations can create an environment that fosters diverse participation and harnesses the collective intelligence of all contributors. As we move towards an increasingly digital future, prioritizing digital inclusivity will not only enhance collaboration but also drive innovation and social change across various sectors.

Cognitive and Psychological Effects

The integration of virtual collaboration tools and environments has profound cognitive and psychological effects on users. Understanding these impacts is essential for optimizing the design and implementation of virtual collaboration spaces, as well as for ensuring the well-being and productivity of participants. This section explores several key areas of cognitive and psychological effects, including cognitive load, social presence, emotional responses, and the implications for team dynamics.

Cognitive Load Theory

Cognitive Load Theory (CLT), developed by Sweller (1988), posits that the human brain has a limited capacity for processing information. In virtual collaboration settings, participants may experience varying levels of cognitive load due to the complexity of the tasks at hand and the design of the virtual environment. Cognitive load can be categorized into three types:

- **Intrinsic Load:** The inherent difficulty of the material being learned or the task being performed. For instance, a complex engineering design task in a virtual environment may result in high intrinsic load.

- **Extraneous Load:** The load imposed by the way information is presented. Poorly designed virtual interfaces or excessive visual stimuli can increase extraneous load, detracting from the learning and collaboration experience.

- **Germane Load:** The load dedicated to the process of learning itself. Effective virtual collaboration tools should aim to maximize germane load by facilitating meaningful interactions and promoting deep learning.

An equation representing the total cognitive load (CL) can be expressed as:

$$CL = IL + EL + GL$$

Where IL is intrinsic load, EL is extraneous load, and GL is germane load.

To mitigate cognitive overload in virtual environments, designers should focus on creating intuitive interfaces, minimizing distractions, and providing clear guidance to users. For example, utilizing virtual reality (VR) environments that allow for natural interactions can help reduce extraneous load and enhance user engagement.

Social Presence Theory

Social Presence Theory (SPT) emphasizes the importance of perceived social presence in communication and collaboration. Social presence refers to the degree to which participants feel psychologically present with each other in a virtual environment. Higher levels of social presence can lead to improved communication, collaboration, and overall satisfaction in virtual spaces.

Research has shown that the use of avatars and immersive environments can enhance social presence. For instance, a study by Biocca et al. (2003) indicated that users who interacted through avatars in a virtual meeting reported higher levels of social presence compared to those using video conferencing without avatars. This sense of presence can foster trust and rapport among team members, which is crucial for effective collaboration.

However, the absence of social cues, such as body language and eye contact, in virtual environments may hinder the development of social presence. Designers of virtual collaboration tools should aim to incorporate features that enhance the perception of social presence, such as real-time body tracking and facial expression recognition.

Emotional Responses

Virtual collaboration can evoke a range of emotional responses, which can significantly influence team dynamics and individual performance. Emotions such as frustration, anxiety, excitement, and satisfaction can arise from various aspects of the virtual collaboration experience.

For example, the phenomenon of *collaboration fatigue* can occur when participants feel overwhelmed by the constant demands of virtual meetings and interactions. A study by Raghuram et al. (2019) found that excessive virtual collaboration can lead to emotional exhaustion, negatively impacting both individual performance and team morale.

Conversely, positive emotional responses can enhance creativity and innovation. When team members feel supported and engaged in a virtual environment, they are more likely to contribute ideas and collaborate effectively. Tools that promote positive emotional experiences, such as gamification elements or collaborative brainstorming sessions, can lead to more productive outcomes.

Implications for Team Dynamics

The cognitive and psychological effects of virtual collaboration extend to team dynamics, influencing how teams function and interact. The following factors are particularly relevant:

- **Trust Building:** Trust is a critical component of effective collaboration. Virtual environments that facilitate open communication and transparency can foster trust among team members. For example, regular check-ins and feedback loops can enhance trust and collaboration.

- **Conflict Resolution:** The lack of non-verbal cues in virtual settings can complicate conflict resolution. Teams may benefit from structured approaches to conflict management, such as employing mediators or establishing clear communication protocols.

- **Diversity and Inclusion:** Virtual collaboration can help bridge geographical and cultural gaps, promoting diversity and inclusion. However, it is essential to be mindful of potential biases that may arise in virtual interactions. Training programs that emphasize cultural competence can help mitigate these biases.

In conclusion, the cognitive and psychological effects of virtual collaboration are multifaceted and have significant implications for the design and implementation of virtual collaboration spaces. By understanding and addressing these effects, organizations can create more effective and engaging virtual environments that enhance collaboration and support the well-being of participants. Future research should continue to explore these dynamics, particularly as technology evolves and virtual collaboration becomes increasingly prevalent in various industries.

Virtual Collaboration and Social Interaction

The advent of virtual collaboration tools has fundamentally altered the landscape of social interaction in professional environments. As organizations increasingly rely on digital platforms to facilitate teamwork, understanding the nuances of social interaction in virtual spaces becomes crucial. This section examines the interplay between virtual collaboration and social interaction, exploring relevant theories, challenges, and practical examples.

Theoretical Framework

Theories of social presence and media richness provide a foundational understanding of how virtual collaboration affects interpersonal interactions. Social presence theory posits that the degree of salience of the other person in a communication interaction influences the quality of the interaction. In virtual collaboration, social presence can be affected by factors such as the medium used (e.g., video conferencing vs. text chat) and the level of interactivity available.

$$SP = f(M, I) \tag{31}$$

Where:

- SP = Social Presence
- M = Medium of communication
- I = Interactivity level

Media richness theory suggests that different communication media have varying capacities to convey information. Rich media, such as video calls, allow for nuanced communication through visual and auditory cues, fostering stronger social interactions compared to lean media, such as emails or instant messages.

Challenges in Virtual Social Interaction

Despite the potential benefits of virtual collaboration, several challenges hinder effective social interaction:

- **Lack of Non-Verbal Cues:** Virtual environments often limit the ability to read body language and facial expressions, which are critical components of effective communication. This can lead to misunderstandings and reduced empathy among team members.

- **Digital Disconnection:** The absence of physical presence can create a sense of isolation among team members. This digital disconnection may lead to feelings of disengagement and reduced motivation.

- **Cultural Barriers:** Virtual collaboration often involves diverse teams from various cultural backgrounds. Differences in communication styles and social norms can complicate interactions and lead to conflict.

- **Collaboration Fatigue:** Prolonged use of virtual collaboration tools can result in fatigue, often referred to as "Zoom fatigue." This phenomenon can diminish the quality of social interactions and overall productivity.

Practical Examples

To illustrate the impact of virtual collaboration on social interaction, consider the following examples:

- **Virtual Team Building Activities:** Companies like Zoom and Microsoft Teams have introduced features that allow teams to engage in virtual team-building exercises. These activities, such as online trivia games or virtual escape rooms, promote social bonding and foster a sense of community among remote workers.

- **Video Conferencing vs. Text-Based Communication:** A study conducted by the University of California found that participants in video conferencing settings reported feeling more connected and engaged compared to those communicating via text-based platforms. The visual and auditory cues present in video calls enhance social presence and facilitate richer interactions.

- **Cultural Sensitivity Training:** Organizations that implement cultural sensitivity training can mitigate misunderstandings arising from cultural differences. Such training equips team members with the skills to navigate diverse communication styles, fostering a more inclusive environment.

Strategies for Enhancing Social Interaction in Virtual Collaboration

To overcome the challenges of virtual social interaction, organizations can implement several strategies:

- **Encourage Video Use:** Promoting the use of video during meetings can enhance social presence and foster a more engaging atmosphere. Encouraging team members to turn on their cameras can help simulate in-person interactions.

- **Regular Check-Ins:** Scheduling regular one-on-one check-ins can help team members feel more connected. These informal conversations provide an opportunity to discuss not only work-related matters but also personal experiences and challenges.

- **Utilize Collaborative Tools:** Leveraging collaborative tools like virtual whiteboards (e.g., Miro or MURAL) can enhance interactivity during brainstorming sessions, making discussions more dynamic and engaging.

- **Create a Virtual Water Cooler:** Establishing informal channels for social interaction, such as dedicated chat rooms for non-work-related conversations, can help replicate the spontaneous social interactions that occur in physical office spaces.

Conclusion

In conclusion, while virtual collaboration presents unique challenges to social interaction, it also offers opportunities to innovate and adapt. By understanding the theoretical underpinnings of social presence and media richness, organizations can implement strategies to enhance social interactions in virtual environments. As the future of work continues to evolve, fostering meaningful social connections in virtual collaboration spaces will be essential for maintaining team cohesion and productivity.

Virtual Collaboration and Cyberbullying

In the realm of virtual collaboration, the advent of digital communication platforms has revolutionized how individuals and teams interact. However, this transformation has also given rise to significant challenges, particularly concerning cyberbullying. Cyberbullying, defined as the intentional and repeated harm inflicted through digital means, poses unique threats in collaborative environments, affecting individuals' psychological well-being and overall productivity.

Theoretical Framework

Cyberbullying can be understood through several theoretical lenses, including Social Learning Theory, which posits that individuals learn behaviors by observing others. In virtual collaboration spaces, the anonymity and distance provided by technology can lead to aggressive behaviors that individuals might not exhibit in face-to-face interactions. This theory suggests that when individuals witness cyberbullying, they may perceive it as an acceptable form of communication, perpetuating a cycle of abuse.

Additionally, the General Strain Theory (GST) provides insight into the motivations behind cyberbullying. GST posits that individuals who experience negative emotions or stressors may resort to harmful behaviors as a coping mechanism. In collaborative settings, high-pressure environments can lead to increased tensions, making members susceptible to engaging in or becoming victims of cyberbullying.

Problems Associated with Cyberbullying in Virtual Collaboration

The implications of cyberbullying in virtual collaboration are profound. The following issues highlight the extent of the problem:

- **Psychological Impact:** Victims of cyberbullying often experience anxiety, depression, and a decline in self-esteem. A study by Kowalski et al. (2014) found that individuals who were bullied online reported higher levels of psychological distress compared to their non-bullied counterparts.

- **Decreased Productivity:** Cyberbullying can lead to disengagement from collaborative tasks. Research indicates that victims may reduce their participation in team activities, leading to decreased overall productivity (Boulton, 2016).

ETHICAL CONSIDERATIONS AND SOCIAL IMPACT

- **Workplace Culture:** A culture that tolerates or overlooks cyberbullying can foster a toxic work environment. This not only affects the targeted individuals but can also impact team cohesion and morale (Hinduja & Patchin, 2010).

- **Legal and Ethical Considerations:** Organizations face potential legal repercussions if they fail to address cyberbullying effectively. Ethical responsibilities to ensure a safe working environment extend to virtual spaces, necessitating clear policies and interventions.

Examples of Cyberbullying in Virtual Collaboration

Real-world examples illustrate the prevalence and impact of cyberbullying in virtual collaboration:

1. **Anonymous Messaging Platforms:** In many organizations, anonymous feedback tools are used to promote openness. However, these platforms can be misused for harassment. For instance, employees may receive derogatory comments about their performance or personal characteristics, leading to significant emotional distress.

2. **Social Media and Professional Networks:** Instances of cyberbullying have been reported on platforms like LinkedIn and Slack, where individuals may publicly criticize or belittle colleagues. Such behavior not only harms the targeted individuals but also creates a hostile environment for others.

3. **Virtual Team Meetings:** During video conferences, individuals may face ridicule or mocking comments from peers. A notable case involved a team meeting where one member was consistently interrupted and belittled, leading to their withdrawal from future collaborative efforts (Smith, 2021).

Strategies for Mitigating Cyberbullying in Virtual Collaboration

To combat cyberbullying in virtual collaboration spaces, organizations can implement several strategies:

- **Establish Clear Policies:** Organizations should develop comprehensive policies that define cyberbullying and outline the consequences for engaging in such behavior. These policies should be communicated effectively to all team members.

- **Promote a Positive Culture:** Encouraging a culture of respect and inclusivity can help mitigate the risk of cyberbullying. Training sessions focused on emotional intelligence and conflict resolution can equip team members with the skills to communicate effectively.

- **Provide Support Systems:** Organizations should offer resources for individuals affected by cyberbullying, such as counseling services or anonymous reporting mechanisms. Providing a safe space for victims to share their experiences can empower them to seek help.

- **Monitor Digital Interactions:** Implementing monitoring tools to track interactions in collaborative platforms can help identify patterns of bullying behavior. While respecting privacy, organizations should be vigilant in addressing any signs of cyberbullying.

Conclusion

As virtual collaboration continues to evolve, addressing the challenges of cyberbullying is paramount. By understanding the theoretical underpinnings, recognizing the problems, and implementing effective strategies, organizations can foster healthier collaborative environments. Ultimately, ensuring that virtual spaces remain safe and supportive is essential for the well-being of all participants, promoting not only individual growth but also the success of collaborative efforts.

Bibliography

[1] Kowalski, R. M., Giumetti, G. W., & Schroeder, A. N. (2014). Bullying in the Digital Age: A Critical Review and Meta-Analysis of Cyberbullying Research Among Youth. *Psychological Bulletin*, 140(4), 1073-1137.

[2] Boulton, M. J. (2016). The Impact of Cyberbullying on Young People: A Review of the Literature. *International Journal of Adolescence and Youth*, 21(1), 1-15.

[3] Hinduja, S., & Patchin, J. W. (2010). Bullying Beyond the Schoolyard: A Critical Review and Meta-Analysis of Cyberbullying Research Among Youth. *Psychological Bulletin*, 136(2), 277-306.

[4] Smith, J. (2021). The Effects of Cyberbullying in Virtual Teams: A Case Study. *Journal of Business Communication*, 58(3), 345-367.

Bibliography

The Challenges and Opportunities of Virtual Collaboration

Technical Challenges

Bandwidth and Connectivity

In the realm of virtual collaboration, bandwidth and connectivity serve as foundational elements that can significantly influence the effectiveness of communication and the overall user experience. As organizations increasingly adopt virtual collaboration tools, understanding the intricacies of bandwidth and connectivity becomes paramount.

Theoretical Framework

Bandwidth refers to the maximum rate of data transfer across a network, typically measured in bits per second (bps). It determines how much information can be sent and received simultaneously. Higher bandwidth allows for more data to be transmitted, which is particularly important in virtual collaboration environments that utilize video conferencing, real-time document editing, and immersive virtual reality experiences.

The relationship between bandwidth and latency—defined as the time it takes for data to travel from the source to the destination—plays a crucial role in determining the quality of a virtual collaboration session. The following equation illustrates the relationship between bandwidth, latency, and data transfer:

$$\text{Effective Throughput} = \frac{\text{Bandwidth}}{\text{Latency}} \qquad (32)$$

This equation suggests that as latency decreases (i.e., the connection becomes faster), the effective throughput increases, allowing for smoother interactions in virtual environments.

Problems Associated with Bandwidth and Connectivity

Despite advancements in technology, various challenges persist regarding bandwidth and connectivity in virtual collaboration:

- **Network Congestion:** High traffic on a network can lead to congestion, resulting in reduced bandwidth availability for individual users. This is especially prevalent during peak usage times, such as during business hours when many employees are accessing the same network resources.

- **Limited Infrastructure:** In some regions, particularly rural or underdeveloped areas, the existing network infrastructure may not support high bandwidth requirements. Users in these locations may experience slow connections, leading to frustration and decreased productivity.

- **Quality of Service (QoS):** Virtual collaboration tools often require prioritization of data packets to ensure quality. Without QoS mechanisms, critical data may be delayed or lost, leading to interruptions during meetings or collaborative sessions.

- **Latency Issues:** High latency can result in delays that disrupt the flow of conversation, making it difficult for participants to engage effectively. This is particularly problematic in video conferencing, where timing is crucial for natural dialogue.

Examples of Bandwidth Challenges in Virtual Collaboration

To illustrate the impact of bandwidth and connectivity issues on virtual collaboration, consider the following scenarios:

- **Video Conferencing Failures:** In a multinational organization, a team meeting is scheduled with participants from various countries. If one participant is located in an area with limited bandwidth, their video feed may freeze or lag, leading to miscommunication and disengagement from the discussion.

TECHNICAL CHALLENGES 147

- **Collaborative Document Editing:** When multiple users attempt to edit a document simultaneously, low bandwidth can hinder the real-time updates necessary for seamless collaboration. Users may encounter delays in seeing changes made by others, which can lead to confusion and version control issues.

- **Virtual Reality Experiences:** In a virtual reality training session, high bandwidth is essential for rendering realistic environments and ensuring smooth interactions. If the connection is insufficient, users may experience choppy visuals or disconnections, diminishing the training's effectiveness.

Strategies for Overcoming Bandwidth and Connectivity Challenges

Organizations can implement several strategies to mitigate bandwidth and connectivity issues in virtual collaboration:

- **Upgrading Infrastructure:** Investing in higher bandwidth solutions, such as fiber-optic connections, can provide the necessary speed and stability for effective virtual collaboration.

- **Utilizing Cloud Services:** Cloud-based collaboration tools can optimize data transfer and storage, reducing the burden on local networks. By leveraging the cloud, organizations can enhance accessibility and scalability while minimizing bandwidth strain.

- **Implementing QoS Protocols:** Organizations can prioritize traffic for virtual collaboration tools through QoS settings, ensuring that critical data packets receive the necessary bandwidth allocation during peak usage times.

- **Educating Users:** Providing training on best practices for optimizing bandwidth usage—such as minimizing video quality when not necessary or closing unnecessary applications during virtual meetings—can help improve overall performance.

Conclusion

In conclusion, bandwidth and connectivity are critical components of successful virtual collaboration. By understanding the theoretical underpinnings, recognizing the challenges, and implementing effective strategies, organizations can enhance their virtual collaboration experiences. As technology continues to evolve, addressing these issues will be vital for fostering productive, engaging, and efficient virtual work environments.

Hardware and Device Compatibility

In the realm of virtual collaboration, hardware and device compatibility is a critical factor that can significantly impact the user experience and effectiveness of collaborative efforts. As virtual reality (VR) and augmented reality (AR) technologies advance, the diversity of hardware options available to users has expanded. This section explores the theoretical underpinnings of hardware compatibility, the challenges that arise, and practical examples of these issues in real-world applications.

Theoretical Framework

Hardware compatibility refers to the ability of various devices to work together seamlessly within a virtual collaboration environment. This encompasses a range of devices, including head-mounted displays (HMDs), motion controllers, computers, and even mobile devices. Theoretical models of compatibility often draw upon the principles of systems integration, which emphasize the importance of interoperability among components to create a cohesive user experience.

One foundational theory relevant to hardware compatibility is the *Technology Acceptance Model* (TAM). TAM posits that perceived ease of use and perceived usefulness significantly influence user acceptance of technology. In the context of virtual collaboration, if users encounter compatibility issues, their perception of the technology's usefulness diminishes, leading to reduced engagement and productivity.

Challenges of Hardware Compatibility

Despite advancements in technology, several challenges persist regarding hardware and device compatibility in virtual collaboration:

- **Diverse Hardware Ecosystems:** Different manufacturers produce a wide array of devices with varying specifications. For instance, VR headsets from Oculus, HTC, and Valve may require different software and drivers, complicating the integration process.

- **Operating System Variability:** Compatibility issues can arise due to differing operating systems (e.g., Windows, macOS, Linux) and their respective support for VR/AR applications. Each OS may handle drivers and hardware differently, leading to inconsistencies in performance.

TECHNICAL CHALLENGES

- **Performance Discrepancies:** The performance of VR applications can vary significantly based on the hardware used. For example, a high-end gaming PC may run a VR application smoothly, while a lower-spec machine may experience lag or crashes, negatively affecting collaboration.

- **Latency Issues:** In collaborative environments, latency can hinder real-time interactions. Devices with slower processing capabilities may introduce delays, disrupting the flow of communication and collaboration.

Examples of Compatibility Issues

Several real-world examples illustrate the challenges of hardware and device compatibility in virtual collaboration:

1. **Cross-Platform Collaboration:** A team using different VR headsets (e.g., Oculus Rift and HTC Vive) may face challenges when attempting to collaborate in a shared virtual space. The need for specific software versions and updates can lead to compatibility issues, resulting in some team members being unable to participate fully.

2. **Software Updates:** Frequent updates to VR software can create temporary incompatibilities with existing hardware. For instance, a new version of a VR collaboration platform may require updated drivers that not all users have installed, leading to fragmented experiences.

3. **Mobile Device Limitations:** While many VR applications are designed for high-end PCs, there is a growing trend toward mobile VR. However, the limited processing power and graphical capabilities of mobile devices can restrict the functionality of collaborative applications, leading to a subpar experience compared to desktop counterparts.

Addressing Compatibility Challenges

To mitigate hardware and device compatibility issues, several strategies can be employed:

- **Standardization Efforts:** Industry-wide standards can facilitate compatibility across devices. Organizations such as the *Virtual Reality Developers Conference* (VRDC) and the *OpenXR* initiative aim to create frameworks that promote interoperability among VR and AR devices.

- **Modular Hardware Design:** Manufacturers can adopt modular designs that allow for easier upgrades and compatibility with a wider range of devices. This approach can help users maintain their systems without needing to replace entire setups.

- **Comprehensive Testing:** Rigorous testing of software across various hardware configurations can identify compatibility issues before deployment. Developers should prioritize compatibility testing to ensure a smooth user experience across different platforms.

- **User Education:** Providing users with clear guidelines on hardware requirements and compatibility can help them make informed decisions about their setups. Training sessions or documentation can assist users in troubleshooting common compatibility issues.

Conclusion

In conclusion, hardware and device compatibility is a fundamental aspect of successful virtual collaboration. As the landscape of VR and AR technologies continues to evolve, addressing compatibility challenges will be essential for maximizing the potential of virtual collaboration spaces. By understanding the theoretical foundations, recognizing the challenges, and implementing effective solutions, organizations can foster a more inclusive and productive virtual collaboration environment.

Performance and Latency

The performance of virtual collaboration spaces is critically influenced by latency, which is defined as the time delay experienced in a system. In the context of virtual reality (VR) and augmented reality (AR), latency can significantly affect user experience, interaction quality, and overall effectiveness of collaboration. This section explores the theoretical foundations of performance and latency, the problems associated with high latency, and practical examples illustrating these concepts.

Theoretical Foundations

Latency in virtual collaboration can be categorized into several types: network latency, rendering latency, and input latency. Understanding these components is essential for optimizing performance in VR environments.

TECHNICAL CHALLENGES

Network Latency Network latency refers to the time taken for data to travel from the source to the destination over a network. It can be influenced by several factors, including:

- **Distance:** The geographical distance between users and servers can introduce significant delays.

- **Congestion:** High traffic on a network can lead to packet loss and increased latency.

- **Routing:** The number of hops data must take through routers can also affect latency.

Mathematically, network latency can be expressed as:

$$L_{network} = T_{transmission} + T_{propagation} + T_{queuing} \tag{33}$$

where:

- $T_{transmission}$ is the time taken to push all the packet's bits into the wire,

- $T_{propagation}$ is the time taken for the signal to travel through the medium,

- $T_{queuing}$ is the time spent waiting in queues at routers.

Rendering Latency Rendering latency is the delay between the input from the user and the corresponding visual output in the VR environment. This latency arises from the time taken to process user inputs, update the virtual scene, and render the graphics. A critical aspect of rendering latency is the frame rate, which is the number of frames displayed per second (FPS). A higher FPS generally results in a smoother experience, while lower FPS can lead to motion sickness and disorientation.

The relationship between frame rate and latency can be expressed as:

$$L_{rendering} = \frac{1}{FPS} \tag{34}$$

where a frame rate of 60 FPS corresponds to a rendering latency of approximately 16.67 milliseconds.

Input Latency Input latency is the delay between a user's action (e.g., moving a controller or making a gesture) and the system's response. This latency can significantly impact user experience, as immediate feedback is crucial for effective interaction in virtual environments. Input latency can be affected by the quality of tracking systems, the responsiveness of controllers, and the processing speed of the software.

Problems Associated with High Latency

High latency in virtual collaboration can lead to several problems, including:

Reduced User Experience In VR environments, high latency can cause a disconnect between user actions and system responses, leading to frustration and a diminished sense of presence. Users may experience delays in their movements being reflected in the virtual space, which can disrupt the flow of collaboration.

Motion Sickness Latency can induce motion sickness in users, especially in immersive environments where visual and vestibular systems must be synchronized. When there is a significant delay between a user's movement and the visual feedback, it can lead to disorientation and discomfort.

Ineffective Communication In collaborative settings, high latency can hinder effective communication. For instance, if one user is speaking while others are experiencing a lag in audio or visual feedback, it can lead to misunderstandings and misinterpretations.

Examples Illustrating Performance and Latency Issues

Example 1: Remote Team Collaboration Consider a remote team using a VR platform for a brainstorming session. If the network latency is high (e.g., 200 milliseconds), team members may experience delays in seeing each other's avatars move or respond. This lag can disrupt the natural flow of conversation, making it difficult to build on each other's ideas effectively.

Example 2: Virtual Training Simulations In a virtual training simulation for healthcare professionals, input latency can be particularly detrimental. If a trainee is practicing a surgical procedure and experiences a delay in the response of the virtual instruments, it can lead to improper technique and potentially dangerous outcomes in real-life scenarios.

TECHNICAL CHALLENGES   153

Example 3: Gaming Environments   In VR gaming, high rendering latency can lead to a poor gaming experience. For instance, if a player is engaged in a fast-paced action game and experiences a frame rate drop to 30 FPS, the rendering latency increases to approximately 33.33 milliseconds, which can result in missed actions and a frustrating gameplay experience.

Mitigating Latency Issues

To enhance performance and reduce latency in virtual collaboration spaces, several strategies can be employed:

Optimizing Network Infrastructure   Improving network infrastructure, such as using high-speed fiber-optic connections and minimizing the number of hops between users and servers, can significantly reduce network latency.

Enhancing Rendering Techniques   Utilizing advanced rendering techniques, such as foveated rendering, which adjusts the resolution based on where the user is looking, can help maintain a high frame rate and reduce rendering latency.

Improving Input Devices   Investing in high-quality input devices with low latency tracking can enhance user experience and reduce input latency, leading to more effective collaboration.

In conclusion, performance and latency are critical factors influencing the effectiveness of virtual collaboration spaces. By understanding the theoretical foundations and addressing the associated challenges, organizations can create more immersive and productive virtual environments that foster collaboration and innovation.

Software Integration

In the realm of virtual collaboration, software integration plays a pivotal role in ensuring seamless communication and productivity among team members. As organizations increasingly rely on various software solutions to facilitate collaboration, the ability to integrate these tools becomes essential. This section explores the theoretical foundations of software integration, the challenges that arise, and practical examples of successful implementations.

Theoretical Foundations

Software integration refers to the process of connecting different software applications to work together as a unified system. This can involve combining functionalities, sharing data, and enabling communication between applications. The primary goal is to enhance efficiency, reduce redundancy, and improve the overall user experience.

The integration of software can be categorized into three main types:

- **Data Integration:** Involves consolidating data from multiple sources into a single view. This is crucial for decision-making processes where data from various departments must be analyzed together.

- **Functional Integration:** Focuses on combining the functionalities of different applications to streamline workflows. For instance, integrating project management tools with communication platforms can facilitate real-time updates and discussions.

- **Process Integration:** Refers to the alignment of business processes across different software systems. This ensures that workflows are consistent and efficient, regardless of the tools used.

The integration of software solutions can be achieved through various methods, including Application Programming Interfaces (APIs), middleware, and custom-built solutions. APIs, in particular, have become a cornerstone of modern software integration, allowing different applications to communicate and share data in real time.

Challenges in Software Integration

Despite its advantages, software integration poses several challenges:

- **Compatibility Issues:** Different software applications may use varying data formats, protocols, and architectures, making it difficult to integrate them seamlessly. Organizations must ensure that the tools they choose are compatible or invest in middleware solutions to bridge the gaps.

- **Data Security and Privacy:** Integrating multiple systems can expose sensitive data to vulnerabilities. Organizations must implement robust security measures, such as encryption and access controls, to protect data during transmission and storage.

- **Cost and Resource Allocation:** The integration process can be resource-intensive, requiring significant investment in time and money. Organizations must weigh the benefits of integration against the costs involved, which can include software licensing, development, and training.

- **User Resistance:** Employees may resist changes to their workflows, particularly if they are accustomed to using specific tools. Effective change management strategies, including training and communication, are essential to facilitate a smooth transition.

Examples of Successful Software Integration

Numerous organizations have successfully implemented software integration strategies to enhance their virtual collaboration efforts. Below are a few notable examples:

- **Slack and Google Drive:** The integration of Slack, a popular communication platform, with Google Drive allows users to share files directly within chat conversations. This integration streamlines workflows, as team members can access and collaborate on documents without leaving the Slack interface.

- **Trello and Zapier:** Trello, a project management tool, can be integrated with Zapier to automate workflows between different applications. For instance, a new card created in Trello can automatically trigger an email notification or update in another tool, reducing manual effort and ensuring timely communication.

- **Zoom and Microsoft Teams:** The integration of Zoom with Microsoft Teams enables users to schedule and join Zoom meetings directly from the Teams interface. This integration enhances the user experience by reducing the need to switch between applications, thereby promoting a more cohesive virtual collaboration environment.

Conclusion

In conclusion, software integration is a critical component of effective virtual collaboration. While it presents various challenges, the benefits of streamlined workflows, enhanced communication, and improved productivity far outweigh the difficulties. Organizations that prioritize software integration and invest in the necessary tools and training will be better positioned to thrive in an increasingly digital and collaborative world. By addressing compatibility issues, ensuring data security, and managing user resistance, teams can harness the full potential of integrated software solutions to drive success in their collaborative efforts.

$$\text{Integration Success} = \frac{\text{Benefits}}{\text{Challenges}} \qquad (35)$$

The equation above illustrates that the success of software integration is a function of the benefits gained relative to the challenges faced. A successful integration strategy will maximize benefits while minimizing challenges, leading to enhanced virtual collaboration outcomes.

Accessibility and Usability

The integration of virtual collaboration spaces into everyday workflows has transformed how teams interact, yet it raises significant concerns regarding accessibility and usability. These two concepts are critical to ensuring that all users, regardless of their physical abilities or technological proficiency, can effectively engage in virtual environments.

Accessibility in Virtual Collaboration

Accessibility refers to the design of products, devices, services, or environments for people with disabilities. In the context of virtual collaboration, it is essential to create spaces that accommodate various disabilities, including visual, auditory, motor, and cognitive impairments.

Theoretical Framework The Web Content Accessibility Guidelines (WCAG) provide a foundational framework for creating accessible digital content. These guidelines emphasize four principles: Perceivable, Operable, Understandable, and Robust (POUR). Each principle plays a crucial role in designing virtual collaboration spaces:

- **Perceivable:** Information and user interface components must be presented to users in ways they can perceive. For instance, visual content should have alternative text descriptions for users with visual impairments.

- **Operable:** User interface components must be operable through various means, such as keyboard navigation for users who cannot use a mouse.

- **Understandable:** Information and operation of the user interface must be understandable. This includes clear instructions and consistent navigation.

TECHNICAL CHALLENGES

- **Robust:** Content must be robust enough to be interpreted reliably by a wide variety of user agents, including assistive technologies.

Challenges in Accessibility Despite the frameworks in place, many virtual collaboration tools fail to meet accessibility standards. Common issues include:

- **Inadequate Alternative Text:** Many platforms do not provide sufficient alternative text for images, making it difficult for screen reader users to understand visual content.

- **Keyboard Navigation:** Some virtual environments require mouse use, excluding users who rely on keyboard navigation.

- **Complex Interfaces:** Overly complicated user interfaces can overwhelm users with cognitive impairments, leading to frustration and disengagement.

Usability in Virtual Collaboration

Usability focuses on how effectively, efficiently, and satisfactorily users can interact with a system. In virtual collaboration, usability impacts user engagement and productivity.

Theoretical Framework The ISO 9241-11 standard outlines three key components of usability:

- **Effectiveness:** The accuracy and completeness with which users achieve their goals in a particular environment.

- **Efficiency:** The resources expended in relation to the accuracy and completeness of goals achieved.

- **Satisfaction:** The comfort and acceptability of the work system to its users and other people affected by its use.

Challenges in Usability Virtual collaboration tools often face usability challenges that can hinder user experience:

- **Learning Curve:** New users may struggle to adapt to complex virtual environments, leading to decreased productivity and satisfaction.

- **Inconsistent User Interfaces:** Variability in design across different tools can confuse users, especially when switching between platforms.

- **Technical Issues:** Performance problems such as lag and crashes can frustrate users, undermining their ability to collaborate effectively.

Examples of Accessibility and Usability in Practice

Several organizations have made strides in improving accessibility and usability in virtual collaboration:

Example 1: Microsoft Teams Microsoft Teams has implemented various accessibility features, including live captions, screen reader support, and keyboard shortcuts. These features enhance the platform's usability for individuals with disabilities, allowing them to participate fully in virtual meetings.

Example 2: Zoom Zoom has introduced accessibility options such as the ability to enable closed captioning and sign language interpretation during meetings. These features demonstrate a commitment to inclusivity and enhance the overall user experience.

Conclusion

Addressing accessibility and usability in virtual collaboration spaces is essential for fostering inclusive environments. By adhering to established guidelines and focusing on user-centered design, organizations can create virtual spaces that accommodate diverse user needs, ultimately enhancing collaboration and productivity.

To summarize, the integration of accessibility and usability principles into virtual collaboration tools is not merely a regulatory requirement but a fundamental aspect of creating equitable and effective digital workspaces. As technology continues to evolve, it is imperative that developers prioritize these aspects to ensure that all users can thrive in virtual environments.

Virtual Collaboration and Green IT

In an era where environmental sustainability is paramount, the intersection of virtual collaboration and Green IT presents both opportunities and challenges. Green IT refers to the environmentally sustainable use of technology, particularly in the management of IT resources and the reduction of the ecological footprint associated with technology use. As organizations increasingly adopt virtual

TECHNICAL CHALLENGES

collaboration tools and spaces, it is crucial to examine how these practices align with Green IT principles.

Theoretical Framework

The theoretical foundation for Green IT is rooted in several key concepts:

- **Sustainability:** The ability to meet present needs without compromising the ability of future generations to meet their own needs. In the context of IT, this involves minimizing waste, reducing energy consumption, and promoting the use of renewable resources.

- **Lifecycle Assessment (LCA):** A systematic approach to evaluating the environmental impacts associated with all stages of a product's life, from raw material extraction through production, use, and disposal. This framework can be applied to virtual collaboration technologies to assess their ecological footprint.

- **Energy Efficiency:** The goal of using less energy to provide the same service. In virtual collaboration, this can involve optimizing data centers, improving software efficiency, and reducing the energy consumption of end-user devices.

Benefits of Virtual Collaboration for Green IT

Virtual collaboration technologies offer several benefits that align with Green IT principles:

- **Reduction of Carbon Footprint:** By enabling remote work and virtual meetings, organizations can significantly reduce the need for travel, which is a major contributor to carbon emissions. For instance, a study by *Global Workplace Analytics* found that remote work can reduce an employee's carbon footprint by an average of 54% per year.

- **Decreased Resource Consumption:** Virtual collaboration reduces the demand for physical office space and resources, such as paper, furniture, and utilities. This not only lowers operational costs but also minimizes waste generation and resource depletion.

- **Enhanced Energy Efficiency:** Many virtual collaboration tools are designed to be energy-efficient, utilizing cloud computing resources that can be scaled based on demand, thus optimizing energy use. For example, cloud service providers often implement advanced energy management systems to reduce their overall energy consumption.

Challenges in Implementing Green IT in Virtual Collaboration

Despite the benefits, several challenges hinder the full realization of Green IT in virtual collaboration:

- **Data Center Energy Consumption:** While virtual collaboration can reduce travel-related emissions, the energy consumption of data centers that host these tools can be substantial. According to the *International Energy Agency*, data centers accounted for about 1% of global electricity demand in 2020, and this figure is expected to grow.

- **E-Waste:** The rapid advancement of technology often leads to increased electronic waste (e-waste). Virtual collaboration tools require various hardware, and as devices become obsolete, they contribute to e-waste, which poses significant environmental challenges.

- **User Behavior:** The effectiveness of virtual collaboration in promoting Green IT is also contingent on user behavior. For instance, if employees do not adopt energy-saving practices while using virtual collaboration tools, the potential environmental benefits may be diminished.

Examples of Green IT Practices in Virtual Collaboration

Several organizations have successfully integrated Green IT practices into their virtual collaboration efforts:

- **Salesforce:** The cloud computing giant Salesforce has committed to achieving 100% renewable energy for its global operations. Their virtual collaboration tools are designed with energy efficiency in mind, and they actively promote remote work to reduce travel-related emissions.

- **Cisco:** Cisco's WebEx platform not only facilitates virtual meetings but also incorporates energy-efficient features. The company has implemented initiatives to reduce the energy consumption of its data centers and promotes remote work to minimize its carbon footprint.

- **Microsoft:** Microsoft has taken significant steps to ensure that its virtual collaboration tools, such as Microsoft Teams, are environmentally sustainable. The company has pledged to be carbon negative by 2030 and invests in renewable energy projects to offset its emissions.

Conclusion

In conclusion, the integration of virtual collaboration and Green IT represents a promising avenue for organizations seeking to enhance sustainability while maintaining operational efficiency. By reducing travel, minimizing resource consumption, and promoting energy efficiency, virtual collaboration can significantly contribute to a greener future. However, organizations must also address the challenges associated with data center energy consumption, e-waste, and user behavior to fully realize the environmental benefits. As technology continues to evolve, embracing Green IT principles in virtual collaboration will be essential for fostering a sustainable digital workspace.

Human Factors

Adaptability and Acceptance

In the rapidly evolving landscape of virtual collaboration, adaptability and acceptance emerge as critical factors influencing the success of virtual teamwork. As organizations increasingly leverage virtual collaboration tools, understanding the psychological and behavioral dimensions of adaptability becomes essential for fostering a productive virtual environment. This section explores the theoretical underpinnings of adaptability, the challenges faced by individuals and teams, and practical examples that illustrate successful adaptation in virtual collaboration settings.

Theoretical Framework

Adaptability in the context of virtual collaboration refers to the ability of individuals and teams to adjust their behaviors, strategies, and tools in response to changing circumstances and demands. Theories such as the *Adaptive Structuration Theory* (AST) provide a framework for understanding how individuals interact with technology and how these interactions shape organizational processes. AST posits that technology is not merely a tool, but a dynamic entity that influences social structures and practices. The interplay between technology and human behavior can lead to either reinforcement of existing practices or the emergence of new collaborative norms.

Furthermore, the *Technology Acceptance Model* (TAM) posits that perceived ease of use and perceived usefulness significantly impact users' acceptance of technology. According to Davis (1989), when individuals believe that a technology enhances their performance and is easy to use, they are more likely to adopt it. This model is particularly relevant in virtual collaboration, where the effectiveness of tools can directly affect team dynamics and outcomes.

Challenges of Adaptability

Despite the theoretical frameworks that support adaptability, several challenges can hinder individuals and teams from fully embracing virtual collaboration tools:

- **Resistance to Change:** Many individuals exhibit resistance to adopting new technologies due to comfort with existing processes. This resistance can stem from fear of the unknown, lack of familiarity with new tools, or a perceived threat to job security.

- **Cognitive Overload:** The introduction of multiple collaboration tools can lead to cognitive overload, where individuals struggle to manage their attention and resources effectively. This overload can reduce productivity and lead to frustration.

- **Lack of Training and Support:** Insufficient training on new technologies can result in a lack of confidence in using virtual collaboration tools. Without proper support, individuals may revert to familiar methods, stifling innovation and collaboration.

- **Cultural Differences:** In diverse teams, cultural attitudes towards technology and collaboration can vary significantly. These differences can create barriers to acceptance and hinder effective communication.

Strategies for Enhancing Adaptability and Acceptance

To overcome these challenges, organizations can implement several strategies to enhance adaptability and acceptance among team members:

- **Comprehensive Training Programs:** Providing thorough training that emphasizes the benefits of virtual collaboration tools can help alleviate fears and build confidence. Training should be tailored to different learning styles and include hands-on practice.

- **Fostering a Culture of Innovation:** Encouraging a culture that values experimentation and innovation can help reduce resistance to change. Leaders should model adaptability by demonstrating their willingness to embrace new tools and processes.

- **Feedback Mechanisms:** Establishing channels for feedback allows team members to express concerns and suggest improvements. Actively listening to feedback can help organizations refine their collaboration tools and processes.

- **Gradual Implementation:** Introducing new technologies gradually can help team members adjust without feeling overwhelmed. Pilot programs can provide valuable insights and allow for adjustments before a full rollout.

Examples of Successful Adaptation

Numerous organizations have successfully navigated the challenges of adaptability in virtual collaboration. For instance, a multinational technology company implemented a phased approach to adopting a new virtual collaboration platform. Initially, they identified early adopters within teams who were enthusiastic about the change. These individuals received advanced training and served as champions for the new platform, helping to mentor their peers. This approach not only facilitated smoother adoption but also fostered a sense of community and support among team members.

Another example can be seen in a global consulting firm that faced resistance when introducing a new project management tool. To address this, the firm organized a series of interactive workshops that allowed employees to explore the tool's features and benefits. By involving employees in the decision-making process and providing hands-on experience, the firm successfully increased acceptance and usage of the tool across teams.

Conclusion

In conclusion, adaptability and acceptance are vital components of successful virtual collaboration. By understanding the theoretical frameworks that inform these concepts and addressing the challenges that hinder adaptability, organizations can create an environment conducive to effective virtual teamwork. Through comprehensive training, fostering a culture of innovation, and learning from successful adaptation examples, teams can enhance their ability to navigate the complexities of virtual collaboration, ultimately leading to improved performance and outcomes in the digital workspace.

Virtual Collaboration Skills

In the rapidly evolving landscape of virtual collaboration, specific skills are essential for individuals and teams to thrive. As organizations increasingly rely on virtual environments for teamwork, understanding and developing these skills becomes paramount. This section explores the key competencies required for effective virtual collaboration, the challenges faced by individuals in acquiring these skills, and strategies to overcome these challenges.

Key Competencies for Virtual Collaboration

The following skills are crucial for successful virtual collaboration:

- **Communication Skills:** Clear and effective communication is the cornerstone of successful collaboration. In virtual settings, where non-verbal cues may be limited, individuals must be adept at using various communication tools (e.g., video conferencing, chat platforms, and collaborative documents) to convey ideas, provide feedback, and resolve conflicts.

- **Technical Proficiency:** Familiarity with the tools and technologies that facilitate virtual collaboration is critical. This includes understanding software for project management, file sharing, and real-time editing. Technical proficiency ensures that team members can navigate the virtual workspace efficiently and troubleshoot common issues.

- **Cultural Awareness:** Virtual teams often comprise members from diverse cultural backgrounds. Understanding and respecting cultural differences can enhance collaboration and foster a more inclusive environment. This skill involves being open to different perspectives and adapting communication styles accordingly.

- **Self-Management:** In a virtual environment, individuals often have more autonomy over their schedules and workspaces. Self-management skills, including time management, organization, and self-discipline, are essential to maintain productivity and meet deadlines without direct supervision.

- **Problem-Solving Abilities:** Virtual collaboration frequently involves addressing challenges that arise in real-time. Team members must be equipped with strong problem-solving skills to identify issues, brainstorm solutions, and implement strategies collaboratively.

- **Emotional Intelligence:** The ability to recognize and manage one's emotions, as well as the emotions of others, is vital in virtual collaboration. High emotional intelligence can lead to better teamwork, improved relationships, and enhanced conflict resolution.

- **Adaptability:** The virtual collaboration landscape is dynamic, with tools and technologies continually evolving. Team members must be willing to adapt to new platforms, workflows, and communication styles to remain effective.

Challenges in Developing Virtual Collaboration Skills

Despite the importance of these skills, several challenges can impede their development:

- **Limited Interaction:** Virtual environments can reduce opportunities for spontaneous interactions and informal conversations, which are often essential for developing communication and relationship-building skills.

- **Technological Barriers:** Not all team members may have equal access to technology or the internet, leading to disparities in their ability to participate fully in virtual collaboration.

- **Cultural Misunderstandings:** Without face-to-face interactions, cultural nuances may be overlooked, leading to miscommunication and potential conflicts within diverse teams.

- **Isolation and Loneliness:** Remote work can lead to feelings of isolation, which may hinder individuals' motivation to engage and collaborate effectively.

Strategies for Overcoming Challenges

To address these challenges and foster the development of virtual collaboration skills, organizations can implement several strategies:

- **Training and Development Programs:** Organizations should invest in training programs that focus on enhancing communication, technical skills, and emotional intelligence. Workshops, webinars, and online courses can provide team members with the necessary tools to succeed in virtual collaboration.

- **Encouraging Informal Interactions:** Creating opportunities for informal interactions, such as virtual coffee breaks or team-building activities, can help build relationships and improve communication skills.

- **Providing Technology Support:** Ensuring that all team members have access to the necessary technology and resources is crucial. Organizations should offer technical support and training to help individuals navigate collaboration tools effectively.

- **Fostering an Inclusive Culture:** Promoting cultural awareness and sensitivity within teams can help mitigate misunderstandings. Organizations can encourage team members to share their cultural backgrounds and experiences, fostering a more inclusive environment.

- **Encouraging Feedback and Reflection:** Regular feedback sessions can help team members identify areas for improvement in their collaboration skills. Encouraging reflection on collaborative experiences can also promote learning and growth.

Conclusion

In conclusion, virtual collaboration skills are essential for navigating the complexities of remote teamwork. By focusing on key competencies, recognizing challenges, and implementing targeted strategies, individuals and organizations can enhance their collaborative capabilities in virtual environments. As the future of work continues to evolve, the ability to collaborate effectively in virtual spaces will be a critical determinant of success.

$$Success_{\text{virtual collaboration}} = \text{Communication} + \text{Technical Proficiency} + \text{Cultural Awareness} \tag{36}$$

Trust and Relationship Building

In the realm of virtual collaboration, trust and relationship building are fundamental components that underpin effective teamwork and productivity. The absence of physical cues in virtual environments can complicate the establishment of trust, making it imperative to explore strategies that foster strong interpersonal connections among team members. This section delves into the theoretical foundations of trust in virtual settings, the challenges faced in building relationships, and practical examples that illustrate successful trust-building strategies.

Theoretical Foundations of Trust

Trust is a multifaceted construct that has been extensively studied in organizational behavior and psychology. According to Mayer, Davis, and Schoorman's (1995) model of trust, three key factors influence trustworthiness: ability, benevolence, and integrity. These elements can be translated into the virtual collaboration context as follows:

- **Ability:** In virtual teams, members must demonstrate competence in their roles. This can be assessed through past performance, skill assessments, and shared experiences.

- **Benevolence:** Team members need to show concern for one another's interests. This can be fostered through open communication and supportive behaviors, such as offering help and recognizing contributions.

- **Integrity:** Trust is built when team members adhere to shared values and ethical standards. Consistency in actions and transparency in decision-making are critical for establishing integrity in virtual environments.

Challenges in Building Trust

Despite the theoretical frameworks available, several challenges hinder the development of trust in virtual collaboration:

- **Limited Nonverbal Communication:** Virtual environments often lack the rich nonverbal cues present in face-to-face interactions, making it difficult for team members to gauge emotions and intentions.

- **Cultural Differences:** Global teams may encounter varying cultural norms regarding communication styles, conflict resolution, and expressions of trust, complicating relationship-building efforts.

- **Technology Barriers:** Technical issues such as poor connectivity or unfamiliarity with collaboration tools can lead to frustration and misunderstandings, eroding trust.

- **Geographical Distance:** Physical separation can lead to feelings of isolation among team members, making it harder to form bonds and establish rapport.

Strategies for Trust and Relationship Building

To overcome these challenges, organizations can implement several strategies to cultivate trust and foster relationships in virtual collaboration:

1. **Establish Clear Communication Norms:** Setting guidelines for communication frequency, preferred channels, and response times can help manage expectations and promote transparency among team members.

2. **Utilize Team-Building Activities:** Engaging in virtual team-building exercises can create opportunities for members to connect on a personal level. For instance, icebreaker activities or virtual coffee breaks can help break down barriers and foster camaraderie.

3. **Encourage Feedback and Recognition:** Providing regular feedback and recognizing individual contributions can enhance feelings of appreciation and trust. Tools such as virtual shout-outs or recognition platforms can facilitate this process.

4. **Promote Collaborative Decision-Making:** Involving team members in the decision-making process fosters a sense of ownership and accountability, which can strengthen trust. Techniques such as consensus-building or participatory planning can be effective.

5. **Leverage Technology Wisely:** Selecting appropriate collaboration tools that enhance communication and engagement is crucial. For example, using video conferencing platforms can simulate face-to-face interactions, while collaborative documents can facilitate real-time input and feedback.

Examples of Successful Trust-Building Initiatives

Several organizations have successfully implemented trust-building initiatives in their virtual collaboration efforts:

- **Company A:** A global tech firm introduced a virtual mentorship program pairing experienced employees with newer team members. This initiative not only facilitated knowledge sharing but also fostered personal connections, enhancing trust across geographical boundaries.
- **Company B:** An international non-profit organization utilized regular virtual town hall meetings to provide updates and gather input from team members. This practice promoted transparency and inclusivity, leading to increased trust and morale within the organization.
- **Company C:** A remote-first startup integrated a virtual recognition platform where team members could publicly acknowledge each other's contributions. This approach cultivated a culture of appreciation, reinforcing trust and collaboration.

Conclusion

In conclusion, trust and relationship building are critical for the success of virtual collaboration. By understanding the theoretical foundations of trust, recognizing the challenges inherent in virtual environments, and implementing effective strategies, organizations can create a collaborative culture that thrives on mutual respect and support. As remote work continues to shape the future of collaboration, prioritizing trust will be essential for fostering productive and resilient teams.

Overcoming Cultural Differences

Cultural differences can pose significant challenges in virtual collaboration spaces, impacting communication, teamwork, and overall productivity. Understanding these differences is crucial for creating inclusive and effective virtual environments. This section explores the theoretical frameworks relevant to cultural differences, identifies common problems, and provides examples of successful strategies for overcoming these challenges.

Theoretical Frameworks

One widely recognized theory in understanding cultural differences is Hofstede's Cultural Dimensions Theory. This framework identifies six dimensions that can influence how individuals from different cultures communicate and collaborate:

- **Power Distance Index (PDI):** The degree to which less powerful members of a society defer to more powerful members. High PDI cultures may expect hierarchical structures, while low PDI cultures may favor egalitarian approaches.

- **Individualism vs. Collectivism (IDV):** Individualistic cultures prioritize personal achievements, whereas collectivist cultures emphasize group harmony and collective goals.

- **Masculinity vs. Femininity (MAS):** This dimension addresses the distribution of roles between genders, where masculine cultures value competitiveness and achievement, while feminine cultures prioritize care and quality of life.

- **Uncertainty Avoidance Index (UAI):** Cultures with high UAI prefer structured situations and clear rules, while those with low UAI are more comfortable with ambiguity and uncertainty.

- **Long-Term vs. Short-Term Orientation (LTO):** Long-term oriented cultures focus on future rewards and persistence, while short-term oriented cultures value immediate results and traditions.

- **Indulgence vs. Restraint (IVR):** This dimension reflects the extent to which a society allows free gratification of basic and natural human desires related to enjoying life and having fun.

By applying Hofstede's dimensions, virtual teams can better understand each other's cultural backgrounds and adapt their communication styles accordingly.

Common Problems in Virtual Collaboration

Despite the theoretical frameworks available, cultural differences can lead to several practical problems in virtual collaboration:

- **Miscommunication:** Differences in language, idioms, and non-verbal cues can result in misunderstandings. For instance, a direct communication style common in individualistic cultures may be perceived as rude in collectivist cultures.

- **Conflict Resolution:** Approaches to conflict vary culturally. Some cultures may prefer direct confrontation, while others may avoid conflict altogether, leading to unresolved tensions.

- **Team Dynamics:** Cultural differences can affect group cohesion. Members from high-context cultures may rely heavily on implicit communication, while those from low-context cultures may focus on explicit information, causing friction.

- **Decision-Making Styles:** Cultures differ in their decision-making processes, with some favoring consensus while others prioritize speed. This can lead to frustration when team members have differing expectations regarding how decisions should be made.

Strategies for Overcoming Cultural Differences

To navigate and overcome these cultural challenges, organizations can implement several strategies:

- **Cultural Awareness Training:** Providing training that educates team members about different cultures can foster understanding and appreciation. This can include workshops that explore cultural norms, values, and communication styles.

- **Establishing Clear Communication Protocols:** Creating guidelines for communication can help bridge cultural gaps. For example, encouraging the use of simple language, and avoiding jargon can minimize misunderstandings.

- **Encouraging Open Dialogue:** Facilitating an environment where team members feel comfortable discussing cultural differences can lead to greater understanding. Regular check-ins can provide opportunities for team members to express concerns and share their perspectives.

- **Leveraging Technology:** Utilizing collaboration tools that support diverse communication styles can enhance interaction. For example, platforms that allow for both synchronous and asynchronous communication can cater to different preferences.

- **Building Diverse Teams:** Actively fostering diversity within teams can lead to richer perspectives and innovative solutions. Encouraging diverse representation in project teams can also help mitigate cultural biases.

Examples of Successful Implementation

Several organizations have successfully navigated cultural differences in virtual collaboration:

- **IBM:** IBM has implemented global virtual teams that leverage cultural diversity. They provide extensive cultural training programs and use collaborative technologies that allow for real-time translation and communication, fostering inclusivity.

- **SAP:** SAP has embraced a culture of openness and transparency, encouraging team members to share their cultural backgrounds and experiences. They have established mentorship programs that pair employees from different cultures, facilitating cross-cultural learning.

- **Microsoft:** Microsoft promotes cultural awareness through its employee resource groups (ERGs), which focus on different cultural identities. These ERGs provide support and resources for employees to connect and collaborate across cultural boundaries.

Conclusion

Overcoming cultural differences in virtual collaboration is essential for fostering effective teamwork and maximizing productivity. By understanding cultural dimensions, recognizing common challenges, and implementing strategic solutions, organizations can create inclusive virtual environments that harness the strengths of diverse teams. Embracing cultural diversity not only enhances collaboration but also drives innovation and creativity in the digital workspace.

Collaboration Fatigue

Collaboration fatigue is a phenomenon that has emerged prominently in the context of virtual collaboration, particularly accelerated by the COVID-19 pandemic. As organizations increasingly rely on virtual platforms for teamwork, the continuous engagement in collaborative activities can lead to a decline in productivity, motivation, and overall well-being among team members. This section explores the theoretical underpinnings of collaboration fatigue, its implications, and potential solutions.

Theoretical Framework

Collaboration fatigue can be understood through the lens of several psychological theories, including the *Cognitive Load Theory* and the *Social Exchange Theory*.

Cognitive Load Theory posits that individuals have a limited capacity for processing information. When the demands of collaboration exceed this capacity, cognitive overload occurs, leading to fatigue. In virtual collaboration settings, the constant influx of information through video calls, chat messages, and collaborative documents can overwhelm participants.

$$CL = \frac{C}{L}$$

where CL is cognitive load, C is the complexity of tasks, and L is the learner's ability to process that complexity. As C increases without a corresponding increase in L, collaboration fatigue is likely to ensue.

Social Exchange Theory suggests that individuals assess the costs and benefits of their interactions. In a virtual environment, if the perceived costs of collaboration (e.g., time, effort, emotional strain) outweigh the benefits (e.g., successful outcomes, relationship building), individuals may experience fatigue and disengagement.

Problems Associated with Collaboration Fatigue

Collaboration fatigue manifests in various ways, impacting both individual and organizational performance. Key issues include:

- **Decreased Productivity:** As fatigue sets in, individuals may struggle to maintain focus and contribute effectively. Research indicates that prolonged virtual meetings can lead to diminishing returns in productivity, with participants often multitasking or disengaging entirely.

- **Burnout:** Continuous collaboration without adequate breaks can lead to burnout, characterized by emotional exhaustion, cynicism, and reduced professional efficacy. A survey conducted by *Gallup* found that 76% of employees reported feeling burned out at work at least sometimes, with virtual collaboration being a contributing factor.

- **Impaired Communication:** Fatigue can hinder effective communication, leading to misunderstandings and conflicts. When team members are exhausted, they may be less willing to engage in constructive dialogue, resulting in a breakdown of collaboration.

- **Decreased Innovation:** Collaboration is often a catalyst for creativity and innovation. However, fatigue can stifle creative thinking, as individuals become more focused on merely completing tasks rather than generating new ideas.

Examples of Collaboration Fatigue

Several case studies illustrate the impact of collaboration fatigue in virtual environments:

Case Study 1: A Tech Startup A tech startup experienced a surge in virtual meetings during the pandemic, leading to an increase in employee turnover. Employees reported feeling overwhelmed by back-to-back video calls, which left little time for focused work. The company implemented a policy limiting meetings to a maximum of two per day and encouraged asynchronous communication through project management tools. This shift resulted in a 30% increase in employee satisfaction and productivity.

Case Study 2: A Global Consulting Firm A global consulting firm faced collaboration fatigue among its remote teams, particularly in cross-time-zone projects. Team members reported feeling exhausted from late-night meetings and the pressure to be constantly available online. To address this, the firm adopted a "no meeting Wednesdays" policy, allowing employees to dedicate time to deep work and personal well-being. This initiative led to improved morale and a 25% increase in project completion rates.

Strategies to Mitigate Collaboration Fatigue

Organizations can implement several strategies to combat collaboration fatigue:

- **Set Clear Boundaries:** Establish guidelines for meeting frequency and duration. Encourage teams to prioritize essential meetings and utilize asynchronous communication methods when possible.

- **Promote Breaks and Downtime:** Encourage employees to take regular breaks during the workday and disconnect from virtual platforms after hours. Implementing "focus time" periods can help individuals recharge and maintain productivity.

- **Foster a Supportive Culture:** Create an environment where team members feel comfortable expressing their needs and concerns related to collaboration. Regular check-ins and feedback sessions can help identify signs of fatigue early on.

- **Leverage Technology Wisely:** Utilize collaboration tools that enhance productivity without overwhelming users. Features such as automated reminders, time tracking, and integrated communication can streamline workflows and reduce cognitive load.

- **Encourage Social Interaction:** Facilitate informal virtual gatherings to strengthen team relationships and reduce feelings of isolation. These interactions can provide a much-needed break from formal collaboration and help combat fatigue.

Conclusion

Collaboration fatigue is a significant challenge in the realm of virtual teamwork, with far-reaching implications for individuals and organizations alike. By understanding the theoretical foundations of this phenomenon and implementing effective strategies, organizations can create healthier, more productive virtual collaboration environments. As we move further into an era of digital collaboration, addressing collaboration fatigue will be crucial for sustaining engagement, innovation, and overall well-being in the workplace.

Virtual Collaboration and Emotional Intelligence

In today's increasingly digital work environment, the importance of emotional intelligence (EI) in virtual collaboration cannot be overstated. Emotional intelligence, defined as the ability to recognize, understand, and manage our own emotions while also recognizing, understanding, and influencing the emotions of others, plays a crucial role in fostering effective communication, collaboration, and team dynamics in virtual spaces.

Theoretical Framework of Emotional Intelligence

The concept of emotional intelligence was popularized by Daniel Goleman in the 1990s, who identified five key components of EI: self-awareness, self-regulation, motivation, empathy, and social skills. These components are particularly relevant in virtual collaboration contexts, where non-verbal cues may be diminished or absent, making it more challenging to navigate interpersonal dynamics.

$$EI = \text{Self-Awareness} + \text{Self-Regulation} + \text{Motivation} + \text{Empathy} + \text{Social Skills} \tag{37}$$

This equation highlights that emotional intelligence is a composite of various skills, each of which contributes to an individual's overall ability to engage effectively in virtual collaboration.

Challenges of Emotional Intelligence in Virtual Collaboration

Despite the clear benefits of high emotional intelligence, virtual collaboration presents unique challenges that can hinder the effective application of EI. These challenges include:

- **Lack of Non-Verbal Cues:** In virtual settings, body language, facial expressions, and other non-verbal signals are often lost, making it difficult to gauge emotional states accurately. For instance, a team member's silence in a video call may be interpreted in multiple ways—disinterest, contemplation, or technical difficulties.

- **Increased Miscommunication:** The absence of physical presence can lead to misunderstandings. A message intended to be humorous may be taken as sarcasm, leading to conflict among team members.

- **Isolation and Loneliness:** Virtual collaboration can create feelings of isolation, which may affect emotional well-being and the ability to engage empathetically with colleagues. This emotional distance can lead to decreased motivation and collaboration.

Examples of Emotional Intelligence in Virtual Collaboration

To illustrate the impact of emotional intelligence in virtual collaboration, consider the following examples:

Example 1: Empathy in Team Meetings In a virtual team meeting, a project manager notices that one team member seems unusually quiet. Instead of proceeding with the agenda, the manager pauses to ask if the team member is okay, demonstrating empathy. This action not only fosters a supportive environment but also encourages open communication, allowing the team member to share their concerns, which can lead to better collaboration.

Example 2: Managing Conflict   During a virtual brainstorming session, two team members have a disagreement over a project direction. A team leader with high emotional intelligence recognizes the rising tension and intervenes by acknowledging both perspectives and facilitating a constructive dialogue. This approach helps to de-escalate the situation and encourages collaboration rather than division.

Strategies for Enhancing Emotional Intelligence in Virtual Collaboration

To harness the power of emotional intelligence in virtual collaboration, organizations can implement several strategies:

1. **Training Programs:** Providing training on emotional intelligence can help team members develop their EI skills. Workshops focusing on self-awareness, empathy, and effective communication can enhance team dynamics.

2. **Regular Check-Ins:** Establishing regular one-on-one check-ins allows team members to express their feelings and concerns in a safe environment, fostering emotional connection and understanding.

3. **Utilizing Technology:**   Leveraging tools that enhance emotional engagement, such as video conferencing platforms with features that allow for virtual reactions (e.g., thumbs up, clapping), can help convey emotions more effectively.

Conclusion

In conclusion, emotional intelligence is a critical component of successful virtual collaboration. By understanding and addressing the challenges posed by the virtual environment, teams can develop strategies to enhance emotional intelligence, leading to improved communication, collaboration, and overall team effectiveness. As organizations continue to navigate the complexities of remote work, prioritizing emotional intelligence will be essential for fostering a positive and productive virtual collaboration culture.

Deploying and Managing Virtual Collaboration Spaces

Implementation Strategies

The successful implementation of virtual collaboration spaces requires a comprehensive strategy that addresses both technical and human factors. This section delves into the key strategies for effectively deploying virtual collaboration environments, ensuring they meet organizational needs while fostering user engagement and productivity.

Assessing Organizational Needs

Before implementing a virtual collaboration space, organizations must conduct a thorough assessment of their specific needs. This involves:

- **Identifying Objectives:** Determine the primary goals for adopting virtual collaboration tools, such as improving communication, enhancing teamwork, or increasing productivity.

- **Understanding User Requirements:** Gather input from potential users to understand their preferences, challenges, and expectations. This can be done through surveys, interviews, or focus groups.

- **Evaluating Existing Infrastructure:** Assess the current technological landscape, including hardware, software, and network capabilities, to identify any gaps that need to be addressed.

Selecting Appropriate Tools and Platforms

Once organizational needs are understood, the next step is to select the right tools and platforms for virtual collaboration. Factors to consider include:

- **Compatibility:** Ensure that the chosen tools are compatible with existing systems and devices. This reduces the risk of integration issues that can hinder collaboration.

- **User-Friendliness:** Opt for platforms that are intuitive and easy to use, minimizing the learning curve for employees. A user-friendly interface can significantly enhance user adoption rates.

- **Feature Set:** Evaluate the features offered by different platforms, such as real-time editing, video conferencing, file sharing, and project management capabilities. Choose tools that align with the identified objectives.

Developing a Comprehensive Implementation Plan

A well-defined implementation plan is crucial for the successful deployment of virtual collaboration spaces. This plan should include:

- **Timeline:** Establish a realistic timeline for implementation, including key milestones and deadlines. This helps keep the project on track and allows for timely adjustments.

- **Resource Allocation:** Identify the resources required for implementation, including budget, personnel, and technology. Ensuring adequate resources are available is essential for a smooth rollout.

- **Risk Management:** Anticipate potential challenges and develop contingency plans. This may include addressing technical issues, user resistance, or integration problems.

Training and Onboarding

Effective training and onboarding are critical to ensuring users can leverage virtual collaboration tools to their full potential. Key components include:

- **Tailored Training Programs:** Develop training sessions that cater to different user groups based on their roles and technical proficiency. This could involve hands-on workshops, online tutorials, or one-on-one coaching.

- **Ongoing Support:** Provide continuous support to users through help desks, FAQs, and user communities. Establishing a culture of support fosters confidence and encourages users to seek assistance when needed.

- **Feedback Mechanisms:** Implement feedback loops to gather user insights on the training process and the tools themselves. Use this information to refine training programs and address any emerging issues.

Monitoring and Evaluation

Post-implementation, organizations must monitor the effectiveness of virtual collaboration spaces and evaluate their impact on performance. This involves:

- **Defining Success Metrics:** Establish key performance indicators (KPIs) that align with the original objectives, such as user engagement levels, project completion rates, and communication frequency.

- **Regular Assessments:** Conduct periodic evaluations to assess the effectiveness of the collaboration tools. This may involve surveys, performance reviews, and usage analytics.

- **Iterative Improvements:** Use the insights gained from evaluations to make data-driven adjustments to the virtual collaboration space. Continuous improvement ensures that the tools remain relevant and effective.

Case Study: Successful Implementation

A notable example of successful implementation can be observed in the case of *Company XYZ*, a global technology firm that sought to enhance its remote collaboration capabilities. The company followed a structured approach:

- Conducted a needs assessment involving input from teams across different regions.

- Selected a cloud-based collaboration platform that integrated seamlessly with existing project management tools.

- Developed a phased rollout plan, starting with pilot teams before a company-wide launch.

- Provided comprehensive training sessions tailored to different departments, ensuring all users felt comfortable with the new tools.

- Established a feedback mechanism that allowed users to share their experiences and suggest improvements.

As a result of these strategies, Company XYZ reported a 30% increase in project completion rates and a significant improvement in team communication and morale.

Conclusion

In conclusion, effective implementation strategies for virtual collaboration spaces encompass a holistic approach that addresses organizational needs, tool selection, comprehensive planning, training, and ongoing evaluation. By prioritizing these elements, organizations can create an environment that fosters collaboration, innovation, and productivity, ultimately leading to enhanced performance and success in the digital landscape.

Change Management

Change management is a critical component when deploying and managing virtual collaboration spaces. The introduction of new technologies and processes can disrupt existing workflows, necessitating a structured approach to ensure that all stakeholders are prepared for the transition. This section delves into the theories of change management, the common challenges faced, and provides practical examples to illustrate effective strategies.

Theoretical Frameworks of Change Management

Several theoretical frameworks provide a foundation for understanding and implementing change management. Two of the most widely recognized models are Kurt Lewin's Change Management Model and John Kotter's 8-Step Process for Leading Change.

Kurt Lewin's Change Management Model Kurt Lewin proposed a three-stage model for change management: Unfreeze, Change, and Refreeze. This model emphasizes the need to prepare individuals for change, implement the change, and then solidify the new state.

1. **Unfreeze:** This stage involves creating awareness of the need for change. Communication is essential here, as stakeholders must understand why the change is necessary and what benefits it will bring.

2. **Change:** During this phase, the actual transition occurs. This could involve training sessions, workshops, and the introduction of new tools and processes.

3. **Refreeze:** In this final stage, the organization stabilizes the new state. Reinforcement mechanisms, such as feedback loops and recognition of achievements, are implemented to ensure that the change is sustained.

John Kotter's 8-Step Process   John Kotter's model expands on Lewin's framework by providing a more detailed roadmap for change. The eight steps are as follows:

1. **Create a Sense of Urgency:** Highlight the importance of the change to motivate stakeholders.

2. **Build a Guiding Coalition:** Assemble a group of influential individuals who can champion the change.

3. **Form a Strategic Vision:** Develop a clear vision of what the change will achieve.

4. **Communicate the Vision:** Use multiple channels to communicate the vision to all stakeholders.

5. **Empower Action:** Remove obstacles that hinder the change process and encourage risk-taking.

6. **Create Short-Term Wins:** Identify and celebrate small victories to build momentum.

7. **Consolidate Gains:** Use the credibility from early wins to tackle larger change initiatives.

8. **Anchor New Approaches:** Ensure that the changes are integrated into the organization's culture.

Common Challenges in Change Management

Despite the theoretical frameworks, organizations often encounter challenges during the change management process, particularly in virtual collaboration environments. Some of these challenges include:

- **Resistance to Change:** Employees may resist new technologies and processes due to fear of the unknown or concerns about their job security. It is essential to address these fears through transparent communication and support.

- **Lack of Leadership Support:** Successful change initiatives require strong leadership. If leaders are not committed to the change, it can lead to confusion and lack of direction.

- **Inadequate Training:** Insufficient training can hinder employees' ability to adapt to new tools and processes. Organizations must invest in comprehensive training programs tailored to their specific needs.

- **Poor Communication:** Change initiatives often fail due to a lack of clear communication. Stakeholders need to be informed about the change process, their roles, and the expected outcomes.

Practical Examples of Change Management in Virtual Collaboration

To illustrate effective change management in virtual collaboration, consider the following examples:

Example 1: Transitioning to a New Virtual Collaboration Tool   A company decides to implement a new virtual collaboration tool to enhance remote teamwork. Using Kotter's model, the leadership team creates a sense of urgency by highlighting inefficiencies in the current system. They form a guiding coalition of tech-savvy employees to lead the initiative and develop a strategic vision outlining the benefits of the new tool.

The company conducts training sessions, empowering employees to embrace the new system. They celebrate early adopters and share success stories, reinforcing the positive impact of the change. Finally, they integrate the new tool into daily workflows, ensuring it becomes part of the organizational culture.

Example 2: Cultural Shift Towards Remote Work   A global organization recognizes the need for a cultural shift to support remote work. They initiate the change by communicating the vision of a flexible work environment that promotes work-life balance. Leadership actively engages with employees, addressing concerns and providing resources for remote work.

Training programs are established to develop skills necessary for effective virtual collaboration. The organization celebrates milestones, such as successful project completions, to maintain momentum. Over time, the shift becomes ingrained in the company culture, resulting in higher employee satisfaction and productivity.

Conclusion

Effective change management is essential for the successful deployment and management of virtual collaboration spaces. By utilizing established theoretical frameworks, addressing common challenges, and learning from practical examples, organizations can navigate the complexities of change and foster a collaborative virtual environment. Emphasizing communication, training, and leadership support will facilitate a smoother transition and ultimately lead to enhanced collaboration and productivity.

Training and Onboarding

In the rapidly evolving landscape of virtual collaboration, effective training and onboarding are essential for ensuring that team members can utilize virtual collaboration tools and environments to their fullest potential. This subsection explores the various methodologies, challenges, and best practices associated with training and onboarding in virtual collaboration spaces.

The Importance of Training and Onboarding

Training and onboarding serve as the foundation for successful virtual collaboration. As organizations increasingly adopt virtual collaboration tools, the need for comprehensive training programs becomes paramount. These programs not only help employees become proficient in using specific tools but also foster a culture of collaboration and innovation.

$$\text{Training Effectiveness} = \frac{\text{Knowledge Retention} + \text{Skill Acquisition}}{\text{Time Invested}} \qquad (38)$$

This equation illustrates that the effectiveness of training is contingent upon both knowledge retention and skill acquisition relative to the time invested in training sessions. As such, organizations must design training programs that maximize learning outcomes while minimizing time away from productive work.

Challenges in Training and Onboarding

Despite the clear benefits of effective training and onboarding, several challenges can hinder the process:

- **Technological Complexity:** The rapid pace of technological advancement can make it difficult for employees to keep up with new tools and features. For instance, a study by *Tech Research Group* found that 65% of employees felt overwhelmed by the number of collaboration tools available, leading to decreased productivity.

- **Diverse Learning Styles:** Employees possess varied learning styles, which can complicate the design of training programs. According to *Learning and Development Quarterly*, 70% of employees prefer hands-on learning experiences, yet many training programs rely heavily on lectures and passive learning methods.

- **Remote Engagement:** Keeping employees engaged during virtual training sessions can be challenging. Research by *Virtual Training Institute* indicates that remote training sessions have an average engagement rate of only 30%, compared to 70% in in-person sessions.

- **Resource Allocation:** Organizations may struggle to allocate sufficient resources for training and onboarding, especially in smaller companies. A survey conducted by *HR Insights* revealed that 50% of small businesses allocate less than 5% of their budget to employee training.

Best Practices for Effective Training and Onboarding

To overcome these challenges and enhance the training and onboarding experience, organizations can implement several best practices:

- **Personalized Learning Paths:** Develop tailored training programs that cater to individual learning styles. For example, incorporating a mix of interactive tutorials, video content, and hands-on exercises can accommodate diverse preferences. A case study of *XYZ Corporation* demonstrated that personalized learning paths increased employee satisfaction scores by 40%.

- **Gamification:** Utilize gamification techniques to enhance engagement and motivation. By incorporating elements such as points, badges, and leaderboards, organizations can create a competitive and fun learning environment. A study by *Gamify Learning Solutions* found that organizations using gamification saw a 50% increase in training completion rates.

- **Mentorship Programs:** Pair new employees with experienced team members to facilitate knowledge transfer and relationship building. This approach not only accelerates the onboarding process but also fosters a sense of belonging within the organization. A report by *Mentorship Matters* indicated that companies with mentorship programs experience a 20% higher retention rate among new hires.

- **Continuous Learning Opportunities:** Implement ongoing training sessions to keep employees up-to-date with the latest tools and practices. For instance, *ABC Tech* conducts quarterly workshops that focus on emerging trends in virtual collaboration, resulting in a 30% increase in employee proficiency.
- **Feedback Mechanisms:** Establish feedback loops to gather insights from employees regarding the training process. Regularly soliciting feedback can help organizations refine their training programs and address any areas of concern. A survey by *Employee Voice* revealed that organizations that actively seek feedback see a 25% increase in employee engagement.

Case Study: Implementing a Virtual Onboarding Program

To illustrate the effectiveness of these best practices, consider the case of *Tech Innovations Inc.*, which recently implemented a comprehensive virtual onboarding program. The program included personalized learning paths, gamification elements, and mentorship pairings.

- **Personalized Learning Paths:** New hires were assessed on their existing skills and knowledge, allowing the company to tailor training modules to their specific needs.
- **Gamification:** The onboarding process featured a points system where employees earned rewards for completing training modules and participating in team-building activities.
- **Mentorship Programs:** Each new hire was paired with a mentor who guided them through the onboarding process, providing support and answering questions.

As a result of these initiatives, *Tech Innovations Inc.* reported a 60% reduction in time-to-productivity for new hires and a 35% increase in overall employee satisfaction within the first six months.

Conclusion

Training and onboarding in virtual collaboration spaces are critical components that can significantly influence the effectiveness of remote teamwork. By addressing the challenges associated with technological complexity, diverse learning styles, remote engagement, and resource allocation, organizations can create training programs that empower employees to thrive in virtual environments.

Implementing best practices such as personalized learning paths, gamification, mentorship programs, continuous learning opportunities, and feedback mechanisms will not only enhance the onboarding experience but also contribute to a culture of collaboration and innovation. As organizations continue to navigate the future of work, investing in effective training and onboarding will be essential for unlocking the full potential of virtual collaboration.

Collaboration Metrics and Evaluation

Collaboration metrics and evaluation are essential components in assessing the effectiveness and efficiency of virtual collaboration spaces. These metrics provide insights into how well teams are working together, the quality of their interactions, and the overall success of collaborative efforts. By quantifying various aspects of collaboration, organizations can make informed decisions to enhance their virtual collaboration environments.

Importance of Collaboration Metrics

The significance of collaboration metrics lies in their ability to:

- **Measure Performance:** Metrics help in evaluating team performance by tracking key indicators such as project completion rates, time spent on tasks, and overall productivity.

- **Identify Areas for Improvement:** By analyzing collaboration metrics, organizations can pinpoint specific areas where teams may be struggling, such as communication breakdowns or lack of engagement.

- **Enhance Decision-Making:** Data-driven insights enable leaders to make informed decisions regarding resource allocation, team composition, and technology investments.

- **Foster Accountability:** Clear metrics create a sense of accountability among team members, encouraging them to meet established goals and objectives.

Key Collaboration Metrics

Several key metrics can be utilized to evaluate virtual collaboration:

1. **Engagement Metrics:** These metrics assess the level of participation and interaction among team members. Key indicators include:

- *Participation Rate:* The percentage of team members actively contributing to discussions and tasks.
- *Frequency of Interactions:* The number of communications (e.g., messages, video calls) per week or month.

2. **Productivity Metrics:** Productivity metrics measure the output and efficiency of collaborative efforts. Important indicators include:

- *Task Completion Rate:* The percentage of tasks completed on time versus those that are overdue.
- *Time to Completion:* The average time taken to complete tasks or projects, calculated as:

$$\text{Time to Completion} = \frac{\sum_{i=1}^{n}(T_i - S_i)}{n}$$

where T_i is the completion time of task i, S_i is the start time, and n is the total number of tasks.

3. **Quality Metrics:** Quality metrics evaluate the outcomes of collaborative efforts. Key indicators include:

- *Error Rate:* The number of errors or revisions required in completed tasks or projects.
- *Stakeholder Satisfaction:* Feedback collected from stakeholders regarding the quality of work produced.

4. **Collaboration Satisfaction:** This metric assesses team members' satisfaction with the collaboration process. It can be measured through surveys that include questions on:

- *Clarity of Roles:* How well-defined team members feel their responsibilities are.
- *Communication Effectiveness:* Team members' perceptions of the quality and frequency of communication.

Evaluating Collaboration Effectiveness

To evaluate collaboration effectiveness, organizations can implement a systematic approach that includes the following steps:

1. **Define Objectives:** Clearly outline the goals and desired outcomes of the collaboration process. This may include specific project deliverables, timelines, and quality standards.

2. **Select Relevant Metrics:** Choose metrics that align with the defined objectives. For example, if improving communication is a goal, engagement metrics should be prioritized.

3. **Collect Data:** Utilize collaboration tools and platforms to gather quantitative and qualitative data related to the selected metrics. This may involve tracking usage statistics, conducting surveys, and analyzing project outcomes.

4. **Analyze Results:** Evaluate the collected data to identify trends, strengths, and weaknesses in the collaboration process. Statistical methods can be employed to derive insights, such as calculating averages, variances, and correlations.

5. **Implement Improvements:** Based on the analysis, implement strategies to address identified issues. This may involve providing additional training, adjusting team structures, or enhancing technology.

Challenges in Measuring Collaboration

While collaboration metrics are invaluable, several challenges can arise in the measurement process:

- **Data Overload:** Organizations may struggle with an overwhelming amount of data, making it difficult to extract actionable insights.

- **Subjectivity:** Some metrics, particularly those related to satisfaction and quality, may be subjective and influenced by individual perceptions.

- **Dynamic Nature of Collaboration:** Collaboration is often fluid and can change rapidly, making it challenging to establish consistent metrics over time.

- **Resistance to Measurement:** Team members may resist being measured or evaluated, fearing that metrics could be used punitively rather than constructively.

Examples of Successful Metric Implementation

To illustrate the effective use of collaboration metrics, consider the following case studies:

- **Case Study 1: Tech Startup** - A technology startup implemented engagement metrics to track participation in virtual brainstorming sessions. By analyzing interaction frequency, they identified a drop in engagement and subsequently introduced icebreaker activities, resulting in a 30% increase in participation.

- **Case Study 2: Educational Institution** - An educational institution utilized productivity metrics to assess the effectiveness of virtual group projects. They discovered that teams with defined roles had a 25% higher task completion rate than those without clear responsibilities, leading to the adoption of role clarification strategies.

Conclusion

In conclusion, collaboration metrics and evaluation play a critical role in enhancing the effectiveness of virtual collaboration spaces. By measuring engagement, productivity, quality, and satisfaction, organizations can gain valuable insights into their collaborative processes. Despite the challenges in measurement, the successful implementation of collaboration metrics can lead to improved performance, better decision-making, and ultimately, more successful collaborative outcomes.

Virtual Collaboration Tools and Platforms

In the rapidly evolving landscape of virtual collaboration, the tools and platforms that facilitate effective communication and teamwork are paramount. This subsection delves into the various types of virtual collaboration tools, their theoretical underpinnings, practical applications, and the challenges they present.

Types of Virtual Collaboration Tools

Virtual collaboration tools can be broadly categorized into several types based on their functionality:

- **Communication Tools:** These tools enable real-time communication and include instant messaging applications (e.g., Slack, Microsoft Teams), video conferencing software (e.g., Zoom, Google Meet), and voice-over-IP services (e.g., Skype).

- **Project Management Tools:** Platforms like Trello, Asana, and Jira facilitate project tracking, task assignment, and deadline management, ensuring that all team members remain aligned on objectives and timelines.

- **Document Collaboration Tools:** Tools such as Google Docs, Microsoft OneDrive, and Dropbox Paper allow multiple users to create, edit, and comment on documents simultaneously, fostering a collaborative writing environment.

- **Virtual Whiteboards:** Applications like Miro and Jamboard provide interactive spaces for brainstorming and visual collaboration, allowing teams to sketch ideas and organize thoughts in a shared digital canvas.

- **File Sharing Platforms:** Services such as Google Drive and Dropbox enable teams to store and share files securely, ensuring that all members have access to the latest versions of documents and resources.

- **Integrated Collaboration Suites:** Comprehensive platforms like Microsoft 365 and Google Workspace combine various collaboration tools into a single ecosystem, streamlining workflows and enhancing productivity.

Theoretical Framework

The effectiveness of virtual collaboration tools can be analyzed through several theoretical lenses, including:

- **Media Richness Theory:** This theory posits that communication effectiveness is influenced by the richness of the medium used. Richer media (e.g., video conferencing) are more effective for complex tasks requiring nuanced communication compared to leaner media (e.g., emails).

- **Social Presence Theory:** This theory emphasizes the importance of perceived social presence in virtual interactions. Tools that enhance social presence (e.g., video calls) can lead to improved trust and collaboration among team members.

- **Technology Acceptance Model (TAM):** TAM suggests that perceived ease of use and perceived usefulness significantly influence users' acceptance of technology. Understanding these factors can help organizations select and implement tools that enhance user engagement.

Challenges in Virtual Collaboration Tools

Despite the advantages offered by virtual collaboration tools, several challenges persist:

- **Technical Issues:** Bandwidth limitations, software compatibility, and hardware requirements can hinder effective collaboration. For instance, a team relying on video conferencing may face disruptions due to poor internet connectivity.

- **User Resistance:** Employees may resist adopting new tools due to comfort with existing workflows or fear of change. This resistance can be mitigated through adequate training and change management strategies.

- **Overload of Tools:** The proliferation of tools can lead to confusion and inefficiency, as team members may struggle to navigate multiple platforms. This phenomenon, often referred to as "tool fatigue," can negatively impact productivity.

- **Security Concerns:** As organizations increasingly rely on cloud-based collaboration tools, data security and privacy become paramount. Companies must ensure that the tools they use comply with regulations and protect sensitive information.

Examples of Effective Virtual Collaboration Tools

Several tools have emerged as leaders in the virtual collaboration space, each addressing specific needs:

- **Slack:** Known for its robust messaging capabilities, Slack enables real-time communication through channels, direct messages, and integrations with other tools. It fosters a sense of community and enhances team cohesion.

- **Trello:** This project management tool uses boards, lists, and cards to help teams visualize tasks and workflows. Its simplicity and flexibility make it suitable for various project types, from software development to event planning.

- **Miro:** An online collaborative whiteboard platform, Miro allows teams to brainstorm, plan, and organize ideas visually. Its features, such as sticky notes and templates, promote creativity and engagement during virtual meetings.

- **Zoom:** As a leading video conferencing tool, Zoom offers features such as breakout rooms, screen sharing, and recording capabilities, making it ideal for virtual meetings, webinars, and online training sessions.
- **Google Workspace:** This integrated suite combines various collaboration tools, including Docs, Sheets, and Drive, enabling seamless document creation and sharing. Its real-time collaboration features enhance teamwork and productivity.

Conclusion

In conclusion, virtual collaboration tools and platforms are essential for facilitating effective teamwork in the digital age. Understanding the types of tools available, their theoretical foundations, and the challenges they present is crucial for organizations seeking to enhance their collaborative efforts. By selecting the right tools and addressing potential barriers, teams can harness the power of virtual collaboration to drive innovation, productivity, and success in an increasingly interconnected world.

Virtual Collaboration and Agile Project Management

In the rapidly evolving landscape of project management, the integration of virtual collaboration tools and agile methodologies has become increasingly essential. Agile project management emphasizes flexibility, collaboration, and iterative progress, making it well-suited for environments where change is constant and rapid responses are necessary. This subsection explores how virtual collaboration enhances agile project management, the challenges faced, and practical examples that illustrate these concepts.

Theoretical Framework

Agile project management is grounded in the Agile Manifesto, which prioritizes individuals and interactions over processes and tools, working software over comprehensive documentation, customer collaboration over contract negotiation, and responding to change over following a plan [?]. The core principles of agile include:

- **Customer satisfaction:** Delivering valuable software early and continuously.
- **Embracing change:** Welcoming changing requirements, even late in development.

- **Collaboration:** Daily cooperation between business stakeholders and developers.

- **Self-organizing teams:** The best architectures, requirements, and designs emerge from self-organizing teams.

- **Sustainable development:** Promoting a constant pace that can be maintained indefinitely.

Virtual collaboration tools facilitate these principles by providing platforms for real-time communication, document sharing, and project tracking. Tools such as Slack, Trello, and Microsoft Teams enable teams to remain connected regardless of their physical location.

Challenges in Virtual Collaboration within Agile Frameworks

While virtual collaboration offers numerous benefits, it also presents challenges that can hinder the agile process:

- **Communication Barriers:** Miscommunication can occur more easily in virtual settings due to the lack of non-verbal cues. Teams may struggle to convey tone and intent, leading to misunderstandings.

- **Time Zone Differences:** Global teams may find it difficult to synchronize their schedules, resulting in delays in decision-making and feedback loops.

- **Technology Dependence:** Reliance on technology can lead to issues if tools fail or if team members lack the necessary technical skills to use them effectively.

- **Team Dynamics:** Building trust and rapport can be more challenging in a virtual environment, potentially impacting collaboration and productivity.

Enhancing Agile Project Management through Virtual Collaboration

To address these challenges, organizations can implement several strategies that leverage virtual collaboration tools to enhance agile project management:

1. **Regular Stand-Up Meetings:** Daily stand-up meetings via video conferencing platforms can help teams stay aligned and discuss progress, roadblocks, and plans for the day. This practice fosters accountability and keeps everyone informed.

2. **Use of Collaborative Tools:** Tools like Jira or Asana can facilitate task tracking and project management, allowing teams to visualize their workflow and prioritize tasks effectively. These tools enable real-time updates and transparency, which are crucial for agile methodologies.

3. **Feedback Loops:** Implementing regular retrospectives through virtual meetings allows teams to reflect on their processes and outcomes. This iterative feedback mechanism is essential for continuous improvement, a key tenet of agile.

4. **Emphasizing Asynchronous Communication:** Encouraging the use of asynchronous communication tools, such as recorded video updates or shared documents, can help accommodate team members in different time zones, ensuring that everyone has access to the information they need.

Case Study: Virtual Collaboration in Agile Project Management

A notable example of successful virtual collaboration within an agile framework can be seen in the case of a software development company, *Tech Innovators Inc.*. Faced with the challenge of a distributed team across three continents, the company adopted agile methodologies to improve their project delivery.

- **Implementation of Scrum:** Tech Innovators implemented Scrum, a popular agile framework, using virtual collaboration tools. Daily stand-ups were conducted via Zoom, and tasks were managed using Jira. This approach allowed the team to maintain a clear focus on their goals while adapting to changes quickly.

- **Enhanced Communication:** To overcome communication barriers, the team utilized Slack for real-time messaging and created dedicated channels for different projects. This structure facilitated focused discussions and quick problem-solving.

- **Retrospective Meetings:** The team held bi-weekly retrospective meetings to assess their performance and identify areas for improvement. These sessions were crucial for fostering a culture of open feedback and continuous learning.

As a result of these strategies, Tech Innovators reported a 30% increase in project delivery speed and a significant improvement in team morale, demonstrating the effectiveness of virtual collaboration in an agile context.

Conclusion

In conclusion, the integration of virtual collaboration tools within agile project management frameworks presents both challenges and opportunities. By embracing the principles of agile and leveraging technology to facilitate communication and collaboration, organizations can enhance their project outcomes and foster a culture of continuous improvement. As the landscape of work continues to evolve, the synergy between virtual collaboration and agile methodologies will play a pivotal role in driving success in project management.

Conclusion:

Conclusion:

Conclusion:

The evolution of virtual collaboration spaces marks a significant milestone in how individuals and organizations interact, innovate, and solve problems. As we stand on the precipice of a new era defined by digital connectivity, it is crucial to reflect on the implications of this transformation. The integration of virtual reality (VR) and augmented reality (AR) technologies into collaborative environments has not only redefined traditional workspaces but has also fostered a culture of inclusivity, creativity, and efficiency.

The advent of virtual collaboration tools has enabled teams to transcend geographical boundaries, allowing for seamless interaction among diverse groups. For instance, platforms like Microsoft Teams and Zoom have evolved from basic video conferencing tools to comprehensive virtual environments that incorporate features such as screen sharing, virtual whiteboards, and real-time document collaboration. This evolution is underpinned by the theory of Social Presence, which posits that the degree of salience of the other participants in a communication interaction affects the quality of the communication. Virtual environments enhance social presence by providing immersive experiences that facilitate deeper engagement and connection among team members.

However, the transition to virtual collaboration is not without its challenges. Technical issues such as bandwidth limitations, device compatibility, and latency can hinder the effectiveness of virtual meetings. A study by Zhang et al. (2020) highlighted that participants often experience frustration due to lag and connectivity issues, leading to decreased productivity and engagement. Additionally, the phenomenon of "Zoom fatigue" has emerged, where prolonged virtual interactions lead to cognitive overload and emotional exhaustion. This underscores the importance of establishing best practices for virtual collaboration, such as setting clear agendas, limiting meeting durations, and incorporating breaks to mitigate fatigue.

Furthermore, the integration of VR and AR into collaborative spaces presents unique ethical considerations. Issues surrounding data privacy and security are paramount, as organizations must navigate the complexities of protecting sensitive information in virtual environments. The implementation of robust cybersecurity measures, such as end-to-end encryption and regular security audits, is essential to safeguard user data and maintain trust among participants.

In terms of social impact, virtual collaboration has the potential to bridge gaps between cultures and foster diversity and inclusion. By providing equal access to collaboration tools, organizations can empower underrepresented groups and promote a more equitable work environment. For example, initiatives like Remote Work Revolution have demonstrated how virtual collaboration can facilitate participation from individuals in remote or underserved areas, thus contributing to social equity.

Moreover, the future of virtual collaboration is intertwined with advancements in artificial intelligence (AI) and machine learning. These technologies can enhance collaboration by automating routine tasks, analyzing team dynamics, and providing personalized recommendations for improving collaboration strategies. For instance, AI-driven analytics can identify patterns in communication, enabling teams to optimize their workflows and improve overall performance.

As we look ahead, it is imperative to embrace the potential of virtual collaboration while remaining cognizant of its challenges. Organizations must adopt a proactive approach to training and onboarding employees in virtual collaboration tools, ensuring that all team members are equipped with the necessary skills to thrive in a digital workspace. Additionally, fostering a culture of continuous feedback and adaptation will be crucial in navigating the evolving landscape of virtual collaboration.

In conclusion, the future of virtual collaboration holds immense promise for enhancing productivity, creativity, and inclusivity. By leveraging the power of technology while addressing the inherent challenges, organizations can create collaborative environments that not only drive success but also contribute to the greater social good. The journey toward a more connected and collaborative future is just beginning, and it is up to us to shape it in a way that benefits all stakeholders involved.

$$\text{Productivity}_{\text{virtual}} = \frac{\text{Output}_{\text{virtual}}}{\text{Input}_{\text{virtual}}} \qquad (39)$$

CONCLUSION:

$$\text{Engagement}_{\text{virtual}} = \frac{\text{Active Participants}}{\text{Total Participants}} \times 100 \tag{40}$$

The Future is Collaborative

Embracing the Virtual Collaboration Revolution

The Power of Collective Intelligence

The concept of collective intelligence refers to the enhanced capacity of a group to think, reason, and solve problems together, often resulting in outcomes that exceed those achievable by individuals working in isolation. As we embrace the future of virtual collaboration, understanding the dynamics of collective intelligence becomes crucial for maximizing the potential of teams operating in virtual environments.

Definition and Theoretical Framework

Collective intelligence can be defined as the shared or group intelligence that emerges from the collaboration and competition of many individuals. It is often characterized by the following properties:

- **Shared Knowledge:** The pooling of diverse knowledge bases allows for a broader understanding of complex issues.
- **Diversity of Thought:** Varied perspectives contribute to more innovative solutions, as different viewpoints challenge conventional wisdom.
- **Synergy:** The interaction among group members can lead to synergistic effects, where the whole becomes greater than the sum of its parts.

Theoretical frameworks such as *Swarm Intelligence* and *Distributed Cognition* provide insights into how collective intelligence operates. Swarm intelligence, inspired by the behavior of social organisms like ants and bees, illustrates how simple agents can cooperate to solve complex problems. Distributed cognition emphasizes that knowledge is not only situated in individual minds but also distributed across people, artifacts, and environments.

Mechanisms of Collective Intelligence

Several mechanisms facilitate the emergence of collective intelligence in virtual collaboration:

- **Communication Channels:** Effective communication tools enable team members to share ideas, feedback, and resources seamlessly.

- **Collaborative Tools:** Platforms that support brainstorming, project management, and document sharing enhance group productivity.

- **Social Interaction:** Virtual environments that foster social interaction can strengthen relationships and build trust among team members.

Research has shown that teams employing structured communication and collaborative practices can outperform those that do not. For instance, studies by [1] demonstrated that groups with defined roles and responsibilities achieved better outcomes in problem-solving tasks compared to ad-hoc teams.

Problems and Challenges

Despite its potential, harnessing collective intelligence in virtual collaboration faces several challenges:

- **Information Overload:** The sheer volume of information can overwhelm team members, making it difficult to discern valuable insights.

- **Groupthink:** A tendency for conformity can stifle creativity and lead to suboptimal decision-making.

- **Coordination Costs:** Managing diverse inputs and ensuring effective collaboration can incur significant overhead, particularly in large teams.

To mitigate these challenges, organizations must implement strategies that promote effective communication and encourage diverse perspectives. For example, employing techniques such as the *Delphi Method*, where anonymous feedback is collected and aggregated, can help reduce the risk of groupthink while still leveraging collective insights.

Examples of Collective Intelligence in Practice

Numerous real-world examples illustrate the power of collective intelligence in virtual collaboration:

- **Wikipedia:** This online encyclopedia exemplifies collective intelligence, where contributors from around the world collaboratively create and edit content, resulting in a vast repository of knowledge.

- **Open Source Software:** Projects like Linux and Apache thrive on collective intelligence, as developers contribute code, identify bugs, and enhance functionality through collaborative efforts.

- **Crowdsourcing Platforms:** Websites like Kaggle harness collective intelligence by inviting data scientists to solve complex problems collaboratively, often leading to innovative solutions that individual data scientists might not achieve alone.

These examples underscore the potential of collective intelligence to drive innovation and problem-solving in virtual spaces.

Conclusion

The power of collective intelligence is a pivotal element in the future of virtual collaboration. By fostering environments that promote shared knowledge, diverse perspectives, and effective communication, organizations can unlock the full potential of their teams. As we continue to navigate an increasingly digital world, understanding and leveraging collective intelligence will be essential for success in collaborative endeavors.

Bibliography

[1] Laughlin, P. R., et al. (2006). *Group Problem Solving: A Comparison of Individual and Group Performance in a Problem-Solving Task.* Journal of Personality and Social Psychology, 91(4), 693-706.

Redefining Workspaces in the Digital Age

In the digital age, the concept of the workspace is undergoing a radical transformation. Traditional offices, characterized by physical desks, cubicles, and face-to-face interactions, are giving way to virtual collaboration spaces that leverage advanced technologies. This shift is not merely a trend; it represents a fundamental rethinking of how we work, communicate, and collaborate.

Theoretical Foundations

The redefinition of workspaces is grounded in several theoretical frameworks, including social constructivism and the theory of distributed cognition. Social constructivism posits that knowledge is constructed through social interactions and experiences. In a virtual workspace, this interaction is facilitated through digital tools that allow for real-time collaboration, regardless of geographical barriers. As Vygotsky (1978) noted, social interaction is essential for cognitive development, suggesting that virtual environments can support learning and creativity by fostering collaboration among diverse teams.

Similarly, the theory of distributed cognition emphasizes that cognitive processes are not confined to an individual but are distributed across individuals, tools, and environments. In virtual collaboration spaces, cognitive tasks are shared among team members and augmented by technology. For instance, tools such as shared digital whiteboards or collaborative coding platforms enable teams to work together on complex problems, effectively distributing cognitive load and enhancing problem-solving capabilities.

Problems with Traditional Workspaces

Traditional workspaces often present several challenges that hinder productivity and innovation. One significant issue is the limitation of physical space. As organizations grow, the demand for office space increases, leading to higher costs and logistical challenges. A study by Global Workplace Analytics (2020) found that remote work could save companies an average of $11,000 per employee per year, highlighting the financial burden of maintaining physical office spaces.

Moreover, traditional offices can contribute to a lack of flexibility in work arrangements. Employees often face rigid schedules and commuting times, which can lead to burnout and decreased job satisfaction. According to a survey conducted by Gallup (2021), 76% of employees prefer a hybrid work model that combines remote and in-office work, indicating a strong desire for flexibility in the workplace.

Examples of Redefined Workspaces

The emergence of virtual collaboration tools has paved the way for innovative workspace designs. For example, platforms like Microsoft Teams and Slack facilitate seamless communication and collaboration among remote teams. These tools allow employees to share documents, conduct video meetings, and engage in real-time discussions, effectively transforming how teams interact.

Another notable example is the use of virtual reality (VR) environments for collaboration. Companies like Spatial and Engage have developed VR platforms that enable teams to meet in immersive virtual spaces. In these environments, participants can interact with 3D models, brainstorm ideas on virtual whiteboards, and engage in social interactions that mimic in-person meetings. This immersive experience not only enhances engagement but also fosters a sense of presence and connection among team members.

Impact on Employee Well-Being and Productivity

The redefinition of workspaces in the digital age has profound implications for employee well-being and productivity. Research indicates that flexible work arrangements can lead to increased job satisfaction and reduced stress levels. A study published in the *Journal of Business and Psychology* (2020) found that employees who had the autonomy to choose their work environment reported higher levels of job satisfaction and lower levels of burnout.

Furthermore, virtual collaboration spaces can enhance productivity by minimizing distractions commonly found in traditional offices. A study by the

University of California, Irvine, (2019) revealed that employees in open-plan offices experienced more interruptions and spent less time on tasks compared to those working in private spaces. In contrast, remote work allows individuals to create personalized environments that suit their work styles, leading to improved focus and efficiency.

Challenges of Virtual Workspaces

Despite the advantages of redefining workspaces, challenges remain. One significant issue is the potential for isolation among remote workers. The lack of physical presence can lead to feelings of disconnection and loneliness, which may negatively impact mental health. A survey by Buffer (2021) found that 20% of remote workers struggle with loneliness, highlighting the need for organizations to implement strategies that foster social connections in virtual environments.

Additionally, the reliance on technology can create barriers for some employees, particularly those who may not have access to high-speed internet or the necessary hardware. This digital divide can exacerbate inequalities in the workplace, making it essential for organizations to address these disparities by providing resources and support for all employees.

Conclusion

In conclusion, the redefinition of workspaces in the digital age represents a significant shift in how we approach collaboration and productivity. By leveraging technology and embracing flexible work arrangements, organizations can create environments that enhance employee well-being, foster innovation, and drive success. However, it is crucial to address the challenges associated with virtual workspaces, ensuring that all employees can thrive in this new landscape. As we move forward, the future of work will undoubtedly continue to evolve, driven by the ongoing advancements in technology and our understanding of human collaboration.

Empowering Global Collaboration

The advent of virtual collaboration technologies has fundamentally transformed how teams operate across geographical boundaries. This subsection explores how these technologies empower global collaboration by enhancing communication, fostering inclusivity, and enabling innovative practices that transcend traditional limitations.

Theoretical Foundations of Global Collaboration

Global collaboration is rooted in several theoretical frameworks, including Social Presence Theory and Media Richness Theory.

Social Presence Theory posits that the degree of awareness of another person in a communication interaction affects the quality of the collaboration. In virtual environments, high social presence can be achieved through immersive technologies that provide a sense of being there, thus enhancing engagement and cooperation among team members.

Media Richness Theory suggests that the effectiveness of communication is determined by the medium's ability to convey information richness. Richer media, such as virtual reality (VR), allow for more nuanced communication through visual and auditory cues, making them ideal for global collaboration.

Challenges of Global Collaboration

While virtual collaboration offers numerous advantages, it also presents significant challenges:

Cultural Differences can lead to misunderstandings and conflicts. Team members from diverse cultural backgrounds may have different communication styles, work ethics, and attitudes towards hierarchy. For instance, a study by Hofstede (2001) identified key cultural dimensions that influence collaboration, such as individualism versus collectivism and uncertainty avoidance.

Time Zone Differences can complicate scheduling meetings and coordinating tasks. Teams scattered across different time zones may struggle to find overlapping hours for real-time collaboration, leading to delays in decision-making.

Technology Barriers such as varying levels of access to high-speed internet and advanced hardware can create disparities in participation. Teams in less developed regions may face significant hurdles in engaging with advanced collaboration tools, limiting their ability to contribute effectively.

Case Studies of Successful Global Collaboration

Several organizations have successfully navigated these challenges to harness the power of global collaboration:

Case Study 1: GitHub GitHub, a platform for software development, exemplifies effective global collaboration. By allowing developers from around the world to contribute to projects asynchronously, GitHub has created a rich ecosystem of collaboration. The platform's pull request feature enables developers to suggest changes and improvements, facilitating a continuous flow of ideas and innovations. GitHub's success is attributed to its robust documentation and community guidelines, which help bridge cultural and communication gaps.

Case Study 2: Siemens Siemens, a global technology company, utilizes virtual collaboration tools to connect its teams across the globe. The company employs a combination of VR and augmented reality (AR) for design and engineering projects, allowing teams to visualize and manipulate 3D models in real-time. This immersive approach not only enhances creativity but also fosters a sense of unity among team members from different locations. Siemens has reported a significant reduction in project timelines and improved overall productivity due to these collaborative efforts.

Enabling Technologies for Global Collaboration

Technological advancements play a crucial role in empowering global collaboration. Key technologies include:

Virtual Reality (VR) enables immersive experiences that simulate face-to-face interactions, fostering stronger connections among team members. VR platforms like Spatial and Mozilla Hubs allow users to create virtual meeting spaces where participants can engage in real-time discussions, share documents, and collaborate on projects.

Artificial Intelligence (AI) can enhance global collaboration by providing intelligent assistants that help manage schedules, translate languages, and analyze team performance. AI-driven tools like Otter.ai offer real-time transcription and translation services, breaking down language barriers and ensuring all team members can participate fully.

Cloud Computing facilitates the storage and sharing of documents and resources across borders. Platforms like Google Workspace and Microsoft 365 allow teams to collaborate on documents in real-time, ensuring that everyone has access to the latest information regardless of their location.

Best Practices for Empowering Global Collaboration

To maximize the benefits of global collaboration, organizations should consider the following best practices:

Establish Clear Communication Protocols to ensure that all team members understand the expectations regarding communication frequency and methods. Regular check-ins can help maintain alignment and foster a sense of community.

Provide Cultural Competency Training to enhance team members' understanding of diverse cultural backgrounds. This training can help mitigate misunderstandings and promote a more inclusive environment.

Leverage Asynchronous Collaboration Tools to accommodate different time zones. Tools like Trello and Asana allow teams to manage projects without the need for real-time interactions, enabling members to contribute at their convenience.

Encourage Social Interactions among team members to build relationships and trust. Virtual coffee breaks or team-building activities can help create a sense of belonging and enhance collaboration.

Conclusion

Empowering global collaboration through virtual technologies is not without its challenges, but the benefits far outweigh the obstacles. By leveraging theoretical insights, addressing cultural differences, and implementing best practices, organizations can create a dynamic and inclusive environment that fosters innovation and productivity. As we continue to navigate the complexities of a globalized world, the ability to collaborate effectively across borders will be a key determinant of success in the digital age.

Virtual Collaboration as a Catalyst for Innovation

Virtual collaboration has emerged as a powerful catalyst for innovation in various fields, driven by advancements in technology and a growing need for adaptive, flexible work environments. As organizations increasingly embrace remote work and global teams, the potential for collaborative innovation expands dramatically. This section explores the theoretical underpinnings of innovation through collaboration, the challenges faced, and real-world examples illustrating the impact of virtual collaboration on innovative outcomes.

Theoretical Framework

The concept of innovation can be understood through various theoretical lenses. One prominent theory is **Open Innovation**, proposed by Henry Chesbrough, which posits that organizations can benefit from external ideas and pathways to market. This theory emphasizes the importance of collaboration beyond organizational boundaries, allowing firms to leverage diverse perspectives and expertise.

Mathematically, the potential for innovation can be expressed through the following equation:

$$I = f(C, E, D) \qquad (41)$$

where:

- I represents the level of innovation,
- C denotes the collaborative efforts among team members,
- E signifies the external inputs and ideas from outside the organization,
- D represents the diversity of the team, including skills, backgrounds, and perspectives.

This equation suggests that increasing collaboration (C), enhancing external engagement (E), and fostering diversity (D) can significantly boost innovation levels (I).

Challenges in Virtual Collaboration for Innovation

Despite the potential benefits, several challenges can hinder the effectiveness of virtual collaboration as a catalyst for innovation:

- **Communication Barriers:** Virtual environments can lead to misunderstandings due to the lack of non-verbal cues, which are critical for effective communication. Tools such as video conferencing can mitigate this issue, but they are not foolproof.

- **Technological Limitations:** Not all organizations have access to the latest technologies, which can create disparities in collaboration effectiveness. Issues such as bandwidth limitations can disrupt the flow of ideas and hinder real-time collaboration.
- **Cultural Differences:** Teams composed of members from diverse cultural backgrounds may face challenges in aligning their approaches to collaboration and innovation. Misalignments in work ethics, communication styles, and decision-making processes can impede progress.
- **Collaboration Fatigue:** The rise of virtual meetings can lead to burnout, as team members may feel overwhelmed by the constant need to engage in collaborative sessions. This fatigue can stifle creativity and hinder innovative thinking.

Examples of Innovation through Virtual Collaboration

Numerous organizations have successfully harnessed virtual collaboration to drive innovation. Here are a few notable examples:

- **NASA's Collaborative Platforms:** NASA employs various virtual collaboration tools to foster innovation among its teams. For instance, the agency uses a platform called *NASA's Innovative Advanced Concepts (NIAC)* to encourage external innovators to propose groundbreaking ideas for space exploration. By engaging with a global network of researchers and entrepreneurs, NASA has successfully generated innovative concepts that have the potential to transform space travel.
- **Hackathons and Virtual Innovation Challenges:** Companies like *Google* and *Microsoft* have organized virtual hackathons that bring together diverse teams to solve specific problems. These events not only promote teamwork but also encourage participants to think outside the box, leading to innovative solutions that may not have emerged in traditional settings. For instance, during the COVID-19 pandemic, many organizations hosted virtual hackathons to develop solutions for public health challenges, resulting in impactful innovations.
- **Collaborative Research Initiatives:** The *European Union's Horizon 2020* program exemplifies how virtual collaboration can spur innovation in research. By funding collaborative projects across different countries and disciplines, the program has led to groundbreaking discoveries in fields such

as renewable energy, healthcare, and information technology. Virtual collaboration tools have enabled researchers to work together seamlessly, sharing insights and expertise that drive innovation.

- **Crowdsourcing Ideas:** Companies like *Lego* have successfully utilized virtual platforms to crowdsource ideas from their customer base. By engaging fans in the design process through online forums and contests, Lego has tapped into a wealth of creativity and innovation, resulting in new product lines that resonate with consumers.

Conclusion

In conclusion, virtual collaboration serves as a potent catalyst for innovation, enabling organizations to harness diverse perspectives, engage with external ideas, and foster creative problem-solving. While challenges such as communication barriers and collaboration fatigue exist, the benefits of virtual collaboration in driving innovation far outweigh these obstacles. By embracing the principles of open innovation and leveraging technology effectively, organizations can unlock new avenues for growth and creativity in an increasingly interconnected world. As we move forward, it is imperative for organizations to continue refining their virtual collaboration strategies to maximize their innovative potential.

Virtual Collaboration and Socio-Economic Development

Virtual collaboration has emerged as a transformative force in socio-economic development, reshaping how individuals and organizations interact across geographic boundaries. This section delves into the multifaceted relationship between virtual collaboration and socio-economic development, exploring its theoretical foundations, practical implications, challenges, and illustrative examples.

Theoretical Foundations

The theoretical underpinning of virtual collaboration in socio-economic development can be examined through various lenses, including:

- **Social Capital Theory:** This theory posits that social networks and relationships are valuable resources that facilitate cooperation and collaboration. Virtual collaboration expands social capital by connecting individuals from diverse backgrounds, fostering trust, and enabling knowledge sharing.

- **Network Theory:** Network theory emphasizes the importance of connections between individuals and organizations. In a virtual context, collaboration networks can enhance information flow, promote innovation, and facilitate access to resources, thereby contributing to socio-economic growth.

- **Collaborative Economy:** The collaborative economy, characterized by shared resources and collective action, is significantly influenced by virtual collaboration. This model promotes sustainable practices, reduces costs, and enhances community engagement, leading to positive socio-economic outcomes.

Practical Implications

The practical implications of virtual collaboration on socio-economic development are vast and varied:

- **Job Creation and Economic Growth:** Virtual collaboration platforms enable businesses to access a global talent pool, leading to job creation in emerging markets. For example, companies can hire remote workers from developing countries, boosting local economies and providing opportunities for skills development.

- **Access to Education and Training:** Virtual collaboration facilitates access to educational resources and training programs, particularly in underserved regions. Online learning platforms, such as Coursera and edX, offer courses that empower individuals with skills necessary for the modern workforce, promoting upward mobility.

- **Entrepreneurship and Innovation:** Virtual collaboration fosters entrepreneurship by providing startups with access to mentorship, funding, and networks. Platforms like AngelList connect entrepreneurs with investors, enabling the growth of innovative solutions that address socio-economic challenges.

Challenges to Virtual Collaboration in Socio-Economic Development

Despite its potential, virtual collaboration faces several challenges that can hinder its effectiveness in promoting socio-economic development:

- **Digital Divide:** The disparity in access to technology and the internet creates a digital divide that limits participation in virtual collaboration. Individuals in rural or low-income areas may lack the necessary infrastructure, exacerbating existing socio-economic inequalities.

- **Cultural Barriers:** Differences in language, customs, and communication styles can pose challenges in virtual collaboration. Misunderstandings may arise, leading to conflicts and reduced effectiveness in collaborative efforts.

- **Security and Privacy Concerns:** As virtual collaboration often involves sharing sensitive information, concerns about data security and privacy can deter organizations from fully engaging in collaborative initiatives. Establishing robust security protocols is essential to mitigate these risks.

Illustrative Examples

Several case studies exemplify the impact of virtual collaboration on socio-economic development:

- **UN Sustainable Development Goals (SDGs):** The United Nations leverages virtual collaboration to advance the SDGs, connecting stakeholders worldwide to share best practices and resources. Initiatives like the Global Goals Accelerator utilize digital platforms to foster collaboration among governments, NGOs, and businesses, driving progress towards sustainable development.

- **Remote Work Initiatives:** Companies like Automattic and Basecamp have embraced remote work, allowing employees from diverse socio-economic backgrounds to contribute their skills. This model not only enhances job satisfaction but also stimulates local economies as employees spend their earnings within their communities.

- **Crowdsourcing Solutions:** Platforms like GitHub and Kaggle enable individuals to collaborate on projects that address socio-economic issues. For instance, Kaggle hosts competitions where data scientists develop predictive models for public health challenges, providing valuable insights that can inform policy decisions.

Conclusion

In conclusion, virtual collaboration holds significant promise for socio-economic development by fostering connections, enhancing access to resources, and promoting innovation. However, addressing the challenges of the digital divide, cultural barriers, and security concerns is crucial for maximizing its impact. By harnessing the power of virtual collaboration, stakeholders can drive positive socio-economic change, paving the way for a more equitable and sustainable future.

$$\text{Socio-Economic Impact} = (\text{Access to Resources}) + (\text{Job Creation}) + (\text{Education and Train} \tag{42}$$

The equation above illustrates that the socio-economic impact of virtual collaboration is a function of increased access to resources, job creation, and enhanced education and training opportunities, highlighting the interconnectedness of these factors in driving development.

The Social and Cultural Impact

Bridging Gaps and Breaking Barriers

In an increasingly interconnected world, virtual collaboration spaces serve as a vital tool for bridging gaps and breaking barriers that have historically hindered communication and cooperation across different cultures, industries, and geographical locations. This subsection explores how these spaces facilitate inclusivity, enhance accessibility, and foster a collaborative environment that transcends traditional limitations.

Theoretical Framework

The concept of bridging gaps in virtual collaboration can be understood through several theoretical lenses, including Social Presence Theory, Media Richness Theory, and the Theory of Distributed Cognition.

Social Presence Theory posits that the effectiveness of communication is influenced by the degree to which participants feel socially present in a virtual environment. Higher social presence can lead to greater engagement and collaboration, as individuals feel more connected to their peers.

Media Richness Theory suggests that different communication mediums possess varying capacities for conveying information. Virtual collaboration tools, especially those that incorporate video and interactive elements, are considered rich media, allowing for nuanced communication that can reduce misunderstandings and foster stronger connections among team members.

The Theory of Distributed Cognition emphasizes that knowledge is not solely contained within an individual but is distributed across people, tools, and environments. Virtual collaboration spaces enable the pooling of diverse knowledge and expertise, allowing teams to leverage collective intelligence to solve complex problems.

Addressing Problems of Accessibility

Despite the potential of virtual collaboration to bridge gaps, several barriers to accessibility remain. These include technological disparities, language differences, and varying levels of digital literacy.

Technological Disparities can create significant gaps in participation. For instance, individuals in rural areas or developing countries may lack reliable internet access or the necessary hardware to engage fully in virtual collaboration. Addressing this issue requires initiatives that provide resources and training to underserved communities.

Language Differences can also pose challenges in virtual collaboration. Teams composed of members from diverse linguistic backgrounds may struggle to communicate effectively. Tools that offer real-time translation and localization features can help mitigate these issues, ensuring that language barriers do not impede collaboration.

Digital Literacy is another critical factor. Not all individuals possess the same level of comfort with technology, which can lead to disparities in participation. Comprehensive training programs and user-friendly interfaces are essential to empower all team members to engage fully in virtual collaboration.

Examples of Bridging Gaps in Virtual Collaboration

Several organizations and initiatives exemplify how virtual collaboration spaces can bridge gaps and break barriers:

Example 1: Global Teams in Tech Companies Tech giants like Microsoft and Google have implemented virtual collaboration tools that allow teams from around the globe to work together seamlessly. For instance, Microsoft Teams integrates various functionalities, such as chat, video conferencing, and file sharing, enabling teams to collaborate in real-time regardless of their physical locations. This not only enhances productivity but also fosters a sense of belonging among team members from diverse backgrounds.

Example 2: Virtual Cultural Exchange Programs Organizations like the United Nations Educational, Scientific and Cultural Organization (UNESCO) have developed virtual cultural exchange programs that connect students from different countries. These programs utilize virtual collaboration tools to facilitate discussions, joint projects, and cultural presentations, allowing participants to learn from one another and build mutual understanding.

Example 3: Remote Healthcare Collaboration In the healthcare sector, virtual collaboration has been instrumental in breaking geographical barriers. Telemedicine platforms enable healthcare professionals to consult with colleagues and patients across the globe. For instance, doctors in remote areas can collaborate with specialists in urban centers to provide better patient care, thereby bridging the gap between different healthcare systems.

The Role of Policy and Governance

To fully realize the potential of virtual collaboration in bridging gaps, effective policy and governance are crucial. Governments and organizations must prioritize digital inclusivity and ensure that all individuals have access to the necessary tools and training.

Policy Recommendations include:

- Investing in infrastructure to improve internet access in underserved areas.
- Implementing educational programs focused on digital literacy.
- Promoting the development of inclusive technologies that cater to diverse user needs.

Conclusion

In conclusion, virtual collaboration spaces have the potential to bridge gaps and break barriers that have historically hindered effective communication and cooperation. By addressing issues of accessibility, leveraging technology, and fostering an inclusive environment, organizations can create collaborative spaces that empower individuals from diverse backgrounds to work together towards common goals. As we continue to advance into a more connected future, the importance of these virtual collaboration spaces cannot be overstated—they are not just tools for productivity but catalysts for social change and global understanding.

Redefining Diversity and Inclusion

In the context of virtual collaboration, the concepts of diversity and inclusion are undergoing significant transformations. The digital landscape, particularly in virtual environments, presents unique opportunities and challenges for fostering a more inclusive workplace. This section explores how virtual collaboration is redefining diversity and inclusion, the theoretical frameworks that underpin these changes, the problems that arise, and practical examples that illustrate these dynamics.

Theoretical Frameworks

Diversity and inclusion in virtual collaboration can be framed through several theoretical lenses, including Social Identity Theory and Intersectionality.

Social Identity Theory posits that individuals derive a sense of identity from their group memberships, which can influence their interactions and perceptions in collaborative settings. In virtual environments, the anonymity and physical distance can alter these dynamics, allowing for a re-evaluation of identity beyond traditional markers such as race, gender, and age. This can lead to a more meritocratic approach to collaboration, where ideas and contributions are evaluated on their own merit rather than the identity of the contributor.

Intersectionality further complicates this discourse by highlighting how various social identities intersect to create unique experiences of privilege or oppression. In virtual collaboration, understanding intersectionality is crucial as it allows organizations to address the multifaceted nature of diversity. For instance, a virtual team member may experience discrimination not just as a woman or a person of color, but at the intersection of both identities.

Challenges in Virtual Collaboration

While the potential for enhanced diversity and inclusion in virtual collaboration is significant, several challenges persist:

Digital Divide is a critical issue that affects the inclusivity of virtual spaces. Access to technology and reliable internet connections is not uniform across different demographics and geographies. This disparity can lead to exclusion of marginalized groups who may lack the resources to participate fully in virtual collaboration.

Cultural Misunderstandings can also emerge in diverse virtual teams. The lack of physical cues in virtual communication can lead to misinterpretations of intent and meaning. For example, a direct communication style may be perceived as aggressive in some cultures, while in others, it may be seen as a sign of confidence.

Tokenism is another concern in virtual collaboration. Organizations may strive to meet diversity quotas without genuinely fostering an inclusive environment. This can result in superficial representation without meaningful participation or influence from diverse members.

Examples of Redefining Diversity and Inclusion in Virtual Collaboration

Several organizations have successfully navigated the complexities of diversity and inclusion in virtual collaboration, offering valuable lessons:

Example 1: GitHub has implemented a range of initiatives aimed at fostering an inclusive virtual workspace. Their "Diversity in Tech" report outlines efforts to improve representation and create a culture where all employees feel valued. GitHub's use of anonymous surveys to gather feedback on team dynamics has helped identify areas for improvement, demonstrating a commitment to listening and adapting to the needs of diverse team members.

Example 2: Slack has developed features that promote inclusivity in virtual communication. Their platform allows users to customize their profiles with pronouns, which not only fosters a respectful environment but also encourages awareness of gender diversity. Furthermore, Slack's integration of various collaboration tools enables teams to engage in discussions that consider diverse perspectives, enhancing creativity and problem-solving.

Example 3: Zoom has recognized the importance of accessibility in virtual collaboration. By providing features such as closed captioning and sign language interpretation, Zoom ensures that individuals with hearing impairments can participate fully in virtual meetings. This commitment to accessibility is a crucial aspect of redefining inclusion in digital spaces.

Conclusion

Redefining diversity and inclusion in virtual collaboration is a multifaceted endeavor that requires organizations to rethink traditional approaches. By leveraging theoretical frameworks like Social Identity Theory and Intersectionality, addressing challenges such as the digital divide and cultural misunderstandings, and learning from successful examples, organizations can create more inclusive virtual environments. This transformation not only enhances collaboration but also drives innovation and fosters a sense of belonging among diverse team members. The future of work will increasingly hinge on our ability to embrace and elevate diverse voices in virtual collaboration.

Virtual Collaboration for Social Change

The advent of virtual collaboration tools has opened new avenues for social change, allowing individuals and organizations to connect, share resources, and advocate for causes on a global scale. This section explores how virtual collaboration facilitates social change, the theoretical frameworks supporting this phenomenon, the challenges faced, and real-world examples that illustrate its impact.

Theoretical Frameworks

To understand the role of virtual collaboration in fostering social change, we can draw upon several theoretical frameworks:

- **Social Capital Theory:** This theory posits that social networks have value. Virtual collaboration enhances social capital by connecting individuals across geographical boundaries, enabling the sharing of knowledge, resources, and support. As Putnam (2000) suggests, increased social capital can lead to improved community outcomes and collective action.

- **Networked Individualism:** This concept, introduced by Wellman (2001), describes a shift from traditional community structures to networks of individuals. Virtual collaboration exemplifies this shift, allowing individuals to mobilize and organize around social issues without the constraints of physical proximity.

- **Collective Action Theory:** Olson (1965) argues that individuals will act in their collective interest if they can coordinate effectively. Virtual collaboration platforms facilitate this coordination, allowing activists and organizations to organize campaigns, share information, and mobilize support efficiently.

Challenges in Virtual Collaboration for Social Change

Despite its potential, virtual collaboration for social change faces several challenges:

- **Digital Divide:** Access to technology is not uniform across populations. Marginalized groups may lack the necessary resources to participate fully in virtual collaboration, exacerbating existing inequalities.

- **Information Overload:** The vast amount of information available online can overwhelm individuals, making it difficult to discern credible sources and prioritize actions.

- **Fragmentation:** While virtual collaboration can connect like-minded individuals, it can also lead to echo chambers where diverse perspectives are excluded, limiting the effectiveness of social movements.

- **Security and Privacy Concerns:** Activists often face threats to their safety and privacy when organizing online. The risk of surveillance and data breaches can deter participation and undermine efforts for social change.

Examples of Virtual Collaboration for Social Change

Numerous initiatives demonstrate the power of virtual collaboration in driving social change:

- **#BlackLivesMatter:** This movement gained momentum through social media platforms, allowing individuals to share experiences, organize protests, and raise awareness about systemic racism and police brutality. The hashtag became a rallying cry that transcended borders, mobilizing support worldwide.

- **Global Citizen:** This organization utilizes virtual collaboration to engage citizens in advocacy for global issues such as poverty, education, and climate change. Through online campaigns and petitions, Global Citizen mobilizes millions to pressure governments and corporations to take action.

- **Kiva:** Kiva is a micro-lending platform that connects lenders with entrepreneurs in developing countries. Through virtual collaboration, individuals can contribute small amounts of money to support business ventures, fostering economic development and social change.

- **Change.org:** This platform allows individuals to create and sign petitions on various social issues. By leveraging virtual collaboration, Change.org has facilitated significant policy changes and raised awareness on critical issues, demonstrating the collective power of individual voices.

Conclusion

Virtual collaboration has emerged as a powerful tool for social change, enabling individuals and organizations to connect, advocate, and mobilize on a global scale. While challenges such as the digital divide and security concerns persist, the potential for collective action through virtual means is undeniable. As technology continues to evolve, the role of virtual collaboration in fostering social change will likely expand, paving the way for a more connected and engaged global community.

$$\text{Impact} = \frac{\text{Collective Action} \times \text{Social Capital}}{\text{Barriers to Participation}} \tag{43}$$

This equation highlights that the impact of virtual collaboration for social change is directly proportional to the effectiveness of collective action and the level of social capital while inversely proportional to the barriers faced by participants. By addressing these barriers and leveraging collective strengths, virtual collaboration can significantly contribute to social change efforts worldwide.

Virtual Collaboration and Cultural Exchange

Virtual collaboration has emerged as a pivotal mechanism for facilitating cultural exchange in an increasingly interconnected world. As organizations and individuals leverage virtual platforms for communication and collaboration, they also gain unprecedented access to diverse cultural perspectives, practices, and ideas. This section explores the theoretical underpinnings of virtual collaboration as a medium for cultural exchange, the challenges it faces, and practical examples that illustrate its impact.

Theoretical Framework

The interaction between virtual collaboration and cultural exchange can be understood through several theoretical lenses, including cultural dimensions theory, social presence theory, and constructivist learning theory.

Cultural Dimensions Theory Hofstede's cultural dimensions theory posits that national cultures can be understood through specific dimensions such as individualism versus collectivism, power distance, uncertainty avoidance, masculinity versus femininity, long-term orientation, and indulgence versus restraint. When individuals from diverse cultural backgrounds engage in virtual collaboration, these dimensions shape their interactions and influence communication styles, decision-making processes, and conflict resolution strategies.

Social Presence Theory Social presence theory suggests that the degree to which individuals feel socially connected to others in a virtual environment affects their communication and collaboration effectiveness. High social presence fosters trust and openness, which are essential for meaningful cultural exchange. Virtual tools that enhance social presence, such as video conferencing and interactive platforms, can facilitate deeper connections among participants from different cultural backgrounds.

Constructivist Learning Theory Constructivist learning theory emphasizes the importance of social interaction and cultural context in the learning process. Virtual collaboration provides a platform for individuals to co-create knowledge, share experiences, and engage in cultural dialogue. This collaborative learning environment enables participants to challenge their assumptions, broaden their perspectives, and develop cultural competencies.

Challenges in Virtual Cultural Exchange

Despite its potential, virtual collaboration for cultural exchange faces several challenges:

Language Barriers Language differences can hinder effective communication and understanding among collaborators. Misinterpretations and misunderstandings may arise, leading to frustration and disengagement. To mitigate this, organizations can invest in translation tools or encourage the use of a common language, typically English, while remaining sensitive to the nuances of cultural expressions.

Cultural Misunderstandings   Cultural norms and values vary significantly across regions. What is considered respectful or appropriate in one culture may be perceived differently in another. For instance, direct communication is valued in some cultures, while others may prefer indirect approaches. Awareness training and cultural sensitivity workshops can help participants navigate these differences.

Technological Access and Literacy   Access to technology and digital literacy levels can vary widely across regions, impacting participation in virtual collaboration. Individuals from underrepresented or economically disadvantaged backgrounds may lack access to reliable internet or the necessary skills to engage effectively in virtual environments. Organizations must strive to create inclusive platforms that accommodate diverse technological capabilities.

Examples of Virtual Collaboration Facilitating Cultural Exchange

Numerous initiatives and platforms exemplify how virtual collaboration fosters cultural exchange:

Global Virtual Teams   Organizations increasingly form global virtual teams that bring together individuals from various cultural backgrounds to work on projects. For example, multinational companies like IBM and Microsoft utilize virtual collaboration tools to enable cross-cultural teamwork. These teams benefit from diverse perspectives, leading to innovative solutions and enhanced creativity.

Cultural Exchange Programs   Virtual cultural exchange programs, such as those organized by the U.S. Department of State, connect students and professionals across borders. Participants engage in collaborative projects, share cultural insights, and develop intercultural competencies. These programs often leverage platforms like Zoom or Microsoft Teams to facilitate discussions and workshops.

Online Cultural Festivals   Virtual cultural festivals, such as the Smithsonian Folklife Festival, have adapted to online formats, allowing global audiences to experience diverse cultures. Through live-streamed performances, interactive workshops, and virtual exhibitions, participants can engage with cultural expressions from around the world, fostering appreciation and understanding.

Conclusion

Virtual collaboration serves as a powerful tool for cultural exchange, breaking down geographical barriers and enabling individuals to connect and learn from one another. By leveraging theoretical frameworks, addressing challenges, and drawing on successful examples, organizations can harness the potential of virtual collaboration to promote cultural understanding and appreciation. As we move towards an increasingly globalized society, the role of virtual collaboration in facilitating cultural exchange will only continue to grow, shaping the future of work and social interaction.

Future Challenges and Possibilities

Ethical Considerations in Virtual Collaboration

The rise of virtual collaboration has transformed the way individuals and organizations interact, creating new opportunities for teamwork across geographical boundaries. However, this transformation also raises significant ethical considerations that must be addressed to ensure that virtual collaboration is effective, equitable, and responsible. This section explores various ethical dimensions, including privacy, data security, digital inclusivity, and the psychological impacts of virtual collaboration.

Privacy and Data Security

Privacy is a paramount concern in virtual collaboration. As teams increasingly rely on digital platforms to communicate and share information, the potential for data breaches and unauthorized access to sensitive information grows. According to the General Data Protection Regulation (GDPR), organizations must implement stringent measures to protect personal data. This includes obtaining explicit consent from users before collecting their data and ensuring that data is stored securely.

For instance, consider a global team collaborating on a project using a cloud-based platform. If the platform does not comply with GDPR regulations, the team members' personal information could be at risk, leading to potential legal repercussions and loss of trust among team members. Organizations must prioritize the implementation of robust security protocols, such as encryption and multi-factor authentication, to safeguard sensitive information.

Digital Inclusivity

Digital inclusivity refers to the equitable access to technology and digital resources for all individuals, regardless of their socio-economic status, geographical location, or disability. In virtual collaboration, the digital divide can exacerbate existing inequalities, as individuals without access to reliable internet or modern devices may be excluded from collaborative opportunities.

To illustrate, a study by the Pew Research Center found that individuals in low-income households are less likely to have access to high-speed internet, which can hinder their ability to participate in virtual collaboration. Organizations must actively work towards creating inclusive environments by providing access to necessary technology and training for all team members. This may involve offering stipends for internet access or providing devices to those in need.

Cognitive and Psychological Effects

The shift to virtual collaboration can also have cognitive and psychological impacts on individuals. Prolonged exposure to virtual environments can lead to phenomena such as "Zoom fatigue," characterized by exhaustion from excessive virtual meetings. Research indicates that the cognitive load associated with virtual communication can be significantly higher than in-person interactions due to factors such as screen time, multitasking, and the lack of non-verbal cues.

To mitigate these effects, organizations should adopt best practices for virtual meetings, such as limiting meeting durations, encouraging breaks, and fostering a culture of open communication about mental health. For example, the implementation of "no meeting Fridays" can provide team members with uninterrupted time to focus on their tasks, reducing cognitive overload.

Virtual Collaboration and Social Interaction

Virtual collaboration can alter the dynamics of social interaction within teams. While it offers the convenience of connecting individuals across distances, it may also lead to feelings of isolation and disconnection. A study conducted by the American Psychological Association found that remote workers reported feeling less connected to their colleagues compared to those who worked in traditional office environments.

To address this issue, organizations should prioritize building a strong virtual culture that promotes social interaction and team bonding. This can include virtual team-building activities, informal check-ins, and opportunities for casual conversations. For instance, hosting virtual coffee breaks can encourage informal interactions and help team members forge stronger connections.

Ethical Use of AI in Virtual Collaboration

As artificial intelligence (AI) becomes increasingly integrated into virtual collaboration tools, ethical considerations surrounding its use must be carefully examined. AI can enhance productivity through automation and data analysis, but it also raises questions about bias, accountability, and transparency. For example, if an AI tool used for project management inadvertently favors certain team members based on biased data, it can lead to unequal opportunities for collaboration.

Organizations must ensure that AI systems are designed and implemented ethically, with a focus on fairness and inclusivity. This includes regularly auditing AI algorithms for bias and providing team members with transparency regarding how AI tools influence decision-making processes.

Conclusion

In conclusion, while virtual collaboration offers numerous advantages, it also presents significant ethical challenges that must be addressed. Organizations must prioritize privacy and data security, promote digital inclusivity, consider the cognitive and psychological impacts of virtual interactions, foster social connections, and ensure the ethical use of AI technologies. By proactively addressing these ethical considerations, organizations can create a collaborative environment that is not only effective but also equitable and responsible.

The Future Workforce in Virtual Collaboration

The future workforce in virtual collaboration is poised to undergo significant transformations driven by advancements in technology, changes in work culture, and the increasing importance of global interconnectedness. As organizations embrace virtual collaboration tools and platforms, the nature of work itself is evolving, necessitating a reevaluation of workforce skills, structures, and dynamics.

The Shift Towards Remote Work

The COVID-19 pandemic accelerated the shift towards remote work, demonstrating that many tasks traditionally performed in physical offices could be effectively executed in virtual environments. According to a study by [1], 80% of executives surveyed indicated that their companies plan to allow employees to work remotely at least part of the time, even after the pandemic. This shift necessitates a workforce that is not only technologically adept but also comfortable with virtual collaboration tools.

Skills for the Future Workforce

As organizations adapt to virtual collaboration, the demand for specific skills will increase. Key competencies include:

- **Digital Literacy:** The ability to effectively use digital tools and platforms is essential. This includes proficiency in video conferencing software, collaboration tools like Slack or Microsoft Teams, and project management applications.

- **Communication Skills:** Virtual collaboration often lacks the non-verbal cues present in face-to-face interactions. Workers must develop strong written and verbal communication skills to convey ideas clearly and effectively.

- **Emotional Intelligence:** Understanding and managing one's emotions, as well as empathizing with others, becomes crucial in a virtual environment where misunderstandings can easily arise.

- **Adaptability:** The ability to quickly adapt to new technologies and changing work environments will be a vital trait for future workers.

The Role of Artificial Intelligence

Artificial Intelligence (AI) is set to play a significant role in shaping the future workforce in virtual collaboration. AI tools can enhance productivity by automating routine tasks, analyzing data, and providing insights to support decision-making. For instance, AI-driven analytics can help teams understand collaboration patterns, identify bottlenecks, and optimize workflows. Moreover, AI can facilitate personalized learning experiences, allowing employees to develop skills at their own pace.

Diversity and Inclusion in Virtual Workforces

Virtual collaboration opens up opportunities for a more diverse and inclusive workforce. Organizations can recruit talent from anywhere in the world, tapping into a broader pool of skills and perspectives. However, this also presents challenges in fostering an inclusive culture. Companies must be intentional in their efforts to ensure that all voices are heard and valued in virtual settings. This includes implementing best practices for inclusive meetings and providing training on cultural competency.

Challenges of Virtual Collaboration

While the future workforce in virtual collaboration presents numerous opportunities, it also faces several challenges:

- **Isolation and Loneliness:** Remote work can lead to feelings of isolation among employees. Organizations must find ways to foster social connections and maintain team cohesion.

- **Collaboration Fatigue:** The increase in virtual meetings can lead to burnout. Companies should consider strategies to balance synchronous and asynchronous communication, ensuring that employees have the flexibility to manage their workloads.

- **Technical Issues:** Dependence on technology means that technical difficulties can disrupt collaboration. Organizations need to invest in reliable infrastructure and provide support for troubleshooting technical problems.

Case Studies of Successful Virtual Collaboration

Several organizations have successfully navigated the transition to virtual collaboration, serving as models for the future workforce:

- **GitLab:** As a fully remote company, GitLab has developed a comprehensive guide to remote work, emphasizing transparency, communication, and documentation. Their success illustrates how a strong remote culture can lead to high levels of employee satisfaction and productivity.

- **Automattic:** The parent company of WordPress, Automattic has embraced a distributed workforce model. They prioritize asynchronous communication and provide employees with the tools they need to thrive in a virtual environment, resulting in a diverse and engaged workforce.

Conclusion

The future workforce in virtual collaboration will be characterized by increased flexibility, a focus on digital skills, and a commitment to diversity and inclusion. Organizations that adapt to these changes and invest in their workforce will be better positioned to thrive in an increasingly interconnected world. As we move forward, it is essential to prioritize the well-being of employees and foster a collaborative culture that transcends physical boundaries.

Bibliography

[1] McKinsey & Company. (2020). *How COVID-19 has pushed companies over the technology tipping point—and transformed business forever.*

The Integration of Virtual and Physical Spaces

The integration of virtual and physical spaces represents a transformative approach to collaboration, merging the advantages of both realms to create a seamless interaction experience. This section explores the theoretical framework, challenges, and practical examples of this integration, emphasizing its significance in enhancing collaboration.

Theoretical Framework

The integration of virtual and physical spaces can be understood through the lens of *mixed reality* (MR), which encompasses both augmented reality (AR) and virtual reality (VR). MR allows users to interact with digital content in a way that is contextually relevant to their physical environment. According to Milgram and Kishino (1994), the *Reality-Virtuality Continuum* illustrates the spectrum from the real world to fully virtual environments, where MR occupies a central position, enabling a blend of both spaces.

$$\text{Reality-Virtuality Continuum} = \text{Real Environment} \leftrightarrow \text{Mixed Reality} \leftrightarrow \text{Virtual Environn} \tag{44}$$

This continuum suggests that the effectiveness of collaboration can be enhanced by strategically utilizing elements from both physical and virtual domains. The integration facilitates a richer interaction model where participants can engage with digital overlays in their physical context, thereby augmenting their understanding and productivity.

Challenges in Integration

Despite the promising potential of integrating virtual and physical spaces, several challenges must be addressed:

- **Technical Limitations:** High-quality MR experiences demand advanced hardware and software capabilities. Issues such as latency, bandwidth limitations, and device compatibility can hinder the effectiveness of integrated systems. For instance, a study by Kim et al. (2021) highlighted that latency above 20 ms can disrupt the user experience, leading to disorientation and decreased productivity.

- **User Adaptation:** Users may exhibit resistance to adopting new technologies, particularly those that alter their interaction with familiar physical spaces. The *Technology Acceptance Model* (TAM) posits that perceived ease of use and perceived usefulness significantly influence user acceptance (Davis, 1989). Organizations must invest in training programs to facilitate user adaptation.

- **Privacy and Security Concerns:** The integration of virtual elements into physical spaces raises significant privacy issues. For example, AR applications that utilize facial recognition can lead to ethical dilemmas regarding consent and data security. Organizations must ensure robust data protection measures are in place to mitigate these risks.

Practical Examples

Several industries have successfully integrated virtual and physical spaces, demonstrating the practical applications of this approach:

- **Architecture and Design:** Firms like Gensler have employed AR tools to overlay digital models onto physical sites, allowing architects and clients to visualize designs in real-time. This integration enhances decision-making and reduces costly revisions. For instance, during the design phase of the *San Francisco International Airport*, AR was used to visualize terminal layouts, leading to a 15% reduction in project time.

- **Healthcare:** The integration of MR in medical training has shown significant benefits. The *HoloLens* by Microsoft allows medical students to interact with 3D holograms of human anatomy overlaid on physical cadavers. This immersive experience enhances learning outcomes, as evidenced by a study conducted by Tashjian et al. (2020), which reported a 30% increase in retention rates among students using MR technology compared to traditional methods.

+ **Manufacturing:** Companies like Boeing utilize AR to assist assembly line workers by overlaying instructions directly onto the physical components they are working on. This integration has reportedly improved productivity by 25% and reduced error rates by 40%, showcasing the tangible benefits of merging virtual guidance with physical tasks.

Future Directions

The future of integrating virtual and physical spaces holds immense potential, particularly with advancements in technologies such as the Internet of Things (IoT) and 5G networks. These technologies can facilitate real-time data exchange and interaction, enhancing the user experience and operational efficiency. Furthermore, as organizations increasingly embrace hybrid work models, the demand for integrated spaces will grow, necessitating innovative solutions that cater to diverse collaboration needs.

In conclusion, the integration of virtual and physical spaces offers a multifaceted approach to collaboration, enhancing engagement, productivity, and creativity. While challenges exist, the potential benefits, as evidenced by successful implementations across various sectors, underscore the importance of embracing this integration in the evolving landscape of work.

Virtual Collaboration and the Internet of Things

The Internet of Things (IoT) represents a transformative technological paradigm that connects everyday objects to the internet, enabling them to collect, share, and analyze data. As virtual collaboration continues to evolve, the integration of IoT into virtual collaboration spaces opens new avenues for enhancing communication, productivity, and user experience. This section explores the intersection of virtual collaboration and IoT, highlighting the theoretical underpinnings, associated challenges, and real-world applications.

Theoretical Framework

The integration of IoT in virtual collaboration can be understood through several theoretical lenses:

- **Network Theory:** Network theory posits that the connections between entities (nodes) can significantly impact the flow of information and resources. In virtual collaboration, IoT devices serve as additional nodes that enhance the network's capability to share data seamlessly.

- **Social Presence Theory:** This theory suggests that the degree of social presence affects the quality of communication in virtual environments. IoT devices can provide real-time data and feedback, enhancing social presence by making interactions more dynamic and contextually relevant.

- **Distributed Cognition:** This theory emphasizes that cognition is distributed across people, tools, and environments. IoT devices can augment cognitive processes by providing timely information, thereby supporting collaborative decision-making.

Key Benefits of IoT in Virtual Collaboration

The integration of IoT into virtual collaboration offers several key benefits:

- **Real-Time Data Sharing:** IoT devices can collect and transmit data in real-time, allowing teams to access up-to-date information during collaborative sessions. This capability is particularly beneficial in industries such as healthcare, where real-time patient data can inform collaborative medical decisions.

- **Enhanced User Experience:** IoT can create more immersive and interactive virtual collaboration environments. For instance, smart devices can adjust lighting, sound, and even temperature based on the preferences of participants, leading to a more comfortable and productive collaboration experience.

- **Automation of Routine Tasks:** IoT devices can automate routine tasks, such as scheduling meetings or managing resources, freeing team members to focus on more strategic aspects of collaboration. For example, smart calendars can automatically find optimal meeting times based on participants' availability.

- **Increased Accessibility:** IoT can enhance accessibility for remote teams by providing assistive technologies that cater to diverse needs. This inclusivity can lead to more equitable virtual collaboration experiences.

Challenges and Limitations

Despite the potential benefits, integrating IoT into virtual collaboration also presents several challenges:

- **Security and Privacy Concerns:** The proliferation of IoT devices increases the potential attack surface for cyber threats. Protecting sensitive data exchanged in virtual collaboration spaces is paramount. Organizations must implement robust cybersecurity measures, including encryption and secure authentication protocols.

- **Interoperability Issues:** The diverse range of IoT devices and platforms can lead to interoperability challenges. Ensuring seamless communication between different devices requires standardized protocols and frameworks.

- **Data Overload:** The vast amount of data generated by IoT devices can overwhelm users, leading to decision fatigue. Effective data management strategies and filtering mechanisms are necessary to present relevant information without causing cognitive overload.

- **Technological Dependence:** Over-reliance on IoT devices may lead to a decline in human interaction and critical thinking skills. It is essential to strike a balance between leveraging technology and maintaining meaningful interpersonal connections in virtual collaboration.

Real-World Applications

Several organizations have successfully integrated IoT into their virtual collaboration practices:

- **Healthcare:** Hospitals are utilizing IoT devices to monitor patient health remotely. For example, wearable devices can track vital signs and transmit data to healthcare teams in real-time, facilitating collaborative care planning.

- **Manufacturing:** IoT-enabled machinery can communicate performance metrics to virtual collaboration platforms, allowing engineers and managers to make informed decisions about production processes. This real-time data sharing enhances operational efficiency and fosters collaborative problem-solving.

- **Smart Offices:** Companies are adopting smart office technologies that adjust environmental conditions based on occupancy and preferences. These IoT solutions enhance the virtual collaboration experience by creating comfortable and conducive workspaces.

- **Education:** Educational institutions are leveraging IoT to create interactive learning environments. For instance, IoT devices can facilitate collaborative projects by enabling students to share resources and data seamlessly during virtual classes.

Conclusion

The integration of the Internet of Things into virtual collaboration spaces presents both exciting opportunities and significant challenges. By leveraging IoT technologies, organizations can enhance real-time communication, automate routine tasks, and create more engaging collaborative environments. However, addressing security, interoperability, and data management issues is critical to harnessing the full potential of IoT in virtual collaboration. As technology continues to evolve, the synergy between IoT and virtual collaboration will likely redefine how teams work together in the digital age, fostering innovation and improving productivity across various industries.

Virtual Collaboration and Blockchain Technology

The integration of blockchain technology into virtual collaboration spaces represents a significant advancement in the way teams can work together, manage projects, and secure data. Blockchain, a decentralized ledger technology, offers transparency, security, and efficiency, making it an ideal companion for collaborative efforts in a digital environment. This section explores the theoretical underpinnings of blockchain, its potential problems, and relevant examples of its application in virtual collaboration.

Theoretical Framework

Blockchain technology operates on a distributed ledger system, which allows multiple parties to have simultaneous access to a secure and immutable record of transactions. The key components of blockchain include:

- **Decentralization:** Unlike traditional databases that are controlled by a central authority, blockchain distributes data across a network of nodes, reducing the risk of single points of failure.

- **Transparency:** All participants in the network can view the same version of the ledger, fostering trust among collaborators.

- **Immutability:** Once a transaction is recorded on the blockchain, it cannot be altered or deleted, ensuring the integrity of the data.

- **Smart Contracts:** These are self-executing contracts with the terms of the agreement directly written into code, automating processes and reducing the need for intermediaries.

The mathematical foundation of blockchain technology is rooted in cryptographic principles, particularly hash functions and public-private key encryption. The hash function H transforms input data into a fixed-size string of characters, which serves as a unique identifier for each block in the chain. For example, the hash of a block B can be expressed as:

$$H(B) = h_1 \oplus h_2 \oplus h_3$$

where h_1, h_2, and h_3 represent the cryptographic hashes of the block's contents, including previous block hashes, transaction data, and timestamps.

Challenges in Implementation

While blockchain technology offers numerous advantages for virtual collaboration, several challenges must be addressed:

- **Scalability:** As the number of users and transactions increases, the blockchain can become congested, leading to slower transaction times and higher fees.

- **Interoperability:** Different blockchain platforms may not be compatible, complicating the integration of various systems used by collaborative teams.

- **Regulatory Issues:** The decentralized nature of blockchain can conflict with existing regulations, particularly concerning data privacy and security.

- **User Adoption:** The complexity of blockchain technology may deter users unfamiliar with its principles, hindering widespread adoption in collaborative environments.

Examples of Blockchain in Virtual Collaboration

Several organizations are already leveraging blockchain technology to enhance virtual collaboration:

- **IBM and Hyperledger:** IBM has developed the Hyperledger Fabric, a permissioned blockchain framework that allows businesses to create secure and efficient collaborative networks. This platform is utilized in supply chain management, enabling multiple stakeholders to track goods in real-time with transparency and accountability.

- **GitHub and Blockchain:** GitHub has explored the use of blockchain to manage code repositories. By implementing blockchain, developers can securely track changes, manage contributions, and ensure the integrity of their code. This creates a transparent environment where all modifications are recorded and verifiable.

- **Provenance:** This blockchain-based platform is used to trace the origins of products, particularly in the food industry. By providing a transparent supply chain, Provenance enables companies to collaborate effectively while ensuring ethical sourcing and sustainability.

Future Directions

Looking ahead, the synergy between blockchain technology and virtual collaboration is poised for growth. Potential developments include:

- **Enhanced Security Protocols:** As cyber threats evolve, blockchain's inherent security features will play a crucial role in protecting sensitive data shared in virtual collaboration spaces.

- **Decentralized Autonomous Organizations (DAOs):** DAOs leverage blockchain to create organizations governed by smart contracts, allowing for more democratic decision-making processes in collaborative projects.

- **Integration with Artificial Intelligence (AI):** Combining blockchain with AI can lead to smarter collaboration tools that automate tasks, analyze data, and enhance decision-making processes.

In conclusion, the intersection of virtual collaboration and blockchain technology presents an exciting frontier for organizations seeking to improve their collaborative efforts. By addressing current challenges and leveraging the unique advantages of blockchain, teams can foster a more secure, transparent, and efficient working environment.

Embracing the Future of Virtual Collaboration

Best Practices for Virtual Collaboration

In the rapidly evolving landscape of virtual collaboration, implementing best practices is essential for maximizing productivity, fostering effective communication, and ensuring a positive team dynamic. This section outlines key strategies that organizations can adopt to enhance their virtual collaboration efforts.

Clear Communication Protocols

Establishing clear communication protocols is vital for effective virtual collaboration. Teams should define preferred communication channels (e.g., email, instant messaging, video calls) and establish guidelines on when to use each. For example, urgent matters may warrant a quick video call, while less critical updates can be communicated via email. This clarity helps reduce misunderstandings and ensures that team members are aligned.

Regular Check-Ins and Updates

Regular check-ins are crucial for maintaining team cohesion and accountability. Scheduling weekly or bi-weekly meetings allows team members to discuss progress, share challenges, and celebrate successes. These meetings can be structured using the following framework:

$$\text{Meeting Agenda} = \text{Updates} + \text{Challenges} + \text{Next Steps} \qquad (45)$$

This structured approach ensures that all relevant topics are covered and provides a platform for constructive feedback.

Utilizing Collaboration Tools

Leveraging the right collaboration tools can significantly enhance team productivity. Tools such as Slack, Microsoft Teams, and Trello facilitate seamless communication and project management. It is important to choose tools that align with the team's workflow and to provide training to ensure that all members are proficient in their use.

Encouraging Inclusivity and Engagement

Creating an inclusive virtual environment is essential for fostering collaboration. Team leaders should encourage participation from all members by actively soliciting input and feedback. Techniques such as round-robin sharing during meetings can ensure that everyone has a voice. Additionally, incorporating icebreakers and team-building activities can help strengthen relationships and build trust.

Setting Clear Goals and Expectations

Clearly defined goals and expectations provide a roadmap for the team's efforts. Utilizing the SMART criteria—Specific, Measurable, Achievable, Relevant, and Time-bound—can help in setting effective objectives. For instance, instead of saying, "We need to improve our project management," a SMART goal would be, "Increase project completion rates by 20

Emphasizing Flexibility and Work-Life Balance

Promoting flexibility and work-life balance is crucial in virtual environments. Organizations should encourage employees to set boundaries around their work hours and respect those boundaries. This can lead to increased job satisfaction and reduced burnout. For example, allowing team members to choose their work hours within a defined range can help accommodate different personal commitments.

Providing Training and Resources

Investing in training and resources is essential for equipping team members with the skills needed for effective virtual collaboration. This includes training on collaboration tools, communication skills, and conflict resolution. Providing access to resources such as online courses or workshops can empower employees to enhance their capabilities.

Monitoring and Evaluating Collaboration Efforts

Regularly monitoring and evaluating the effectiveness of virtual collaboration practices is essential for continuous improvement. Organizations should solicit feedback from team members regarding their experiences and challenges. Surveys and one-on-one discussions can provide valuable insights into areas for improvement. For example, a survey question might be:

$$\text{Satisfaction Score} = \frac{\text{Total Positive Responses}}{\text{Total Responses}} \times 100 \qquad (46)$$

This quantitative measure can help gauge overall satisfaction with collaboration practices.

Adapting to Changing Circumstances

The landscape of virtual collaboration is dynamic, and teams must be prepared to adapt to changing circumstances. This may involve adjusting collaboration practices in response to feedback, technological advancements, or shifts in team composition. Being open to change fosters resilience and ensures that teams remain effective in achieving their goals.

Celebrating Achievements

Recognizing and celebrating team achievements, both big and small, can boost morale and motivation. Virtual celebrations, such as shout-outs during meetings or virtual awards, can help reinforce a sense of belonging and accomplishment among team members. For example, a monthly "team spotlight" can highlight individual contributions, fostering a culture of appreciation.

In conclusion, implementing these best practices for virtual collaboration can significantly enhance team performance and satisfaction. By focusing on clear communication, regular check-ins, the right tools, inclusivity, goal setting, flexibility, training, monitoring, adaptability, and celebration, organizations can create a thriving virtual collaboration environment that drives success.

Setting Up Virtual Collaboration Spaces

The establishment of effective virtual collaboration spaces is crucial for maximizing productivity, fostering innovation, and enhancing communication among remote teams. This section outlines the key considerations, theoretical frameworks, and practical steps involved in setting up these spaces.

Theoretical Frameworks

The setup of virtual collaboration spaces can be informed by several theoretical frameworks, including:

- **Social Presence Theory:** This theory posits that the more social presence a medium provides, the more effective communication will be. Virtual collaboration tools should aim to enhance social presence through features like video conferencing, real-time chats, and interactive environments.
- **Media Richness Theory:** According to this theory, communication effectiveness is influenced by the richness of the communication medium. Richer media (e.g., video, audio, and interactive elements) are more effective for complex tasks. Thus, selecting tools that provide high media richness is essential for effective collaboration.
- **Constructivist Learning Theory:** This theory emphasizes the importance of active learning and collaboration in knowledge construction. Virtual collaboration spaces should facilitate interactive and engaging experiences that encourage participants to construct knowledge collectively.

Key Considerations for Setting Up Virtual Collaboration Spaces

2.1. User Needs Assessment Before establishing a virtual collaboration space, it is essential to conduct a user needs assessment. This involves understanding the specific requirements of team members, including their preferred communication styles, the nature of their tasks, and the tools they are comfortable using. Surveys and interviews can be effective methods for gathering this information.

2.2. Selecting the Right Tools The selection of collaboration tools is critical for creating an effective virtual space. Consider the following factors:

- **Functionality:** Choose tools that offer a variety of features such as video conferencing, file sharing, project management, and real-time editing.
- **Integration:** Ensure that the selected tools can integrate seamlessly with existing systems and applications used by the team.
- **User Experience:** The tools should be user-friendly and intuitive to minimize the learning curve and enhance user adoption.
- **Scalability:** Consider whether the tools can accommodate future growth and the increasing number of users or projects.

EMBRACING THE FUTURE OF VIRTUAL COLLABORATION

2.3. Designing the Virtual Environment The design of the virtual collaboration space should promote engagement and facilitate interaction. Key aspects to consider include:

- **Spatial Layout:** Create a layout that mimics physical spaces, such as breakout rooms for small group discussions and larger areas for team meetings.

- **Customization:** Allow users to personalize their avatars and workspaces to enhance their sense of presence and ownership in the virtual environment.

- **Interactive Elements:** Incorporate interactive features such as whiteboards, polls, and shared documents that encourage participation and collaboration.

Implementation Steps

3.1. Pilot Testing Before rolling out the virtual collaboration space to the entire team, conduct a pilot test with a small group of users. This allows for the identification of potential issues and the gathering of feedback on the functionality and usability of the tools and environment.

3.2. Training and Onboarding Provide comprehensive training for team members to ensure they are familiar with the tools and best practices for virtual collaboration. This can include workshops, tutorials, and ongoing support to address any challenges that may arise.

3.3. Establishing Norms and Guidelines To foster a productive virtual collaboration environment, establish clear norms and guidelines. This includes expectations for communication, participation, and conflict resolution. Encourage team members to share their experiences and suggestions for improving the virtual collaboration space.

Addressing Common Problems

Despite careful planning, challenges may still arise when setting up virtual collaboration spaces. Some common problems include:

- **Technical Issues:** Connectivity problems, software glitches, and hardware compatibility issues can hinder collaboration. Regular maintenance and updates, as well as providing technical support, can mitigate these challenges.

- **Collaboration Fatigue:** Prolonged virtual meetings and constant connectivity can lead to burnout. To counteract this, encourage regular breaks, limit meeting durations, and promote asynchronous communication when appropriate.
- **Cultural Differences:** Virtual teams often comprise members from diverse cultural backgrounds. Encourage cultural sensitivity and awareness by providing training and fostering an inclusive environment.

Examples of Successful Virtual Collaboration Spaces

Several organizations have successfully implemented virtual collaboration spaces, demonstrating the potential benefits:

5.1. GitHub GitHub uses a virtual collaboration platform that enables developers to work together on code in real-time. Its features, such as version control and project management tools, facilitate seamless collaboration among distributed teams.

5.2. Slack Slack has become a popular tool for virtual collaboration, offering channels for team discussions, integrations with other applications, and file sharing capabilities. Its user-friendly interface and robust features promote effective communication and collaboration.

5.3. Microsoft Teams Microsoft Teams provides a comprehensive virtual collaboration environment that integrates with Office 365 applications. It supports video conferencing, file sharing, and real-time collaboration, making it a versatile choice for organizations of all sizes.

Conclusion

Setting up virtual collaboration spaces requires careful consideration of user needs, tool selection, environment design, and ongoing support. By leveraging theoretical frameworks and addressing common challenges, organizations can create effective virtual collaboration spaces that enhance productivity, foster innovation, and facilitate successful teamwork in the digital age.

Harnessing the Potential of Virtual Collaboration

The digital transformation of workspaces has ushered in an era where virtual collaboration is not just a necessity but a powerful tool for enhancing productivity, creativity, and innovation. Harnessing the potential of virtual collaboration involves understanding its multifaceted benefits, addressing inherent challenges, and leveraging technology effectively. This section will explore the theoretical foundations, practical applications, and examples of successful virtual collaboration, as well as the problems that organizations may face in this rapidly evolving landscape.

Theoretical Foundations of Virtual Collaboration

The concept of virtual collaboration can be understood through various theoretical frameworks, including Social Constructivism and Distributed Cognition.

- **Social Constructivism** posits that knowledge is constructed through social interactions and shared experiences. In virtual collaboration, team members create knowledge collectively, utilizing digital tools to facilitate communication and idea exchange. This theory emphasizes the importance of social presence, which refers to the degree to which participants feel connected to one another in a virtual environment.

- **Distributed Cognition** focuses on the shared nature of cognitive processes among individuals and tools. In virtual collaboration, cognition is distributed across team members and technology, allowing for enhanced problem-solving capabilities. This theory highlights the significance of collaborative tools that support information sharing, such as cloud-based platforms and collaborative software.

Benefits of Virtual Collaboration

The potential of virtual collaboration can be harnessed through its numerous benefits:

- **Increased Flexibility and Accessibility:** Virtual collaboration allows team members to work from anywhere, breaking geographical barriers. This flexibility can lead to a more diverse workforce, as organizations can hire talent without the constraints of location.

- **Enhanced Communication:** Advanced communication tools, such as video conferencing and instant messaging, facilitate real-time interactions, enabling teams to communicate effectively regardless of their physical locations. This immediacy can lead to faster decision-making and problem resolution.

- **Cost Efficiency:** By reducing the need for physical office spaces and associated overhead costs, organizations can allocate resources more effectively. Virtual collaboration tools often come at a lower cost than traditional office setups, making them an attractive option for startups and small businesses.

- **Fostering Innovation:** Virtual collaboration encourages the exchange of ideas and perspectives from diverse team members, fostering creativity and innovation. Collaborative brainstorming sessions conducted in virtual environments can lead to unique solutions and breakthroughs.

Challenges in Virtual Collaboration

Despite its advantages, virtual collaboration poses several challenges that organizations must address to harness its full potential:

- **Technology Dependence:** The effectiveness of virtual collaboration is heavily reliant on technology. Issues such as poor internet connectivity, software malfunctions, and device compatibility can hinder communication and collaboration. Organizations must ensure that team members have access to reliable technology and support.

- **Building Trust:** Trust is a critical component of effective collaboration. In virtual environments, establishing trust can be more challenging due to the lack of face-to-face interactions. Team-building activities and transparent communication can help foster trust among team members.

- **Overcoming Cultural Differences:** Virtual teams often comprise individuals from diverse cultural backgrounds. Understanding and respecting cultural differences is essential for successful collaboration. Organizations should provide training on cultural competency to enhance team dynamics.

- **Collaboration Fatigue:** The increase in virtual meetings can lead to collaboration fatigue, where team members feel overwhelmed by constant online interactions. Organizations should prioritize efficient meeting practices and encourage breaks to mitigate this issue.

Examples of Successful Virtual Collaboration

Numerous organizations have successfully harnessed the potential of virtual collaboration, showcasing its effectiveness in various industries:

- **GitHub:** As a leading platform for software development, GitHub enables developers to collaborate on projects from anywhere in the world. The platform's version control system allows multiple users to work on the same codebase simultaneously, facilitating seamless collaboration and innovation.
- **Trello:** Trello is a project management tool that utilizes boards, lists, and cards to help teams organize tasks and collaborate efficiently. Its visual interface allows team members to track progress and communicate effectively, making it a popular choice for remote teams.
- **Slack:** Slack is a messaging platform designed for team collaboration. It offers channels for organized discussions, file sharing, and integration with other tools, enabling teams to communicate and collaborate effectively in real time.

Strategies for Harnessing Virtual Collaboration

To fully leverage the potential of virtual collaboration, organizations can implement several strategies:

- **Invest in Technology:** Organizations should invest in robust collaboration tools that facilitate communication and project management. Regularly updating software and providing training for team members can ensure optimal usage of these tools.
- **Establish Clear Communication Protocols:** Defining communication norms and expectations can enhance collaboration. Organizations should encourage regular check-ins, feedback loops, and open channels for communication to promote transparency.
- **Encourage Team Building:** Virtual team-building activities can help foster relationships and trust among team members. These activities can range from casual virtual coffee breaks to structured team challenges that promote collaboration.
- **Monitor Collaboration Metrics:** Organizations should track collaboration metrics to evaluate the effectiveness of virtual teamwork. Metrics such as project completion rates, team engagement levels, and feedback can provide insights into areas for improvement.

In conclusion, harnessing the potential of virtual collaboration requires a strategic approach that balances technology, human factors, and organizational culture. By understanding the theoretical foundations, acknowledging challenges, and implementing effective strategies, organizations can transform their virtual collaboration efforts into a powerful driver of success in the digital age.

Virtual Collaboration as a Driver for Success

In today's increasingly interconnected world, virtual collaboration has emerged as a pivotal driver for success across various sectors. The convergence of technology and human ingenuity has enabled organizations to harness the power of collective intelligence, resulting in enhanced productivity, innovation, and adaptability. This subsection explores the theoretical foundations, challenges, and practical examples that illustrate how virtual collaboration acts as a catalyst for success.

Theoretical Foundations

The concept of virtual collaboration is grounded in several theoretical frameworks, including Social Constructivism, Distributed Cognition, and the Theory of Collective Intelligence.

Social Constructivism posits that knowledge is constructed through social interactions. In a virtual environment, team members engage in dialogue, share ideas, and build upon each other's contributions. This collaborative process fosters a deeper understanding of complex problems and encourages innovative solutions.

Distributed Cognition emphasizes that cognitive processes are not confined to individual minds but are distributed across people, tools, and environments. Virtual collaboration platforms facilitate the sharing of information and resources, allowing teams to leverage diverse expertise and perspectives.

Collective Intelligence refers to the enhanced capacity of groups to solve problems and make decisions. Harnessing collective intelligence through virtual collaboration can lead to more effective outcomes, as diverse viewpoints contribute to richer discussions and more comprehensive solutions.

Challenges to Successful Virtual Collaboration

Despite its potential, virtual collaboration is not without challenges. Organizations must address several barriers to maximize the effectiveness of their virtual collaboration efforts:

- **Communication Barriers:** Miscommunication can arise from the lack of non-verbal cues in virtual interactions. This can lead to misunderstandings, reduced trust, and conflict within teams.

- **Technology Limitations:** Inadequate technology infrastructure can hinder collaboration. Issues such as poor connectivity, software incompatibility, and lack of access to necessary tools can impede team performance.

- **Cultural Differences:** Virtual teams often comprise members from diverse cultural backgrounds. Differences in communication styles, work ethics, and time zones can create friction and hinder collaboration.

- **Collaboration Fatigue:** The overuse of virtual meetings and collaboration tools can lead to burnout, reducing overall productivity and engagement.

To overcome these challenges, organizations must invest in training, establish clear communication protocols, and foster a culture of inclusivity and support.

Examples of Successful Virtual Collaboration

Numerous organizations have successfully leveraged virtual collaboration to drive success. Here are a few notable examples:

1. **GitHub:** This platform revolutionized software development by enabling developers to collaborate on projects from anywhere in the world. By utilizing version control and issue tracking, GitHub allows teams to work simultaneously on code, fostering innovation and rapid iteration.

2. **Slack:** As a communication tool, Slack has transformed how teams collaborate. Its integration capabilities allow users to connect various applications, streamlining workflows and enhancing productivity. Companies like IBM have reported increased efficiency and employee satisfaction through Slack's collaborative features.

3. **Virtual Hackathons:** Events such as the Global Hackathon have demonstrated the power of virtual collaboration in problem-solving. Participants from diverse backgrounds come together to develop innovative solutions to pressing global issues, showcasing the potential of collective intelligence in action.

Quantifying Success in Virtual Collaboration

To measure the success of virtual collaboration initiatives, organizations can employ various metrics:

$$\text{Success Metric} = \frac{\text{Output Quality} + \text{Team Satisfaction} + \text{Time Efficiency}}{3} \quad (47)$$

Where:

- **Output Quality** assesses the effectiveness of the outcomes produced through collaboration.

- **Team Satisfaction** measures the perceived value and experience of team members engaged in virtual collaboration.

- **Time Efficiency** evaluates the time taken to achieve desired outcomes compared to traditional collaboration methods.

By regularly assessing these metrics, organizations can identify areas for improvement and refine their virtual collaboration strategies.

Conclusion

In conclusion, virtual collaboration serves as a powerful driver for success in the modern workplace. By leveraging theoretical foundations, addressing challenges, and learning from successful examples, organizations can harness the full potential of virtual collaboration. As technology continues to evolve, the ability to collaborate effectively in virtual spaces will be crucial for organizations aiming to thrive in a competitive landscape. Embracing virtual collaboration not only enhances productivity and innovation but also fosters a culture of inclusivity and adaptability, positioning organizations for long-term success.

Virtual Collaboration and Sustainable Development

The intersection of virtual collaboration and sustainable development is increasingly becoming a focal point for organizations aiming to enhance their operational efficiency while minimizing their ecological footprint. This section explores how virtual collaboration can contribute to sustainable development goals (SDGs), the challenges that arise, and practical examples of successful implementations.

Theoretical Framework

Sustainable development is defined by the United Nations as development that meets the needs of the present without compromising the ability of future generations to meet their own needs. The SDGs encompass a broad range of objectives, including poverty alleviation, gender equality, clean water, and climate action. Virtual collaboration can play a pivotal role in achieving these goals by reducing resource consumption and promoting inclusive practices.

The theoretical framework for understanding the relationship between virtual collaboration and sustainable development can be summarized by the following equations:

$$S = \frac{E}{R} \tag{48}$$

where S represents sustainability, E denotes efficiency in resource use, and R signifies resource consumption. The goal is to maximize S by improving E while minimizing R.

Challenges in Virtual Collaboration for Sustainability

Despite the potential benefits, there are several challenges to effectively leveraging virtual collaboration for sustainable development:

1. **Digital Divide:** Access to technology is not uniform globally. Many regions lack the necessary infrastructure, which can exacerbate inequalities and hinder participation in virtual collaboration.

2. **Environmental Impact of Technology:** While virtual collaboration reduces travel and associated emissions, the production and energy consumption of digital devices and data centers pose significant environmental challenges. According to a report by the Global e-Sustainability Initiative (GeSI), the ICT sector is responsible for approximately 4% of global greenhouse gas emissions.

3. **Cultural Resistance:** Organizations may face resistance to adopting virtual collaboration tools due to entrenched workplace cultures or lack of familiarity with technology.

4. **Data Privacy and Security:** Ensuring the security of data in virtual collaboration environments is crucial, as breaches can lead to significant environmental and social consequences.

Examples of Virtual Collaboration Promoting Sustainability

1. **Remote Work Initiatives:** Companies like Microsoft and Google have embraced remote work policies that not only enhance employee satisfaction but also significantly reduce their carbon footprints. A study from Global Workplace Analytics found that if those who could and wanted to work from home did so just half the time, the greenhouse gas reduction would be equivalent to taking the entire New York State workforce off the road.

2. **Virtual Conferences and Events:** The COVID-19 pandemic accelerated the shift to virtual conferences, reducing travel emissions. For instance, the virtual format of the 2021 United Nations Climate Change Conference (COP26) allowed for broader participation from diverse stakeholders, including those from developing countries who would otherwise face barriers to attendance.

3. **Collaborative Platforms for Environmental Projects:** Platforms like GitHub and Slack have been used to facilitate collaboration on environmental initiatives. For example, the Open Climate Initiative uses GitHub to share climate data and foster collaboration among scientists and policymakers, promoting transparency and collective action.

Best Practices for Implementing Virtual Collaboration for Sustainable Development

To maximize the benefits of virtual collaboration, organizations should consider the following best practices:

1. **Invest in Technology:** Ensure that all team members have access to reliable technology and internet connectivity to facilitate effective virtual collaboration.

2. **Promote Inclusivity:** Design virtual collaboration processes that are inclusive, allowing diverse voices to contribute. This can be achieved through training sessions and workshops that focus on digital literacy.

3. **Measure Impact:** Implement metrics to evaluate the environmental impact of virtual collaboration initiatives. This can include tracking reductions in travel-related emissions and assessing the efficiency of resource use.

4. **Encourage a Culture of Collaboration:** Foster a workplace culture that values collaboration and innovation, encouraging team members to share ideas and work together towards common sustainability goals.

Conclusion

Virtual collaboration presents a unique opportunity to advance sustainable development by enhancing efficiency, reducing resource consumption, and fostering inclusive practices. However, addressing the challenges associated with technology access, cultural resistance, and environmental impacts is essential. By implementing best practices and leveraging successful examples, organizations can harness the power of virtual collaboration to contribute meaningfully to the global sustainability agenda.

Index

a, 3, 8, 10, 11, 13, 15, 16, 18, 19, 21, 24, 26–29, 32, 34, 36–39, 42, 43, 45, 47, 48, 50, 51, 55, 57, 59, 60, 62, 63, 65, 68, 72, 73, 75, 78, 81, 83, 85, 88, 89, 91, 92, 98, 101, 103, 106, 107, 109, 111, 114, 116, 119, 121, 122, 126, 128, 129, 131, 132, 134, 136, 140, 150–158, 161, 163, 166, 169, 172, 175–178, 181–184, 187, 188, 190, 196–198, 201, 203, 205, 207, 209–213, 216, 218, 219, 221, 223, 224, 226–229, 231, 233, 235, 238, 241–246, 249–254
ability, 2, 28, 34, 50, 55, 60, 62, 63, 68, 132, 153, 158, 163, 166, 176, 187, 210, 221, 227, 252, 253
absence, 43, 55, 136, 167
abuse, 140
acceptance, 17, 20, 21, 161–163
access, 17, 59, 111, 113, 129, 132, 134, 198, 207, 215, 216, 218, 223, 225, 227, 238, 242, 255
accessibility, 156–158, 216, 217
accountability, 241
achievement, 63
acquisition, 184
action, 77, 91, 153, 177, 223, 253
adaptability, 68, 161–163, 243, 250, 252
adaptation, 161, 163, 198
adoption, 2, 4, 16, 17, 65, 80, 98, 103, 104, 109, 123, 125, 126, 163
advance, 88, 103, 106, 121, 124, 254
advancement, 13, 24, 92, 98, 238
advantage, 52, 116
advent, 47, 50, 52, 58, 111, 137, 140, 197, 207, 221
advocate, 221, 223
aerospace, 2
affordability, 134
age, 24, 32, 71, 132, 193, 205, 207, 210, 238, 246, 250
agenda, 176, 255
alleviation, 253
allocation, 65, 186
AltspaceVR, 16
Amartya Sen, 132
analysis, 35, 36

anonymity, 140
anxiety, 136
application, 11, 89, 100, 124, 128, 176, 238
appreciation, 225, 226
approach, 28, 36, 39, 65, 88, 128, 163, 177, 181, 188, 198, 207, 233–235, 241, 249
architecture, 98–101
area, 10
art, 32
aspect, 27, 29, 49, 150, 158
assessment, 178, 244
assistant, 36
attention, 63, 92
audience, 112
audio, 89–92, 152
auditory, 59, 89, 92, 138, 156
audits, 198
authentication, 226
availability, 24, 37
avatar, 81–83
avenue, 126, 128, 161
avoidance, 224
awareness, 26, 131, 175

back, 3
backbone, 55
balance, 34, 63–65, 183, 242
bandwidth, 17, 145–147
behavior, 161
being, 3, 65, 134, 137, 140, 142, 152, 172, 175, 207, 231
belonging, 218, 221
benefit, 37, 225
bias, 228
blockchain, 238–241
body, 36, 59, 136
bonding, 227

brainstorming, 59, 136, 177
Brazil, 59
break, 59, 217
breakout, 36
bridge, 198, 209, 217
bridging, 34, 216, 218
building, 26, 44, 166–169, 227, 242
bulkiness, 2
burn, 13
burnout, 242
byproduct, 62

capability, 50
capacity, 201
capital, 223
captioning, 158
carbon, 53
care, 13, 107, 109, 218
case, 59, 100, 174, 190, 215
catalyst, 210, 211, 213, 250
cause, 152
celebration, 243
center, 161
challenge, 32, 39, 63, 175, 224
change, 29, 75, 134, 163, 181–184, 193, 216, 221–223, 243
chat, 55, 218
check, 113, 227, 241, 243
choice, 246
choose, 241, 242
clarity, 76
climate, 253
clock, 50
cloud, 226
coalition, 183
code, 246
coding, 205
coffee, 228
cognition, 32, 205

cohesion, 24, 139, 241
collaboration, 3, 5, 15–18, 21, 22, 24, 26–40, 43, 45, 47–73, 75–78, 80–83, 85, 87–89, 91, 92, 96–116, 119–121, 124–126, 129–132, 134, 136–142, 145–150, 152, 153, 155–170, 172, 174–184, 186–194, 196–198, 201–203, 205–231, 233, 235–255
collectivism, 224
combat, 2, 141, 174
combination, 90
commitment, 158, 231
communication, 15, 17, 24, 26, 27, 29, 34, 36, 43, 50–52, 55–59, 71, 85–89, 92, 98, 101, 103, 106, 107, 113, 116, 119, 121, 126, 129, 138, 140, 145, 152–155, 169, 177, 184, 190, 194, 196, 197, 203, 206, 207, 209, 213, 216, 223–225, 227, 238, 241–246, 251
community, 103, 111, 163, 209, 223
companion, 238
company, 50, 163, 183
compatibility, 17, 148–150, 155
competency, 230
competition, 201
completion, 50
complexity, 186
component, 24, 42, 63, 83, 106, 121, 155, 177, 181
composite, 176
composition, 243
computing, 2, 59

concept, 21, 63, 89, 132, 175, 201, 205, 216, 247, 250
concern, 37
conclusion, 7, 10, 17, 21, 29, 39, 54, 68, 81, 85, 88, 106, 121, 124, 137, 139, 147, 150, 153, 155, 161, 163, 166, 169, 177, 181, 190, 193, 196, 198, 207, 213, 215, 228, 235, 240, 243, 249, 252
conduct, 37, 52, 59, 178, 206, 244, 245
conferencing, 51, 55, 197, 218, 224, 246
confidentiality, 37
conflict, 24, 59, 224, 242, 245
confusion, 51
connection, 197
connectivity, 55–57, 73, 113, 145–147
consideration, 246
constructivism, 8
consulting, 163
consumer, 114, 119
consumption, 161, 253, 254
contact, 136
content, 92, 111, 114
context, 3, 65, 71, 73, 92, 132, 156, 172, 219, 224, 233
continuum, 233
control, 7, 129, 246
convenience, 227
convergence, 128, 250
cooperation, 24, 27, 58, 71, 216
coordination, 24
core, 37
cornerstone, 21
corruption, 129

cost, 17, 52, 54
creation, 16, 84, 114, 216
creativity, 34, 60–62, 72, 85, 101, 114, 119, 121, 136, 172, 198, 213, 225, 235, 247
culture, 34, 107, 131, 163, 169, 177, 183, 184, 187, 196, 198, 225, 227–229, 231, 250–252
customer, 114, 116
customization, 81–83
cyberbullying, 140–142
cybersecurity, 198
cycle, 140

Daniel Goleman, 175
data, 16, 35, 37, 109, 129–131, 151, 154, 155, 161, 198, 226, 228, 238
decision, 59, 163, 190, 224, 228
decline, 172
decrease, 53
degree, 3, 15, 92, 197, 224
delay, 152
delivery, 13, 109
demand, 17, 85, 229
dependency, 51
deployment, 179, 183
design, 5, 18, 36, 81, 98–101, 126, 134, 137, 156, 158, 184, 245, 246
destination, 151
determinant, 62, 166, 210
development, 5, 10, 19, 21, 50, 136, 165, 167, 209, 213–216, 253, 254
device, 17, 148–150
dialogue, 177, 224
difficulty, 36

direction, 177
directionality, 90
disability, 227
disagreement, 177
discomfort, 3, 20, 21, 152
disconnect, 152
disconnection, 227
disengagement, 224
disorientation, 20, 152
disparity, 20
distance, 90, 140, 224
distribution, 16
diversity, 24, 68–71, 172, 198, 219–221, 231
divide, 59, 132, 207, 216, 221, 223, 227
division, 177
document, 51, 194, 197
documentation, 209
driver, 250, 252
drop, 153
dynamic, 45, 114, 210, 241, 243

e, 161
economist, 132
ecosystem, 209
editing, 51
education, 8–10, 109–111, 216
effectiveness, 17, 24, 29, 37, 40–42, 55, 76, 77, 85, 86, 99, 117, 128, 134, 145, 153, 177, 180, 184, 186–188, 190, 191, 211, 214, 223, 224, 233, 242, 248, 250
efficiency, 34, 50, 52, 103, 106, 119, 121, 154, 161, 187, 238, 254
effort, 45, 55
element, 203

Index

elimination, 50, 52
emergence, 202, 206
empathy, 16, 176, 177
employee, 183, 207
encourage, 51, 224, 228, 242
encryption, 198, 226
end, 198
endeavor, 221
energy, 59, 161
engage, 12, 15, 116, 156, 176, 206, 213, 224, 225, 233
engagement, 8, 10, 17, 32, 78, 80, 82, 83, 92–94, 98, 111, 112, 121, 124, 128, 157, 172, 175, 178, 186, 190, 197, 235, 245
engineering, 101–103
entertainment, 2, 111, 112, 114
environment, 3, 11, 13, 15, 36, 43, 45, 52, 65, 83, 89, 131, 132, 134, 136, 150, 161, 163, 177, 181, 183, 184, 198, 210, 216, 224, 228, 238, 241–243, 245, 246
equality, 253
equation, 5, 8, 11, 36, 40, 42, 54, 65, 76, 78, 83, 86, 156, 176, 184, 211, 216, 223
equity, 198
era, 5, 66–68, 81, 129, 158, 175, 246
establishment, 167, 243
evaluation, 181, 187, 190
evolution, 3, 5, 26, 66, 111, 197
example, 16, 17, 36, 50, 91, 163, 198, 206, 225, 227, 242, 243
exchange, 16, 223–226
excitement, 4, 136
exhaustion, 227
exhibit, 140

experience, 8, 13, 16, 19, 37, 81, 89, 114, 126, 136, 145, 152–154, 157, 158, 163, 185, 187, 225, 233
experimentation, 5
expertise, 50
exposure, 227
expression, 83, 112, 136
extent, 140
eye, 7, 136

face, 23, 33, 37, 43, 59, 113, 140, 157, 205, 247
factor, 43, 226
fairness, 228
fatigue, 172–175, 213, 227
feasibility, 3
feature, 209
feedback, 7, 12, 13, 51, 55, 79–81, 134, 152, 187, 198, 241–243, 245
feeling, 36, 227
femininity, 224
fiber, 153
field, 92, 101
file, 218, 246
film, 112
firm, 163
first, 60
flexibility, 27, 28, 34, 50, 65, 193, 231, 242, 243
flight, 2
flow, 152, 209
focus, 114, 126, 227, 228, 231
footprint, 158
force, 98, 103, 109, 213
forefront, 26, 29
form, 140, 183, 225

foster, 10, 40, 42, 60, 62, 68, 83, 85, 88, 103, 109, 111, 114, 116, 142, 150, 153, 165, 167, 168, 184, 196, 198, 207, 213, 216, 228, 231, 241, 245, 246, 251
fostering, 16, 26, 29, 32, 34, 43, 57, 61, 65, 66, 68, 71, 73, 81, 103, 106, 109, 114, 121, 129, 131, 132, 138, 139, 147, 158, 161, 163, 169, 172, 177, 178, 198, 203, 207, 215, 219, 221, 223, 225, 227, 229, 238, 241–243, 255
foundation, 3, 159, 181, 184
frame, 151, 153
framework, 27, 39, 169, 182, 233, 241, 253
frontier, 240
frustration, 136, 152, 224
function, 136, 156, 216
functionality, 190, 245
future, 3, 5, 7, 13, 17, 18, 26, 29, 34, 55, 65, 68, 78, 81, 85, 88, 94, 97, 98, 103, 106, 111, 114, 121, 124, 128, 134, 139, 161, 166, 169, 187, 198, 201, 203, 207, 216, 221, 226, 228, 230, 231, 253

gain, 190, 223
game, 7, 153
gameplay, 153
gamification, 136, 187
gaming, 5–7, 112, 153
gap, 218
gathering, 244, 245

gender, 132, 253
Germany, 59
gesture, 17
globalization, 29, 71–73
globe, 28, 88, 218
goal, 59, 154, 243
good, 198
governance, 218
groundwork, 5
group, 201, 245
growth, 21, 142, 213, 240

hand, 129
haptic, 7, 13, 80, 81
hardware, 17, 19, 113, 148–150, 207
harm, 140
harness, 28, 42, 52, 60, 94, 121, 126, 156, 172, 177, 193, 208, 213, 226, 248, 250, 252, 255
head, 3, 131
health, 227
healthcare, 11–13, 107–109, 152, 218
hearing, 89
help, 6, 113, 153, 184, 209, 225, 228, 242, 243
hinge, 221
hire, 50, 72
hiring, 50
horizon, 7
human, 89, 178, 207, 249, 250

idea, 78
identification, 245
identity, 81, 83
immersion, 3, 5, 7, 8, 80, 81, 83
impact, 6, 42, 51–53, 58, 66, 75–78, 138, 141, 146, 174, 176,

180, 183, 198, 211, 215, 216, 221, 223
implement, 25, 38, 44, 52, 56, 61, 139, 141, 147, 162, 165, 168, 171, 174, 177, 181, 183, 185, 188, 194, 249
implementation, 5, 10, 12, 18, 26, 84, 89, 97, 109, 134, 137, 178–181, 190, 198, 226, 227
importance, 11, 34, 39, 40, 49, 55, 68, 131, 132, 165, 224, 228, 235
improvement, 196, 242, 243, 252
in, 3, 5–13, 15–17, 21, 24, 26, 27, 29, 32, 34, 36, 37, 40, 42–45, 47, 49, 50, 52, 55–59, 61–63, 65–68, 71–73, 76, 80, 81, 83–85, 87–92, 94, 96–116, 119–121, 125, 126, 128–132, 134, 136, 137, 139–141, 146–150, 152, 153, 155–161, 163, 164, 166–170, 172–177, 181–184, 186, 187, 189, 190, 192, 193, 196–198, 201–203, 206–210, 213, 214, 216, 218–231, 233, 235, 238, 242, 243, 246–248, 250–253
include, 10, 17, 20, 24, 37, 51, 79, 85, 102, 157, 173, 176, 178, 179, 182, 209, 217, 227, 229, 238, 240, 245
inclusion, 68–71, 198, 219–221, 231
inclusivity, 17, 68, 114, 132–134, 158, 198, 207, 216, 218, 226–228, 243, 251, 252
income, 227
incorporation, 96
increase, 8, 49, 229
individual, 36, 65, 88, 136, 142, 173, 176, 205
individualism, 224
individuality, 81
indulgence, 224
industry, 7, 101, 103, 106, 107, 109, 111, 112, 114
influence, 37, 59, 71, 136, 145, 169, 186, 224, 228
information, 35–37, 40, 88, 129, 131, 138, 198, 226, 244
infrastructure, 153
ingenuity, 250
initiative, 183
innovation, 3, 5, 7, 26, 29, 34, 40, 42, 60–62, 65, 68, 71–73, 103, 106, 109, 114, 117, 121, 134, 136, 153, 163, 172, 175, 181, 184, 187, 193, 203, 207, 210–213, 216, 221, 238, 243, 246, 247, 250, 252
input, 50, 150, 152, 153, 242
ins, 113, 227, 241, 243
insight, 29
instance, 11, 17, 36, 50, 72, 152, 153, 163, 197, 205, 218, 225, 226, 228
integration, 9, 12, 13, 34–36, 42, 50, 52, 79, 81, 88, 92, 98, 109, 115, 119, 126, 128, 134, 153–156, 158, 161, 193, 196, 198, 233, 235, 236, 238
integrity, 37, 131

intelligence, 114, 134, 175–177, 201–203, 250
intensity, 8
interaction, 3, 5, 15, 16, 32, 36, 51, 113, 137–139, 197, 224, 226, 227, 233, 245
interconnectedness, 216, 228
interest, 17, 92
interface, 246
internet, 59, 113, 207, 225, 227
interoperability, 109, 238
interplay, 3, 65, 137
interpretation, 158
intersection, 114, 129, 158, 240
introduction, 181
invest, 29, 116, 155, 224, 231, 251
investing, 34, 187
involvement, 92
isolation, 51, 201, 227
issue, 227
it, 5, 10, 13, 16, 26, 37, 42, 43, 48, 52, 60, 62, 66, 71, 73, 88, 91, 92, 107, 111, 113, 120, 121, 129, 139, 140, 152, 155, 156, 158, 159, 167, 176, 183, 193, 194, 198, 205, 207, 208, 213, 223, 227, 228, 230, 231, 238, 244, 246
Ivan Sutherland's, 3

job, 34, 216, 242
John Kotter's, 181, 182
journey, 3, 5, 198

key, 22, 27, 47, 50, 109, 127, 134, 157, 159, 164, 166, 175, 178, 187, 210, 236, 238, 241, 243

keyboard, 158
knowledge, 75, 109, 184, 203, 224
Kurt Lewin, 181
Kurt Lewin's, 181

lack, 59, 113, 225, 227
lag, 152
landscape, 5, 24, 32, 37, 47, 52, 60, 65, 83, 98, 106, 109, 114, 116, 119, 121, 129, 137, 150, 161, 164, 181, 184, 190, 193, 196, 198, 207, 219, 235, 241, 243, 247, 252
language, 17, 36, 59, 136, 158, 217, 225
latency, 17, 150–153
lead, 8, 26, 34, 51, 59, 109, 113, 132, 136, 140, 152, 153, 170, 172, 177, 183, 184, 190, 227, 242
leader, 177
leadership, 183, 184
learning, 8, 21, 29, 36, 39, 42, 60, 94, 109, 111, 114, 127–129, 163, 184, 186, 187, 221, 224, 252
ledger, 238
lens, 37, 112
level, 36, 223
leverage, 18, 21, 36, 71, 83, 88, 161, 179, 194, 205, 223, 225, 249
leveraging, 24, 32, 49, 59, 60, 62, 68, 73, 75, 78, 85, 98, 101, 114, 116, 196, 198, 203, 207, 210, 213, 221, 223, 226, 238, 240, 241, 246, 247, 252, 253, 255

life, 11, 34, 63–65, 152, 183, 242
listener, 89
literacy, 111, 134, 217, 225
live, 112, 158, 225
load, 8, 91, 134, 205, 227
localization, 90
location, 50, 132, 194, 227
loss, 226

machine, 114
magnitude, 76
mainstream, 3
making, 42, 43, 59, 88, 91, 106, 163, 167, 176, 190, 193, 207, 224, 228, 238, 246
management, 13, 47–49, 59, 158, 163, 181–183, 193, 194, 196, 238, 241, 246
manager, 176
manufacturing, 103–106
market, 116
marketing, 119–121
marketplace, 52
masculinity, 224
means, 107, 132, 140, 223
measure, 134, 243, 252
measurement, 189, 190
mechanism, 223
media, 21, 32, 138, 139
medium, 55, 223
meeting, 16, 21–24, 36, 176, 227
member, 176, 177
mentor, 163
mentorship, 187
message, 55
messaging, 51
military, 2
mind, 17
Miro, 59

Misinterpretations, 224
model, 36, 42, 50, 181–183, 233
momentum, 183
monitoring, 242, 243
Morton Heilig's, 3
motion, 3, 5, 152
motivation, 172, 176
motor, 156
movement, 152
multitasking, 227
multitude, 114
music, 112

nature, 228, 244
necessity, 27, 107, 246
need, 47, 53, 54, 65, 101, 107, 181, 183, 184, 210, 227
network, 150, 151, 153
number, 153

offer, 60, 124, 159
office, 53, 54, 227
on, 7, 8, 11, 16, 18, 34–37, 42, 52, 55, 59, 66, 71, 73, 89, 114, 121, 126, 129, 131, 134, 137, 138, 146, 153, 157, 158, 163, 164, 166, 169, 172, 180, 182, 190, 205, 207, 211, 214, 215, 221, 223, 225–228, 230, 231, 238, 242, 243, 245, 246
onboarding, 179, 184–187, 198
online, 225, 242
openness, 224
operating, 71, 201
opportunity, 32, 42, 254
optic, 153
organization, 107, 183
orientation, 224

Osso VR, 13
other, 15, 16, 71, 129, 197, 246
out, 245
output, 50
overload, 51, 88, 227

pain, 13
pandemic, 59, 65–68, 172
paradigm, 26, 101, 109, 111, 116
parallel, 2
part, 183
participation, 134, 198, 225, 242, 245
patient, 13, 107, 109, 218
people, 16, 156
perception, 43, 136
performance, 36, 45, 52, 55, 136, 150, 153, 164, 173, 180, 181, 190, 243
period, 68
person, 15, 52, 59, 227
personnel, 2
phenomenon, 172, 175, 221
physicality, 80
pilot, 245
place, 157
plan, 179
planet, 55
planning, 181, 245
platform, 16, 36, 158, 163, 209, 224, 226, 241, 246
player, 8, 153
policy, 218
pool, 50, 229
pooling, 75
population, 134
positioning, 91, 252
post, 66–68

potential, 5–7, 9, 10, 12, 13, 15–17, 21, 24, 29, 30, 35, 36, 40, 51, 52, 55, 57, 60, 61, 63, 71, 73, 76, 77, 80, 81, 83, 87, 88, 93, 94, 97–99, 101, 106, 109, 111, 113–115, 121, 124–128, 138, 150, 156, 172, 179, 184, 187, 193, 198, 201–203, 210, 211, 213, 214, 217, 218, 220, 222–224, 226, 234, 235, 237, 238, 245–250, 252, 253
poverty, 253
power, 2, 42, 62, 111, 177, 193, 198, 203, 208, 216, 222, 224, 250, 255
practice, 11, 13, 132
presence, 3, 5, 15, 21, 32, 43, 81, 83, 92, 134, 136, 139, 152, 197, 224
present, 15, 190, 193, 253
pressure, 8
prevalence, 141
principle, 36
privacy, 37, 129–131, 198, 226, 228
problem, 16, 40–42, 140, 203, 205, 213
procedure, 152
process, 27, 36, 45, 55, 71, 73, 98, 114, 154, 163, 182, 184, 189, 194, 224
productivity, 24, 29, 34, 40, 43, 50–52, 65, 73, 98, 126, 134, 139, 140, 153, 155, 157, 158, 166, 169, 172, 178, 181, 183, 184, 190, 193, 198, 207, 210, 218, 233, 235, 238, 241, 243,

246, 250, 252
professional, 9, 63, 65, 137
proficiency, 11, 156
progress, 50, 193, 241
project, 47–50, 59, 163, 176, 177, 183, 193, 194, 196, 226, 241, 246
promise, 10, 88, 94, 198, 215
protection, 129, 131
pursuit, 65, 85

quality, 5, 15, 17, 24, 109, 113, 153, 187, 190, 197
question, 243

range, 122, 136, 242, 253
rate, 151, 153
ratio, 51
reader, 158
reality, 3, 126
realization, 160
realm, 55, 81, 140, 145, 153, 166, 175
reason, 201
receiver, 55
recognition, 136
record, 238
redefinition, 207
reduction, 158
redundancy, 154
reevaluation, 228
regulation, 175
rehabilitation, 12
relationship, 5, 83, 107, 151, 166, 169, 213, 253
reliance, 207
remote, 26–29, 32, 34, 47, 49, 59, 60, 63, 72, 166, 169, 177, 183, 186, 198, 206, 210, 218, 227, 243
rendering, 2, 150, 151, 153
request, 209
requirement, 158
research, 10, 126, 137
resilience, 243
resistance, 79, 156, 163, 255
resolution, 24, 59, 153, 224, 242, 245
resource, 161, 186, 253, 254
respect, 169, 242
response, 152, 243
restraint, 224
result, 153
retail, 114–116
retention, 88, 128, 184
rethinking, 205
richness, 21, 32, 59, 138, 139
right, 129, 178, 193, 241, 243
rise, 63, 72, 114, 140, 226
risk, 13, 51, 226
roadmap, 182
robin, 242
role, 13, 55, 59, 71, 73, 81, 85, 88, 114, 119, 153, 190, 196, 209, 221, 223, 226, 253
routine, 238

s, 2, 3, 5, 27, 34, 55, 89, 152, 158, 163, 169, 176, 181–183, 209, 224, 241, 250
safety, 37
salience, 15, 197
satisfaction, 34, 65, 136, 183, 190, 242, 243
scale, 71, 73, 221, 223
screen, 158, 197, 227

section, 24, 27, 29, 32, 43, 47, 52,
    55, 58, 60, 66, 68, 71, 75,
    81, 98, 101, 103, 109, 112,
    114, 119, 129, 134, 137,
    153, 161, 164, 167, 169,
    172, 178, 181, 210, 213,
    219, 221, 223, 226, 233,
    238, 241, 243, 247
sector, 101, 112, 119, 218
security, 34, 37–40, 109, 116, 124,
    129–131, 156, 198, 216,
    223, 226, 228, 238
Sega VR, 5
selection, 181, 244, 246
self, 175
sender, 55
sensation, 3
sense, 8, 15, 32, 81, 92, 152, 163,
    183, 218, 221
sensitivity, 225
Sensorama, 3
sentiment, 36
series, 163
serve, 81, 145, 184, 216
session, 177
set, 72, 242
setting, 243, 245
setup, 244
shape, 68, 106, 169, 198, 224
share, 21, 37, 59, 109, 177, 183, 206,
    221, 224, 225, 241, 245
sharing, 154, 194, 197, 218, 242,
    246
shift, 26, 29, 52, 66, 101, 109, 111,
    114, 116, 119, 183, 205,
    207, 227
sickness, 3, 5, 152
sign, 158
significance, 24, 27, 187, 233

simulation, 2, 152
situation, 177
skill, 11, 184
society, 132, 226
socio, 132, 213–216, 227
software, 17, 19, 50, 55, 153–156,
    209
solving, 16, 40–42, 203, 205, 213
sound, 89, 90
source, 151
South Africa, 59
space, 16, 32, 80, 89, 91, 152, 178,
    192, 244, 245
speaker, 91
speed, 59, 153, 207, 227
stage, 181
standard, 157
start, 71
state, 181
status, 132, 227
step, 178
strategy, 38, 156, 178
streamlining, 114
struggle, 59
student, 111
study, 13, 227
subsection, 21, 89, 184, 190, 193,
    207, 216, 250
success, 5, 24, 32, 43, 45, 49, 62, 65,
    71, 85, 116, 142, 156, 161,
    166, 169, 181, 183, 187,
    193, 196, 198, 203, 207,
    209, 210, 243, 250–252
suite, 51
summary, 52, 94, 111, 129
sun, 50
support, 24, 132, 137, 158, 162,
    163, 169, 183, 184, 207,
    245, 246, 251

surrounding, 4, 198
survey, 243
sustainability, 78, 158, 161, 255
synergy, 128, 196, 238, 240
system, 89, 92, 152, 154, 157, 183, 238

t, 5
talent, 28, 50, 65, 72, 229
tapestry, 3
target, 134
teaching, 111
team, 24, 36, 43, 45, 49, 51, 59, 134, 136, 139, 153, 162, 163, 167, 172, 176, 177, 183, 184, 197, 198, 205, 218, 221, 226–228, 241–246
teamwork, 17, 24–29, 34, 42, 52, 57, 66, 81, 85, 107, 137, 161, 163, 164, 166, 169, 172, 175, 183, 186, 190, 193, 225, 226, 246
tech, 183
technique, 89, 152
technology, 2, 3, 5, 7, 10, 13, 17–21, 24, 27, 29, 32, 37, 42, 51, 55, 57, 60, 62, 63, 65, 75, 78, 83–85, 88, 89, 92, 94, 98, 103, 106, 107, 109, 111, 113, 114, 116, 121, 124, 126, 128, 132, 137, 140, 146–148, 158, 161, 163, 196, 198, 205, 207, 210, 213, 223, 225, 227, 228, 238–240, 247, 249, 250, 252, 255
tension, 177
term, 224, 252
test, 245

texture, 79
theft, 129
theory, 8, 21, 32, 83, 89, 132, 138, 140, 169, 197, 205, 224
time, 12, 16, 17, 32–36, 50, 51, 59, 65, 73, 136, 151, 183, 184, 194, 197, 206, 218, 227, 238, 246
today, 5, 27, 34, 250
tone, 36
tool, 13, 68, 75, 114, 163, 181, 183, 216, 223, 226, 246
tracking, 5, 7, 136, 153, 194
traction, 89
trainee, 152
training, 2, 9–11, 13, 116, 124, 127–129, 152, 155, 163, 179, 181, 183–187, 198, 216, 218, 225, 227, 230, 242, 243, 245, 251
transformation, 47, 50, 107, 114, 140, 205, 221, 226, 246
transition, 181, 184, 230
translation, 17, 224
transparency, 228, 238
travel, 53, 54, 151, 161
treatment, 13
trend, 29, 107, 205
triad, 37
trust, 26, 43–45, 59, 166–169, 198, 224, 226, 242
trustworthiness, 37

uncertainty, 224
underpinning, 213
understanding, 3, 10, 16, 26, 29, 32, 39, 42, 45, 49, 57, 60, 62, 66, 71, 83, 94, 126, 137, 139, 142, 145, 147, 150,

153, 161, 163, 164, 169, 172, 175, 177, 181, 201, 203, 207, 224–226, 233, 244, 247, 250, 253
unit, 50
up, 198, 229, 243, 245, 246
urgency, 183
usability, 156–158, 245
usage, 163
use, 2, 3, 8, 16, 20, 51, 65, 71, 87, 91, 158, 190, 224, 228, 242
user, 3, 17, 18, 36, 37, 80–83, 85, 92–94, 124, 126, 145, 152–154, 156–158, 161, 178, 198, 244, 246

value, 71
variety, 86
version, 246
video, 51, 55, 138, 197, 206, 218, 224, 246
vision, 76, 183
visual, 59, 138, 152, 156
visualization, 16
voice, 17, 36, 242
VR, 15

waste, 161
water, 253
way, 18, 24, 50, 52, 57, 58, 65, 81, 92, 94, 98, 101, 106, 114, 124, 126, 129, 198, 205, 206, 216, 223, 226, 238
weight, 79
well, 65, 134, 137, 140, 142, 172, 175, 179, 187, 193, 207, 231, 247
work, 5, 21, 24, 26, 27, 29, 32, 34, 47, 49, 50, 59, 63–65, 68, 72, 73, 98, 139, 147, 154, 166, 169, 177, 183, 184, 187, 196, 198, 205, 207, 210, 218, 221, 225–228, 235, 238, 242, 246
workflow, 242
workforce, 29, 32, 50, 57, 71, 72, 129, 228–231
working, 27, 59, 187, 201, 241
workplace, 27, 29, 68, 175, 207, 219, 252
workspace, 34, 161, 164, 172, 198, 205, 206
world, 27, 39, 58, 60, 62, 68, 72, 73, 101, 109, 111, 119, 129, 141, 149, 155, 193, 203, 209–211, 213, 216, 221, 223, 225, 229, 231, 250
wound, 13

zone, 73

Milton Keynes UK
Ingram Content Group UK Ltd.
UKHW030745121124
451094UK00013B/967